The Tearaway

The Tearaway

Dean Williams

with

John F. McDonald

**SIMON &
SCHUSTER**

London · New York · Sydney · Toronto · New Delhi

A CBS COMPANY

First published in Great Britain by Simon & Schuster UK Ltd, 2012
A CBS Company

1 3 5 7 9 10 8 6 4 2

Simon & Schuster UK Ltd
1st Floor
222 Gray's Inn Road
London WC1X 8HB

www.simonandschuster.co.uk

Simon & Schuster Australia, Sydney

Simon & Schuster India, New Delhi

A CIP catalogue record for this book is available
from the British Library.

ISBN: 978-1-84983-774-3

Typeset by Hewer Text UK Ltd, Edinburgh
Printed in Great Britain by CPI Group (UK) Ltd, Croydon, CR0 4YY

In loving memory of my pal, Keith Munson

Contents

Chapter One

The North's another country – from the south, I mean. But it's the only country for a boy of two or three years – the only place a kid that age knows about. That's how old I was when the lousy bugger first began to abuse me – I don't mean sexually abuse or nothing like that, I mean physically abuse, like hitting and punching and swinging the boot and screaming and stuff. At least that's as far back as I can remember. I suppose it really started before then, when he threw a chip pan full of boiling oil at my pregnant mother. The man who was to become my father didn't want me even then. That's not in my head, of course, the chip-pan stuff – it's not a memory. It's just something I know, something maybe my mother told me or I heard it from somebody or other who my mother told. He wouldn't admit to it, though – Bob wouldn't admit it if you asked him, even though it's true. I suppose maybe it's not a memory for him neither. Maybe he's blocked it from his head, like a lot of other things he did.

Andrea, my mother, had a nervous breakdown before she had me. I don't know how that showed itself or anything, or even how she got over it – I suppose she never got over it. I don't know if you get over things like nervous breakdowns? I just know it left a mark on her – a nervousness inside her. It made her susceptible to things, if you get my meaning, to little things that made her jump, that made her afraid of shadows, that made her nervous of herself – in case, I suppose, it might come back again. The breakdown. Andrea had other children too, before me – two girls. She had the first one when she was fourteen or fifteen, I'm not sure. Sarah was her name, the first baby girl. She's in Australia now, with the people who adopted her. Nadia was the second baby – she's up in Scotland somewhere with her dad. Bob Williams didn't know about these babies – at least, I don't think he did. If he did, he never said nothing about them when I was listening. Bob Williams became my father and I lived with him in Grimsby.

When I say the North's another country, I mean like abuse is rife up there – rampant. At least, it was when I was a kid. That's not bullshit or anything, it's something I know, not something I was told. Maybe it was the same down south back then, but they just didn't admit it. Maybe they hid it better than they did up north, kept it quieter, suppressed it, swept it under the carpet. Maybe the southerners are better at that kinda thing, more efficient like, cleverer. Up north, they like to think they're straight, honest – about their past and their present and their beer and their ballads and the abuse of their kids. Maybe they thought it made them hard or something, harder than the shower of ponces down south – like that's the way people from the

2

North think. Bob was a sailor, a fisherman who worked out of the Humber estuary and into the North Sea. He worked on the trawlers that sailed up past the Faroes and west through the Norwegian Sea and into the North Atlantic, off the coast of Iceland. Sometimes they'd sail further west when the fish were scarce; north along the coast of Greenland and even over the Arctic Circle. It must have been a dangerous bloody life and I suppose you had to be a hard man to endure it. Bob was a hard man!

Bob was away a lot of the time, which was good for me. Andrea and I were close, the way mothers with only one kid can be close. It's kinda funny, because she didn't really want a baby after the first two kids. She only had me for Bob, and then he went and threw the bloody chip pan at her when she was pregnant with the kid he wanted and she didn't. Makes you wonder, don't it? Anyway, Bob didn't like how Andrea and me were so close; he thought it made me soft, like I was a poncey little mammy's boy and he didn't want to have no sissy for a son. He spent nine months out of the year at sea and, when he came home, he spent the rest of the time drinking and fighting.

He was a big man, six foot two in his socks, like they say. Him and his brother were tough bastards, they got paid to beat people up – I was too young to know why, maybe for money or maybe for revenge or maybe just for the fun of it. It didn't matter to Bob, the reason, he was up for it, him and his brother. They could fight any man – or woman. And if there wasn't any paid work about, he'd come home and hit me and my mother. I wasn't tough enough for him and I suppose he thought, if he punched me about, it would make me harder – like him. Maybe his father did it to him when he was little and it was a family tradition he was just carrying on, down the bloodline. Like a legacy that's handed down from father to son – a family heirloom.

'Man up!'

That's what he'd shout when he punched me.

'Man up, you little prick!'

I was born in 1972 – the year of Watergate and Bloody Sunday and Buffalo Creek and Farrell's Ice Cream Parlour and Rangers winning the Cup Winners' Cup in Barcelona – but, worst of all, it was the year of the Cod Wars off the coast of Iceland. Maybe that's what started the bugger off. Maybe all that hassle up there in the North Atlantic pissed him off so much he had to take it out on someone when he got home. The Icelandic bloody Cod Wars happened between 1972 and 1976, just when I was growing up from nothing to four years old. The bastard Icelandic coastguard cut the fishing nets of British trawlers and harassed the crews by ramming their vessels and confiscating their catches. Iceland then went and won the Cod Wars and the northern Englishmen from places like Grimsby don't like losing to nobody, especially when that loss messes up their fisheries and makes them lose money. I know it seriously pissed Bob off, because he was always in a bad mood when he came ashore.

Andrea was, and still is, a good-looking woman. I suppose this must have contributed to the fact that she got pregnant when she was fourteen. She didn't do it deliberately like – it was the naivety of the time; girls were getting pregnant because they didn't know enough about birth control and didn't see further than their little community or council estate. The older ones did it because they wanted to please their boyfriends, so the younger ones listened to the stupid pop music about love and all that crap and followed in their footsteps. It was a culture thing, like part of being working class in the north of England. The rich didn't get pregnant and neither did the southerners. I'm sure they screwed just as much, maybe even more – but they didn't have babies, because they used contraceptives or had abortions or whatever they did back in them days – coathangers or bottles of gin or stuff like that, I'm sure. My mother was one of those girls, a victim of her time and her class and her environment and her good looks. It's hard for me to talk about Andrea as she was then, before I was born – I didn't know her then and she's a changed women now. It's easy for me to talk about Bob. He never changed!

I suppose I should say something about Grimsby here, before I go on – you should know something about the place. Maybe you already do. Maybe you know Grimsby is a seaport on the Humber estuary and it was founded by a Danish Viking called Grim and that 'by' means village in Old Norse, so Grimsby means Grim's Village. But, unless you were born and brought up there, you won't really know Grimsby at all. When I was growing up, Grimsby was a town full of fishermen – dour, scowling blokes, with sea-washed faces, hardened by the culture and the climate. These men took no bullshit from nobody and there wasn't much they liked about anything. You asked them something about anywhere else other than Grimsby and they snorted through their noses and spat on the ground, like you were talking about something that was as low as dog shit and came from another planet. They looked out through slits in their faces and saw nothing much further than the horizon out past Spurn Head and their skin was as grey as the waves that lapped up against the deep-water walls of the docks.

The women, too, were mainly resigned – stoical in their acceptance of their lot – knowing their place and not trying to get above themselves. If they did, they got talked about and made out to be a whore or a retard or a shit-don't-stink bitch and got spat at and sneered at. Anyone who didn't fit into this mould, who showed any kind of sensitivity or self-awareness, was straight away suspected of being strange – different in a nasty kind of way, soft as a bloody southerner. A good reason for head-shaking and nose-snorting and mouth-shouting –

'Man up, you little prick!'

My birthday was 27th March – it was a leap-year, officially the longest year in history, according to the records, the longest year ever. The reason being, two leap seconds were added to the UTC time-scale in 1972, whatever that means. But it's something that never happened before and it's never happened since. So, the year was special in the greater scheme of things. I read somewhere that my birth sign was Aries the Ram, the first sign of the zodiac after the spring equinox. The first sign – like a new beginning – 'new' meaning different, strange, head-shaking, nose-snorting. The golden bloody ram may have rescued that Greek bloke Phryxos, carrying him away to the land of Colchis, but there was no mythological beast to rescue me, to take me away from the danger. The only beast around when I was born was the human kind, who was determined to sacrifice me to his own bloody god of manhood and manliness. Not that I know much about astrology or anything, but it should have been clear from the beginning – like, if you believe in that stuff, my sign was fire and my ruling planet was Mars. So it was there, right from the start – the violence. What chance did I have?

My very first memories are of living on a cul-de-sac council estate called Springfield Close, in the shitty Scartho area of Grimsby. I can remember this, even though I couldn't have been more than two or three years old. I used to sit on my pillow at night and rock from side to side to make myself fall asleep. As I recall, the rocking motion felt nice, soothing, it made me dizzy and gave me a sense of being somewhere else – you know, like outside myself, looking in. Trouble was, it used to wake Bob up and he'd stand in the doorway in his underpants screaming. I can't remember if he hit me then, when I was two or three, rocking from side to side, I just remember him in the doorway. I can't remember either why I couldn't go to sleep, just that I was shit-scared most of the time I wasn't with my mother.

Andrea would come into the room, try to push past his screaming bulk, his shaking fist, his big shoulders and chest – trying to get to me before his knuckles did, I suppose. She'd push him back, which wasn't easy if he didn't want to be pushed. She'd plead with him, try to cajole him, promise him she'd quieten me. Sometimes he'd go back to bed – and sometimes he wouldn't. When he did, she'd put me lying down and rub my head. She'd sing 'rock-a-bye-baby' to me, whisper it to me, into my ear, so she wouldn't disturb him – Bob. She'd stay with me like that, whispering her song, sobbing her song, until I went to sleep – or until he called her.

Other times she'd run out of the house with me in her arms, down to the nearest telephone kiosk which, as I remember, was always stinking of piss. I'm glad we got mobile phones today and I don't have to go back into those bloody claustrophobic boxes, waiting for my granddad to come get us, her crying and me crying and not knowing whether Bob would follow us down and drag us back. When we did go back, after being at my grandparents for the night, he'd be all quiet, like – until the next time.

In 1975, when I was three, we moved to Bradley Park estate, in an area of west Grimsby close to a notorious old council estate known locally as the 'Nunny'. There was two and a half thousand houses on the Bradley Park and it looked like a brand-new city to me, all shiny and bright, like a new Grimsby. The old Grimsby of the Nunny was narrow streets, terraced houses, alleyways that led to other people's backyards, history on every corner. There was no history here. No old memories of violence. It was a step up from the previous house in social terms, if you know what I mean. Like, there was central heating and everything. We were lucky. A new beginning? That's what I thought and, for a while it was – while Bob was at sea. He was working on a research ship called the *Cirolana* then, but it didn't improve his mood much. When he came home, he still got drunk and violent.

Ninety per cent of jobs were on the docks and the social life, if you could call it social life, revolved round the men coming home from sea. They'd anchor up and start drinking as soon as they set foot on dry land. There would be crates of beer on the docks and then they'd all move on to Freeman Street, which was literally pub after pub all along the whole thoroughfare. It was the old macho thing again – work hard, play hard. You weren't a real man unless you got so drunk you couldn't see or speak or reason or think – unless you could beat up your wife and abuse your children. Real men didn't get sloppy and mushy and tell their women they missed them all the time they were out on the waves. Real men didn't go home and lift their kids up in their arms and kiss them and hug them and tell them they loved them. To do that was to be different – strange – soft-southern – queer-bugger – head-shaking – nose-snorting – fist-flying – 'Man up!'

Like I said, Bob considered me to be a mammy's boy, because I clung to my mother whenever he came home. I didn't know this man, this violent bloke who came into our lives at certain times during the year. My mother changed when he was at home; she didn't love me like she did when he was away. Of course she did love me, even more – but she wasn't allowed to show that love. The old shaky feelings came back to her, the old nervousness, the shadows, the memory of the breakdown. Maybe she thought the bloody thing would come back if she let her real feelings out? Who was this man? I asked myself this in a kids' way – the way kids ask themselves things when they don't understand what's happening to them. Why did he have to come between us like this? Why did he have to come home from the sea and hurt me and Andrea? He was a bully and I wanted him to drown, maybe get swept away out there on a flood tide, or run aground on a sandbar, or be rammed by a gunboat. I wanted never to see him again, never to be beaten up by him for this or that when he was drunk – for nothing, for being me, a mammy's boy. Never to be chased round the bloody house by him for some minor thing like pissing myself with fear of being beaten black and blue when he caught me. But nothing ever happened to him out there on the sea – the bugger always came back.

A lot of things went on back then, but some stick in my mind more than others. Like, how he'd rub butter into my smashed head and make me eat kippers. I hated the stinking things – dark-brown fish shaped like butterflies. I can remember them to this day, along with the Saxa salt in a red container with a flip-top lid. We had a walk-in cupboard and I remember going in there one day when I was just a little kid and pouring the salt into my mouth from the flip-top lid – swallowing it, letting it clog up my throat, smothering me, suffocating me. But I only threw up and had to be taken to the infirmary. I didn't die like I wanted to.

The bastard would scream when I did something that got on his nerves – and most things got on his nerves when he was drunk, which was most of the time.

'Put the little prick in the cupboard!'

She'd be holding me in her arms and I'd be begging her not to let me go, not to put me down, to keep holding on to me through the shouting and the banging of his fists against the walls and the doors. But he'd shout it even louder:

'Put the little prick in the cupboard! Now!'

And she'd have to do it. She'd have no other choice, otherwise he'd beat the living daylights out of her. He'd probably do it anyway, but it would be worse if she didn't do what he told her. I remember the utility cupboard near the kitchen, it was about six foot by two foot and there was no light. There was nothing much in there, only shoes and a blanket and junk stuff. Some light streaked in from outside, through cracks, until he switched it off. Then it was pitch-black. I'd stay in there like that through the violence. I'd hear her screaming and him shouting. I'd hear things breaking – glass, wood, plastic, things being thrown all over the place – everything in the bloody house. I'd sometimes hear him screwing her after the violence and then he'd sleep. Everything would go quiet. I'd wait in the cupboard for her to come to me. She'd open the door, but she couldn't take me out, she didn't dare take me out in case he woke up and came and checked. She'd sing to me through the crack in the door:

'Rock-a-bye-baby, on the treetop . . .'

She'd whisper it to me, sob it to me, until I fell asleep in among the shoes and other shit, on the rotten blanket – or until she heard a floorboard creak or until he called to her.

'Andrea!'

If she had to leave me, I'd cry myself to sleep in the darkness. And it felt like I wasn't there no more, like I'd disappeared from the face of the earth, like I'd never been born. I'd stay in the cupboard for days on end, not knowing whether it was night or day, scared in case he'd come and beat the crap out of me, like he beat the crap out of Andrea. I'd stay there until he went out to get drunk again. Then she'd take me out for a while, but I'd have to go back in as soon as she heard him coming along the street. I didn't want to be in there, I only wanted to be with my mother. Coming out of the cupboard wasn't a relief or nothing, because I never knew when I'd get beaten or when I'd be thrown back into it. But it wasn't a sanctuary either, like you'd think it would be. It wasn't a hiding place from the violence and it wasn't like I was still in the womb, waiting to be born. It was more like an arsehole than a womb and I was stuck in this arsehole and I didn't know what I'd done to deserve it. I hated it like I hated him. It represented him. It was him – it was Bob, the utility cupboard near the kitchen, and I was trapped inside him and I'd never ever be free of the fucker.

People might ask why didn't she leave him. And I suppose it was because she was afraid he'd come after her and probably kill her, that's why. She was afraid of him, so afraid it's hard to explain to anyone who's never been that scared. I know, because I was that scared too. Other people might ask why she married him in the first place. They might say she was crazy. But it's easy to say things like that; it's easy to know things after they've happened. Everybody makes mistakes; it's just that some are worse than others. And the answer to the question Why did she marry him? is because she loved him and because he was handsome and slick and sexy and edgy and some women like to be with men like that – men with an air of danger about them. Until it goes too far. And he was good as gold when he was sober, which wasn't all that often.

He told me once when he was in a rare good mood that he turned the boat round because of me, like he was saying he loved me in the only way he could. He said he turned round because he heard I was sick or something and he made the trawler come back to port so he could make sure I was all right. But I don't believe that story. The only time he turned round and came back was when he heard my mother had finally taken out an injunction against him because she couldn't take no more and he wasn't allowed anywhere near the house. I think I was about five or so.

Injunctions or restraining orders weren't things that stopped Bob Williams. He came off the boat and headed straight for the house. But the police were waiting. I was downstairs and I could see what was happening. It took six policemen to restrain him. He was screaming and shouting about no one keeping him out of his own bloody home. The fists and feet started flying and I was so shit-scared in case the coppers wouldn't be able to handle him – in case he beat them up and got into the house and came after me and my mother. He'd blame me for it, that's for sure. It would be the mammy's boy's fault, like all the other stuff was my fault. I'd be back under the bloody stairs again, but not before he broke my jaw or my arm or my back or my lousy little neck. But the police hung on to him. They handcuffed him and hauled him away shouting and cursing and kicking. He went to prison for seven days and he didn't try to break the restraining order again, although he threatened to do it lots of times.

Don't get me wrong, I'm not whingeing or nothing like that. I know it was as bad for other kids as it was for me – even a lot worse for some. And there were good things about it as well – every time a tooth got knocked out I put it under my pillow and got fifty pence from the tooth fairy. It wasn't the tooth fairy at all, I know that now, it was Andrea. But at the time I thought it was and I thought there was someone else who loved me. And there was the long hot summer of '76, when Bob seemed to be away more than usual and the Jubilee street party of '77 with cakes and lemonade and flags and smiles and singy-songs. There was times like that, little intervals of happiness, little moments when you could forget the rest of the crap. But they didn't last long, eventually normality would resume and the violence would start up again.

And, so, I was born and grew up. It was the longest year in 1972 and the years that followed were just as bloody long for me. Two years, three years, four years, five years – these are supposed to be the very formative time in a kid's life, aren't they? The early, impressionable years when he learns to speak, to think, to play the piano, to dance, to sing – and to hate!

Chapter Two

Anyway, things got a bit quieter in the house after my mother stitched Bob up with the injunction. Before she got herself round to doing that, I'd started out at school and I'd come home sometimes and see chair legs sticking through the front windows and broken furniture thrown out onto the street. He must've smashed the house up, like, maybe a million times and I think she'd probably had enough of putting it back together again before she managed to pep herself up enough to get the restraining order.

You'd think that would've been that, wouldn't you? But old Bob just wouldn't leave my life. The bugger would come home from sea and go straight round my school and make the teachers let him take me out somewhere. He'd have bags of sweets and, believe it or not, it made me feel special because the other kids could see I did have a dad after all and I wasn't really what they kept calling a 'prozzie's kid' and I was just a normal boy from a normal family. And, for a little while at least, I'd forgive him and forget all the bad things he done when he lived with us, until he got drunk and I'd have to make my way home on my own with my bag of Curly Wurlys.

I was five in the summer of 1977 and the Queen had been sitting on her throne for twenty-five years – so they gave her a party and told us we could all join in. It was like nothing I'd ever seen before. We had about ten groves on our bit of the estate – groves were like cul-de-sacs with alleys linking them – and we got given out these cups and mugs and plates at school, with pictures on so we'd know what it was all about. They said a 'street party' and I didn't know what to expect. Then all the adults started hanging up red-white-and-blue bunting and little flags from lamp post to lamp post. They put up wooden trestle-tables and covered them with crêpe paper. Then they brought out chairs and paper plates and cakes and sandwiches and sausage rolls and dandelion and burdock and cherryade, all bought from the Barr man who came round the roads in his old lorry. We called him the 'Barr' man, because that was the brand of the drinks he sold and his truck had 'Eddy's Mobile' printed on the side of it. A little perk for us kids was we could get a couple of pennies back on the empty bottles and we'd go buy chips and scraps in newspaper cones from the local fish and grease-dipper with the money.

There were street parties all over the estate that day and I wandered from one to the other, collecting free gifts and party bags, until it got dark and us kids were sent up to bed, while the adults stayed down on the street, drinking ale and sweet sherry and gin and Guinness. It sticks in my mind, that street party, like it was one of the happy days in the middle of a lot of bloody misery – like, when you look up at night and the stars are like someone's stuck pinholes in the dark sky, to let the little bits of light through. But it was just a single day in the middle of a lot of days and I said 'thank you' to the old Queen for it, and then it passed and the other days came back again.

The thing was, with Bob Williams out of the way, there were other bastards who came along and took liberties. They wouldn't have done it if Bob had been around, because he'd have kicked seven colours of crap out of them if he found out, and probably out of me too. One of these lousy buggers was an old guy called 'Peanut'. He was a seaman, like Bob, a short bloke of about forty, with black hair going bald and long sideburns down the side of his face so he looked like some old rockabilly or something. He was always drunk, or at least it seemed like that to me. I was about six or seven at the time and I used to hang round with Peanut's little nephew, a kid called Mark.

Me and Mark made this den for ourselves, down a dirt track past the allotments. There was lots of trees down there and thick privet bushes and stuff and it was like a place we could go sometimes to get away from all the shit. We'd nick a box of Swan Vestas and light a little fire, surrounded by stones, and we thought we were like the people who used to live back in the ancient times, before there was electricity and stuff. We knew there were monsters all around us, but we were safe as long as we were inside the den. Until Peanut came and found us.

I suppose being around Mark's house when his uncle was docked caused the problem. He became, I suppose, a familiar figure to us and it's like when adults make friends with kids and the kids trust them because they don't think for a minute that there might be more to it.

'I'll give you ten bob.'

That's what the bugger said straight out when he followed us down the dirt track and came into the den after us.

'Just rub it up and down.'

Then he unzipped his trousers and this big popcorn stuck out. I mean, we had dicks too, me and Mark, but not like that bastard. But we wanted the ten bob and I suppose it must've seemed like some sort of naughty game or something – and we didn't know what would happen if we refused. I mean, would we get into trouble if we said no?

'You do it first, Mark.'

'No . . . you.'

Peanut piped up.

'Both together.'

The game didn't last long. This stuff suddenly shot out of the popcorn and then he zipped his trousers back up and gave us the ten bob.

Peanut followed us down to the den a lot after that and he always gave us the ten bob he promised and we always kept our mouths shut about it – like he told us to. I stopped hanging round with Mark after a while, not because of Peanut, but because of something else that I can't remember now. You know what kids are like, one minute they got this bunch of friends, then the next minute it's all change, then they're back with the first lot again. Anyway, I didn't see Peanut around much after that. I never knew what happened to him but, when I was a few years older, I remember seeing a piece in the local paper saying something about how the police were looking for him – they wanted to speak to him urgently about some sexual abuse thing. But I had other things on my mind by then, so I didn't give it much notice.

Because my mam didn't live with her husband, the other kids called her a whore. They mostly called her a whore to me, like to my face, to wind me up, to see what I'd do about it. In winter, they'd throw snowballs at our windows. Every time one hit the pane of glass, I'd jump, even though I knew it was coming, following the ones that came before. That nervousness probably went back to Bob and when he'd come home drunk and slam the door. These weren't the kids I palled around with, these bastards were older than me and I swore I'd get even with them all some day.

I was about seven when I was given the name 'spike-thrower'. I mean, it wasn't even a spike; it was the brake-arm lever from a bicycle that was hanging loose from the handlebar, that's all. You see, we had this neighbour kid called Andrew and he was three or four years older than me and he didn't like me because I had no dad – or maybe he thought he could get away with it because I had no dad. Anyway, I was out in the alley one day and he was standing in my way.

'Your mam's a slag!'

'And you're a bollocks!'

So he cracked me over the head with a conker. This weren't no normal conker, it was a fiver, that had been hardened in the oven and then steeped in nail-varnish. The wanker hit me hard enough to make me cry and I ran indoors. But I could hear him out in the street mocking me, taking the piss.

'Cry babby, arse all scabby.'

He wouldn't stop and it got on my bloody nerves, so I went back out and that's when I looked to my left and noticed the bicycle. I was getting angrier and angrier with the bugger by now. I knew I couldn't match him in a fair fight, so I needed something to even the odds. I saw the L-shaped brake-lever arm and it literally fell into my hand when I pulled at it. He was still laughing at me and taunting me to come and do something about it when I held up the 'spike', as the papers later called it. So I threw it at him and it spun through the air. I watched it fly, round and round like a boomerang in slo-mo, until it pierced his right temple. One end was at a right angle to his head and the other end stuck out his left ear.

I was just a kid, don't forget, but I still knew I'd done something very serious to the lousy bugger. He just stood there, staring at me like a rabbit caught in the headlights of a car. It was like the world had stopped going round and everything was just stood still, without any sound coming from anywhere. Then he put his hand up to feel the metal thing sticking out of his head – and that was like a signal for the blood to start running down his face. Then everything started up again, even faster than before. He began to scream and I turned and sprinted back indoors and ran upstairs and hid under the bed.

What happened next was probably the beginning of the end of my childhood – I mean, like, I was still only seven years old, but things changed. Things change all the time, but now and then something happens and it's like there was a before and an after that moment in time and they were different. I could hear the shouts and screams from outside on the street.

'Jesus Christ!'

'What's he done?'

'He's got a fucking spike sticking out his ear!'

'It was Williams, he done it!'

'Call the police!'

The voices were drowned out by the noise of approaching sirens and my mother's footsteps coming up the stairs.

'Dean, where are you?'

When she brought me back downstairs, there was all sorts outside the bloody door – ambulance, police cars, newspapers, crowds of neighbours – this was bad. Very bad. The coppers interviewed me in our front room, with all the shit-faces gawking in through the window. There was lots of words floating about in the air – and most of them were bloody angry. But I wasn't listening to much, just looking at the ugly mouths moving. I could hear some of what they were saying – phrases and stuff.

'Taken away . . .'

'Put into care . . .'

But it wasn't getting past my eardrums and into my brain. In the end, it was all just white noise – like when the television goes off and there's only that static stuff left. All I kept thinking about was, what's Bob gonna do when he finds out?

They didn't take me away, as it happens, and Bob never got involved, I dunno why – maybe he just didn't give a damn. But it was on the radio and a regional TV news programme, called *Calendar*, and on the streets and in the newspapers – 'Spike Thrown Thru Boy's Skull'. That's when I turned to God, praying that Andrew wouldn't die. I listened to the updates and the whispers – he was blind, he had brain damage, he was deaf, he was critical – and I prayed all the time. I was just a kid, but I knew what would happen if he snuffed it – I'd be a murderer and be sent to some young offender shithole, where I'd be bullied and raped and generally mucked about with. My mother took me out of school for a while, hoping in vain that it would all die down. But it didn't. People looked at me in a strange way, like I had two bloody heads or something, and I wasn't allowed in my mates' houses no more and I didn't get invited to their birthday parties and they weren't allowed round to my house and some were even told to stay away from me completely.

I wandered round on my own for a bit, in the beginning, until some of the kids forgot, like little kids forget things, and started to wander round with me again. Andrew didn't die, but they couldn't remove all the bar from his head, it was too dangerous, and he was never really the same again. We were neighbours, so it was inevitable that we'd bump into each other again. When we did, he just looked at me in a strange way, like he didn't recognise me and I just shrugged back at him. I mean, what the hell can you say to someone you've injured for life? I did go round and apologised to his mother, but she just started crying and shut the door, so I left it like that. The main thing about it was, I'd lost the name 'Dean' and got re-christened 'Spike Thrower'.

This didn't bother me. No, it was good for my street-cred, like they say, and I got accepted into a local gang. The rest of the members were a bit older than me, but they liked having a 'spike thrower' in the ranks, even though I never threw another spike again. It was good being in a gang; nobody picked on me much or asked me to rub their popcorn for ten bob. We didn't do a lot, like you'd think a gang would do, just played music like Madness or the Cure or Thin Lizzy or Squeeze or the Specials up loud on those old music centres that used to double as drinks cabinets, when the adults weren't at home – or make catapults out of laggy bands and old metal mattresses that were dumped in the lanes. We used the Y bit that joined the coiled springs, then we'd Sellotape round the grip to bulk it out a bit and shoot stones at the street lights.

We'd roam the estate after school, walking the walk like we were tough or something, or go up to Devil's Ditch and explore the storm drain – miles and miles of it. In summertime we'd go out to where the farmers were burning the stubble in the fields. We'd make torches and run through the drills, setting light to the unburned corn stalks, not understanding that we could get trapped and burned to bloody death if the wind changed. After heavy rain, some parts of the countryside round Grimsby would turn into bogs of sink-mud and we'd dare each other to walk into the centre – lots of wellies got lost that way and we'd have to walk home in our socks. Daring was part of the gang thing too – climb a tree a bit higher, or go into the graveyard at night, or jump off a garage roof – always pushing it a bit further than the time before.

These were good times, like where bonds were forged with other kids – making bows and arrows out of sticks and fishing line, and egging through the fields and bushes for birds' nests, and catching newts in the ponds and throwing stuff up into the horse-chestnut trees and knocking down the spiky green seed pods then opening them up to find the best brown conkers, and jumping on the back step of the chip van when it drove past, to see who could stay on the longest and not graze your knees on the ground when you fell off. You could probably call them good days, if I remember right.

On the weekends we'd watch Bruce Lee on the Betamax – all the kids would sit in complete silence watching the video and then we'd all pile out onto the green, each kid truly believing he was a champion kung-fu killer, with arms chopping and legs kicking, until someone got accidentally hurt and it would have to stop. Sunday was bath day, so we'd be all clean again for school on Monday. We'd be covered in all sorts of crap – dried-out clay from mud fights and dogshit from playing bob-on-a-stick and hair full of sugar residue from squirting cans and bottles of shaken-up pop and smelling like dead goats in a heatwave.

In winter we'd play catch-a-gritter, which was like skiing, council-estate style – hanging on to the backs of the gritter lorries as they dumped their sand and salt on the roads. Or make slides by pouring water on the footpaths before we went to bed, so it froze overnight and broke a few old fogies' arses when they slipped on it the next day. For some reason, as I remember, everything seemed to be orange in the winter, especially at night, like the street lamps and the piles of swept-up snow and we'd stick our fingers through the silver foil tops of the milk bottles on our way to school in the dark mornings. We didn't have coal fires on the Bradley Park, but you could see the smoke drifting over from the Nunny and smell the burning chimneys and the little children with raggedy arses, like something from Charles Dickens.

My clothes were rarely new, mostly hand-me-downs from some relatives or stuff from jumble sales that smelled like mothballs and school shoes with plastic soles. Once the soles of your shoes wore out, you had to stick cardboard in them, until you could get another second-hand pair from the jumble. But now and then I'd get a decent bit of clobber, like a denim jacket I had once with studs spelling 'Adam' on one shoulder and 'Ant' on the other, or a parka coat with fur trim round the hood, that I zipped all the way up to look sinister. You see, Mam sometimes helped out at the jumble sales and her reward would be that I could come in early, before everyone else, and pick out some of the best stuff. That's how I got hold of some good clothes that I thought made me look cool or something. I liked Bodie, the Lewis Collins character out of *The Professionals* and I once got hold of a leather jacket like his and I wore it everywhere – never took the thing off.

Mam also done some hairdressing and cleaning to make ends meet – until she got a new boyfriend. She used to ride a bicycle everywhere, cleaning houses the size of Buckingham Palace and sometimes I'd go with her and play on their snooker tables or kick a ball round their huge gardens or paddle in their pools and ponds. The boyfriend's name was Mick and he was thick. He must've been, because if Bob had found out about him, the bugger would've been minus an arsebone. I hated him, he spent all his time in bed round my house and I was all the time being told I couldn't do this and I couldn't do that, in case I woke the wanker up. He had a beige Mini with a yellow roof – can you imagine that? I used to jump on top of it, to try to cave in the roof and he'd go mental when he looked out the window and come running out and throw stuff at me to get me off. But he never hit me – I think he was afraid I'd tell Bob. He didn't know that, while Bob might've cared that he was screwing Andrea, he wouldn't have minded much if the tosser was punching me about. And if I told him he'd only have said:

'Man up, you little prick!'

After all the spike-throwing stuff calmed down, this bloke called Harry Wainman set up a 7-Eleven shop on our estate. He was an ex-Grimsby Town football player and he thought he was like some A-list celebrity, but he wasn't. We'd go in there on the way to school to nick packs of Panini stickers. I was a crazy Liverpool supporter back then and the biggest prize I could imagine was to find a silver Liverpool badge, or a King Kenny sticker – the Scousers were winning everything in the seventies and my bedroom was covered in Reds stuff – posters and team pictures and pennants and all sorts. Anyway, that's got nothing to do with what I was talking about. We also went into the shop on the way home from school and, one time, this mate called Scott pinched a pack of 'jawbreakers'. They were like gobstoppers, only bigger. You had to keep sucking them and they turned ten different colours before you got down to the aniseed pip in the middle. Scott was in front of me and I was just messing about, tapping his heel with my foot and pretending to trip him up. But I miscalculated and caught his ankle and he fell to the ground, jawbreaker in his mouth and hands in his pockets and I heard this smashing sound, like when you break a plate or something. When he got up, he had no front teeth and blood was pouring from his mouth. His dad was a nasty bastard, I knew that, so I ran off home, thinking I'd just got over the bloody spike-throwing – and now this!

Next time I went out of the house these kids started shouting so Scott's dad could hear them:

'He's here . . . the spike thrower!'

Then the bloke came out after me and I ran like a rabbit through the alleys, with all the kids following me and calling back to him:

'He went down here!'

'There he is!'

'He ran in there!'

But I gave them the slip and watched when they ran past me; my heart was beating like a bloody drum and it was like I was in a Rambo movie or something. He never got me, the bastard, but he used to scream at me every time he saw me on the street – for a long time after.

Apart from a few things like that, it was a sort of intermediary time for me back then, between the fear and violence of my very young days and the fear and violence of my later years.

Chapter Three

From four to eight years old I went to Crosby Infants School, Grimsby, on the Bradley Park Estate. Now, I know you're not an infant at eight years old, are you? But that's still what they called the place. All the kids got dropped off in the morning by their parents and it looked like I was the only one without a dad. And everyone had brothers and sisters that were being dropped off with them, but I didn't have none of those either, because Andrea gave them away before I was born. In the beginning, I used to cry when my mam left me there – I used to reach out for her hand when she was moving away from me and heading for the door, with the teachers holding on to me so I didn't run after her. Some kids cry when they start school and some don't. I was a crier. Maybe it was because I was so close to my mother and we were both being beaten up by Bob, I dunno. I'm sure every kid who cries at school ain't being beaten up by their dad, but that's what I put it down to. It was like my mother was my whole life – like I never left the womb or something and it was unnatural for me to be away from her.

Once I calmed down and came to terms with the fact that there was nothing I could do about the situation, I'd get on with painting or plasticining or sand-traying, even though I was still higging, and everything would be all right for a while – until we had to do PE. Now, you wouldn't get five- and six-year-olds prancing about outside in their underwear these days, would you? But it was good for the kids back then, even though it ain't good for them now and we had to do it. Anyway, as time went by, I got used to going to infants school and playing war on the hill in the playground and getting the girls to smell the pissy-beds and holding buttercups under our chins and throwing dick-darts and ending up in the corner with the teacher reading us a fairy tale. So, I suppose it wasn't as bad as all that, was it?

From eight to twelve years, I went to Crosby Juniors and there was no more messing around with little kid stuff. One thing that was a laugh, I had an anthology book where I had to write poems and draw a picture on the opposite page that was connected to the poem in some way. Now, I'm no bloody good at drawing, never have been – the best I can do is a matchstick man with a walking stick or a cat's arse – but my mam was really talented. So I'd write out these poems from the English book and she'd do the drawing for me. They looked bloody amazing and I got my first house points and the teacher was practically frothing at the mouth with satisfaction.

'Exquisite, Williams . . . the detail . . .'

This went on for two years and the teachers were keeping my anthology books and entering them into competitions and stuff and I was getting away with not being a great student at much else because I was a great artist. Then one day the headmaster took me out of a lesson and said he'd like me to draw a portrait of him. It was like someone had slapped me across the back of the head with a wet herring. My heart started doing the bloody rumba and tried to jump out my mouth and make its own escape and my chin must've been touching the bloody floor. My hand shot into the air.

'Toilet, sir, please!'

I thought about doing a runner out of the school and over the wall and never coming back. But I knew they'd only come after me and I'd be dragged through the streets like the liars from the olden days. So, after getting to the toilet before I shit myself, I decided that I'd draw the head and maybe he wouldn't notice that the picture was nothing like the ones in the anthology books, or maybe I could convince him that I was in my Picasso period or something. But it didn't work, I was humiliated in front of assembly and my mother received a letter saying I'd probably turn out to be a forger and it'd be all her fault and the buggers kept a close eye on everything I did after that.

We used to go swimming over at Whitgift, which was a posh school in Crosland Road that had its own pool. This is where I learned that acting the fool and being a clown and making people laugh could save you from getting bullied by the bigger kids. But it had its own risks – it might have scored me some points with the bullies, but it didn't do me no good at all with the teachers. Like, one time at the pool when I was pissing in the shower and spraying it round and making the divs laugh, I didn't notice the PE teacher coming up behind to see what the commotion was about, and when I turned round, he got the full blast of the spray, right down his tracksuit bottoms. I got slapped severely round the head and suspended from swimming.

The clowning stuff got me rulers across the knuckles and sannies across the arse and canes and clouts and all sorts of suspensions, but I reckoned it was better than being bullied. So I kept it up, the clowning – singing songs like:

'Mrs Brace thinks she's ace, cos she won the monkey race.'

Then I'd get caned in front of the whole class for being insolent, or I'd be sent to see the head and he'd ask me how many smacks of the sannie the teacher recommended and I'd say 'six' because I knew the bollocks would check later and if I told a lie it'd go harder for me in the future. The bloody sand shoe had laces and it seemed to me like it had a steel toecap too and the sole looked like it was thicker than a housebrick and I'd have to lay across his lap while the tosser hit me with it – and when I got back to class I'd have to keep shifting from one arse cheek to the other until the pain went away.

The other thing about junior school was the sexual thing. I mean, the bigger boys would interfere with the smaller ones and I'm not bullshitting about this. Maybe it's different now, but back in the seventies and eighties, the wankers would be getting their dicks out all over the place. It was like they were fascinated by the things. I know now it was the onset of puberty, but we weren't taught much about it and these kids knew something was happening to their bodies, but they didn't know what. Now, I'd already seen Peanut's popcorn, so it wasn't a great big deal to me – I knew that dicks got hard sometimes and stuff came out for some reason and I didn't really understand why and I wasn't all that interested. There was other things happening that were more important. Looking back now, I suppose I never knew how vulnerable I was or how all this stuff would affect me later on, when I did get to know all about it.

But I think I've said enough about school, except that Andrea decided to go back there while I was at Crosby Juniors. She started studying hairdressing at Grimsby College of Technology and she worked part-time in salons around the Nunny and did cleaning jobs as well, I think I already told you that. But what you don't know is who she really was. I didn't know myself back then and I was thirty-six before I found out. My mother was adopted when she was a young child and, like I said, she got pregnant when she was fourteen and gave her first two babies away to people in Australia and Scotland. She kept herself to herself and didn't socialise with anyone on the estate and she was really a quiet sort of person. She'd probably be called a 'victim' these days and I suppose, looking back, that's what she was. She was just as vulnerable as me. We were like two little kids together and that's what held us close when everything else was angry and hostile around us.

We had an old couple living next door to us, Mr and Mrs Cash. The old boy died soon after they moved in and my mam looked after the old girl when she got sick. So, you can see she was a kind person, a gentle person, even though she was shat on so much in her life. She became careful about who she let get near her, because her carelessness cost her dear so many times and she learned how to keep herself close inside herself. But she was good to the people she did let in and that's why I loved her and why she loved me.

Bob got access rights to me and I had to go stay with him sometimes at Salamander Close, where he shared a house with his brother, Dave. Uncle Dave was just as big and just as violent as my dad, except he wore a stupid wig – and the more he drank, the more the wig turned round on his head. If he got really plastered, it almost went round back to front. It looked like a dead rat and had double-sided sticky tape that didn't work and it was a different colour to his real hair, what was left of his real hair, round his ears. It would've been funny if Dave wasn't so dangerous and violent.

Anyway, my mother had to put in me a taxi and send me off there and Bob would pay the driver at the other end. I had to stay some weekends and the worst thing about it, I suppose, was the food. Bob was one of those blokes who reckoned, if the grub was good enough for him, it was good enough for me. I mean, what kid likes kippers for breakfast? Or salty bacon with plum tomatoes and spicy Lincolnshire sausages and fried bread – all cooked in lard. It tasted like shit and it made me sick, but I had to eat it – or pretend to eat it until the buggers weren't looking, then I'd empty the plate out the window and the dogs would finish it off. When they saw my plate empty they'd ask if I wanted more, but I'd push out my stomach and rub it and say I was full to bursting.

I thought to myself, I dunno which is worse, me mam's breakfasts or me dad's. I mean, we couldn't afford milk after Bob left and she used to buy 'five-pints' – this was powdered milk and you could get five pints from one pint when you mixed it with longlife stuff and water. It tasted like cat's piss and it made the cornflakes or Rice Krispies go soggy in seconds flat and they looked and tasted like wet bloody cardboard. So, it was a toss-up which was the worst, the soggy cereals or the lardy fry-ups.

I liked it when my cousins were round at Dad's place. Then we'd go out playing football or wandering round the streets and the fields. Otherwise, if they weren't there, we went to the pub and I sat outside with a can of Bass shandy, while Bob and Dave went inside. The shandy was probably my first introduction to alcohol. Afterwards, we went back to the house and sometimes other aunts and uncles might come round. Bob and Dave had a minibar and they'd all drink little green bottles of lager that came in cheap on the boats from Europe. They'd be all over the place, the bottles, on the floor and the shelves and the tables – I picked one up once and drank some of it, but it tasted like something that had come out of a dead person's hot water bottle and I swore I'd never drink the stuff again.

Little did I know!

Everyone smoked roll-ups and Dave had these stand-up ash trays and when you pressed the knob down it opened metal flaps that let the ash and butts drop down to the bottom, or the thing would spin round and I used to sit there watching television and spinning it, while the adults got themselves slaughtered on the piss-lager. When they got into that state, they'd give me money and sometimes I could go home with as much as a fiver – so, I suppose, there's a good side to everything.

My mother's idea of a haircut was a modern style, left long and loose, but that was bloody girly to Bob. He'd take me to the barber's on a Saturday and he'd say to the hair-cutter guy:

'Short back and sides!'

Then I'd come out looking like something from Billy Bunter's bloody schooldays and my mother would shriek when I got home:

'What's he done to you now?'

Bob always wore Farah trousers and white T-shirts and loafers, and when he bought clothes for me, which wasn't very often, they were always Farah trousers and white T-shirts and loafers. I was wearing Farahs at seven, for God's sake, and I suppose he wanted to make me a smaller version of himself and not be such a mammy's boy all the time. Farahs were considered to be 'old men's trousers' by the kids, because they had permanent creases in them, but I didn't really care. I cut the gold 'F' off the back and I was glad of clothes that didn't come out of a jumble sale.

You're probably thinking 'What about grandparents?' and I'm gonna tell you right now. I can only tell you about my mam's parents, Fred and Jessie Roberts, because Bob's mother died of cancer when he was twenty-one and his father, George, lived in a home, because he burned down his house in the Nunny with an electric blanket. I visited him sometimes, but I'm not sure he knew who I was. I used to steal his snuff and then snort it at school so I could get out of class – I'd be sneezing all over the place and brown snot would be flying out of my nose. I didn't go see him much after Bob left, because the kids near the home used to lurk behind walls and throw bamboo canes through the front spokes of my bike and I'd go over the bloody handlebars. George died when I was twelve, so that was that, wasn't it?

Anyway, Fred and Jessie gave me the only, like, guidelines I had as a kid. They lived in Alder View and they had a wooden garage at the end of the garden. They had a coal bunker in the garage and I'd be jumping into the coal and coming out like a pit pony, or I'd get hold of Fred's toolbox and make little wooden boats to sail on the water butt. They didn't have no grass in their garden, just vegetables, like potatoes and onions and broad beans and lettuce and stuff and it all changed with the seasons of the year. They also had a summer house that was made of wooden logs and they creosoted it every year. It was like a safe haven for me when I was younger, like the den in the trees with Mark – only no Peanut. Problem was, Andrea would take me there and I'd go down to the summer house and when I came back she'd be gone.

I hated her for that. Every time she took me somewhere, I never knew if I was gonna be left. Looking back now, I suppose she was just trying to live her life and do whatever she had to do, but it was cruel to a kid who loved her so much and who couldn't stand being without her.

Fred and Jessie bought me this vinyl record for my birthday when I was about seven or eight – it had 'Nellie the Elephant' on it and 'Right Said Fred' by Bernard Cribbins and 'Goodness Gracious Me' by Peter Sellers and Sophia Loren and they used to play it for me and I hated the bloody thing. But they thought it was great and I'm sure they bought it for themselves and pretended it was for me, because they never let me take it home and I was thankful for that. When I got a bit older, like, in the days when I was uncontrollable, if I came round there and played up, old Fred would sit me down and say words to me that meant something, not like the other adults who just shouted and screamed all the time. He never lost his temper, just explained how Andrea was doing her best and I shouldn't be making life more unbearable for her than it already was. Now, you might say this is all bullshit and bollocks, but I listened to old Fred for some reason. But then I'd go back home and things would be different and I'd forget what he said to me.

When I think about it, they were fairly strict – in modern terms, that is. If they had people in the house, the rule was kids should be seen and not heard. But they let me play dominoes and Jessie would set the table with a proper cloth and cutlery and everything and there'd be grapefruit and triangle slices of toast in a little silver stand for breakfast and she had this cake holder with doilies on a trolley and she'd wheel it in with fresh cream cakes and it would be like something out of the olden days. And it was all right when I was younger, I suppose, but I felt isolated there as I got older and then I stopped going round altogether. You see, I kinda outgrew my grandparents. I guess that happens a lot to kids and I liked to roam round and not have to stay inside a house. I suppose it was just me growing up.

One thing that was good though, Fred and Jessie used to take me and Andrea away on holidays, mostly to Scotland. They'd pick up my half-sister, Nadia, who lived in Coldstream and we'd go stay in a caravan park in Pitlochry and tour round the place in their Volkswagen Beetle – I can still remember the registration to this day – L389 EBE. Ha ha ha. I liked it up in Scotland, I could go fishing in the lochs and streams, even though I never caught nothing, but it was beautiful and open and quiet. Only problem was the caravan, it was small by today's standards. The shower was a tiny square cupboard thing and there was no room to manoeuvre once you were inside. Once the door was locked, it was as claustrophobic as a coffin. Now, I wasn't the best kid for taking baths under normal circumstances, but I hated this bloody shower and I'd do anything not to have to go in there – I suppose it reminded me in some way of being locked in the cupboard by Bob when I was little. But Jessie was strict and insisted I take a shower every morning – so I decided to teach her a lesson.

The shower was very powerful in the little caravan and Jessie liked to go in, turn it on and let it run to warm up while she put on her shower cap so she wouldn't ruin her hair-do. Anyway, I had a shower first and when I was

finished I aimed the shower-head so it would be just right.
Bear in mind that, once the door was shut, you could barely
move so, when Jessie turned on the water, it struck her
straight in the face and she couldn't turn it off quick enough
before it soaked her stupid hair-do. I could hear this
screaming:

'*Andreaaaaaaa . . .*'

And I jumped into my bunk and pretended to read a
comic, like I was completely innocent. Jessie came out dripping water off her nose and Mam had to re-do her hair. It
was funny – but I still had to shower every morning.

Other times they'd take us to Humberston, to a place
called the 'Fitties'. There was little wooden chalets, two or
three bedrooms, like prefab bungalows but not as sturdy like.
We'd drive around until we found a 'To Let' sign and Fred
would get out of the car and take a look to see how decent
it was on the outside – tapping the walls and stuff, like he was
an engineer or something. Once we got inside, the first thing
that hit you was the smell of Calor gas, the heaters would be
on even though it was summer and it was like they were
drying the place out after the previous holidaymakers –
whatever they'd been doing. And whatever it was, they
must've been doing it every time we went there, because the
heaters were always on. The next thing you'd see was the car
batteries all over the floor, to power up the black-and-white
television and other stuff and it was like the inside of a do-it-
yourself Tardis, but I loved it. The Fitties was massive, with
all these avenues, like 1st Avenue and 2nd Avenue and 3rd
Avenue and 4th Avenue and so on, all the way down to the

Yachting Club. There was an amusement arcade and all the slots were 1p and 2p and I'd go with a bag of coppers and play push-a-penny and one-armed bandits and Pac-Man and the rifle range. The rifle range had paper targets to shoot at and I always imagined Bob's face on them and they gave us the target to bring home with us if we scored good – which I always did. When all the pennies were gone, I'd hang round the bingo hall and cadge money off the old fogies when they had a win and were all happy-like. I loved being away from the council estate and it was always a problem to settle back in when we came home.

Now, every time there was an election and a new government got in, the council would come round and paint our front door – red for Labour and blue for Conservative. Anyway, when I was about ten, Mam would write poems and send them in to the *Evening Telegraph* and *Woman's Own* and stuff, hoping she could get them printed and make a fiver or something. The arsehole editors never took any of her poems, but I used to check to see, just in case. One day, I was checking the *Evening Telegraph*, when I read this notice in the personal columns. It went something like:

'*I'm looking for Andrea Grace Williams, nee Roberts. Age 32. Contact me at PO Box . . .*'

I sat there reading and thinking 'That's my mother', so I took the newspaper into the kitchen and showed it to her. I remember the look of surprise on her face and it wasn't a nice surprise. She took the paper from me and binned it and said it wasn't her. But I knew it was. I mean, Andrea Grace ain't a common name, like Sharon or Tracy – is it?

Anyway, the Conservatives won the election in 1979 and, a while later, this bloke from the council knocked our door to say they were gonna paint it blue. Our house didn't have radiators, just this blower thing and vents in the wall that had a lever so you could direct the blowing heat where you wanted it. I used to sit on a stool near the vent when I was watching TV – maybe *Moomins* or *Grange Hill* or *Tiswas* – stuff like that, and that meant I was closest to the front door. So, when the bloke from the council knocked to say they were gonna repaint it, I answered it before Mam got there. But, five minutes later, the door got knocked again and I thought maybe the council bloke fancied Mam, because she was very good-looking and she always caught blokes' eyes. I got there first again, but it wasn't the council bloke, it was a middle-aged woman.

Mam was busy and didn't get to the door for a while and I started to have a conversation with this woman.

'You must be Dean?'

'Yer.'

'Do you know who I am?'

'No.'

'I'm your grandma.'

'You're not Jessie.'

'Your other grandma.'

'She's dead.'

She tried to touch my face, but I backed away from her, down the hall. I was confused by this stage, wondering how I could have three grandmas. Then I could hear Andrea shouting.

'Who is it?'

'I think it's the woman from the *Telegraph*.'

Next thing, Mam's in the hall, pushing me away from the door and screaming at the woman to go away, that she wanted nothing to do with her and she should never come back. Mam slammed the door and she was really upset for while and it took her a long time to calm down. I asked if she really was my grandma and Mam said no she wasn't, and that was an end of the matter. I only found out years later that Andrea was adopted.

So, now you know about my grandparents.

Chapter Four

Even after all the bullshit about the spike and knocking out Scott's teeth died down, things were never the same again. I felt like every stupid bastard was watching me all the time and I was completely alone, like nobody wanted to be with me. Everyone else on the estate had brothers and sisters and, if they got bullied, their brothers or their fathers or someone would sort it out. I had to fight my own battles, which I usually lost. I'd pretend to myself I was older, dream I was going to work, jump on a bus with my Multirider and pretend I was driving it on the top deck – anything to escape from who I really was. A Multirider was a weekly pass and you could ride the buses all day round Grimsby and Cleethorpes and Immingham and all the villages; it was like travelling round the world.

One thing that could've got a bit serious – the kids on the Bradley Park were always ringing 999 from the phone boxes to get the fire brigade to come round the estate with its siren going and its big ladder on the back and all the firemen in their gear and helmets, until one time when the chippy van caught fire and the firemen thought it was just another hoax call and, by the time they turned up, one of the women was burnt from the chip fat when it all exploded, or the gas that was used to heat it – no one knows the true facts. The van burned to the ground with all the kids dancing round it like some pagan ritual or something and there was an investigation at school the next day, but nobody ever got blamed.

I didn't mind the chippy van getting burned. It was cheaper for me to take a fifteen-minute walk into the Nunny, where the shop sold chips for a couple of pennies less than the van and the bloke would give me extra scraps that'd crackle away when I put the vinegar on them. And you could turn the newspaper they came in upside down and wear it like the kinda hat a navy man would have. The only drawback was if some of the older kids on the Nunny saw me and pulled up on their Grifters and Choppers, with flails outa the handlebars and wooden lolly-sticks wedged into the spokes to make a noise. It was easier to let them take what they wanted than to run and risk getting battered like the chippy's fish, and they'd gob into the bag before they rode off laughing. But I just flicked the gobby ones out and put more vinegar on and stuffed what was left down my neck in case they came back.

Another time was when the Yorkshire Ripper was on the loose and everyone was hunting for him. I know he never came near Grimsby and did all his killing over Leeds and Bradford way, but a rumour started that he'd been seen in the area and all the mothers wouldn't let their kids out to play on the streets and I seemed to be the only one mooching around out there at night-time. It was like all the kids had been abducted by aliens and I was the only one left and they didn't take me because I wasn't worth anything to them. I thought it was stupid, because he wasn't killing kids, was he? He was killing women.

Anyway, my dad and his brother Dave split up and Bob was seeing a woman called Debbie at the time and they moved into a house in Haycroft Street together. They went on to have two kids and I had to babysit for them whenever I went round there, even though I was only about eight or nine myself at the time. Debbie was nice enough, I got on OK with her, but Bob would take her to the Longship pub and get stinking drunk and come back and start wrestling me, like getting me in armlocks and headlocks and all kinda stupid Boston crabs and stuff. He'd keep pressure on me and almost strangle me until I submitted, like it made him a really tough man or he was hardening me up or something. I'd have bruises all over me and Mam would scream 'What's he done now?' when I got home and sometimes I'd have to wear a polo neck to school on account of the marks on my throat.

I remember one time when I was round Debbie's and she went into town with one of her mates and left Bob with the kids. Her mate had a coloured boy called Gordon who was just a toddler really and he started crying and Bob stuck him in the airing cupboard with all the towels and stuff. This stressed the kid out even more and he was screaming and Bob was screaming back at him and I just kept out of the way, because I knew what it was like and I didn't want to have to go in there with Gordon. I worked it out that this was what happened to kids who cried and that's what I must've been doing wrong all those years – if you cry, you get stuck in a cupboard, or even worse.

So, I stopped crying round about this time – like, it was for babies and I wasn't a baby no more and, even if I got beaten up by lousy arseholes older than me, I wouldn't let them make me cry. If I did get beaten, it was usually over something that happened in school, then at bell time I'd have to go fight the bugger who said something about my mother or called me a cry-babby and we'd fight in the garages on the estate. The other kids would gather in a circle and there was no referee and no backing down. I remember always thinking 'You wait till I'm thirteen, then I'll smash you up, you fucker.' I never thought that, by the time I'd get to thirteen they'd be fifteen or sixteen.

Debbie left Bob, like I knew she would, but I still had to go round there. He had access through the court and I had no choice. The stuff he made me eat got worse – like, he'd chop the head off a chicken and make me watch the thing running round the yard before he plucked it and we had to eat it and I kept seeing the bird with the blood coming out of its neck and I'd gag and he'd shout at me:

'Man up, you prick!'

He always had loads of fish from the boats, like plaice and skate and kippers and he'd do stuff like cockles and mussels and roll-mops and snail-bolognese, all cooked in bloody dripping and looking like something the cat vomited up. Then he'd have his trawlermen mates round and they'd play country and western music and get pissed and I'd have to

sleep in his bed and he'd fall in beside me rat-arsed and I'd
be tucked into his stinking armpit all night, too scared to get
up or move away from him. He'd be farting and dribbling
and fighting in his sleep and I'd finally get up in the morning when the church bells across the road sounded. I'd go
downstairs and put the kettle on and listen to him coughing
and gagging and being sick in the bathroom and I thought
it was just the drink – back then. It'd be Sunday and, after a
while, I'd go home.

Round about this time I started getting mouthy with Mam.
I was growing up and I reckoned I could get away with it.
But she had this swingball bat and, every time I told her to
'Fuck off' I'd get a wallop of it. I often wondered why she
didn't wallop Bob with the swingball bat when he said the
same thing to her, but I suppose she knew he'd only take it
from her and break it across her head. We were still very
close, me and Andrea, like since I was a baby. We'd cycle
around together and take sandwiches and ride for miles and
miles. Sometimes we'd ride into town and there was a half-
price shop called Boyes and she used to buy me Hai Karate
aftershave there – God knows why, I wasn't even shaving.
But the smell made me feel all big and grown-up and hard,
like, and I suppose she knew I needed something to set me
apart. Whenever she had a few quid to spare, she'd let me
buy tapes that were called 'made famous by', which meant
they weren't the real bands on there, but some lousy tribute
divs and I couldn't work out why the music that usually
sounded so great always sounded shit on my tape recorder.

So I'd put the machine up close to the radio and try to tape the top twenty without getting any of the DJs speaking on there, which was practically bloody impossible.

Sometimes I'd go fishing. I had a big green box filled with tackle and maggots and I'd take off on my bike and fish for hours on my own. I loved the freedom of fishing and I could just up and go whenever I liked. It didn't matter to me that nobody else wanted to come, I was happy doing it alone. The other thing was football. I loved it when I was a boy. The first team I played for was Yarborough FC – we'd train every Tuesday at the back of the local swimming pool and after that I went to play for Darley Barbarians and this was a team that won everything, loads of trophies and cups and all the kids would have their families there at the final to see them play, except me. Mam came once, but I ended up wishing she hadn't, because she kept screaming every time I got tackled and calling the referee a blind bastard and it was just embarrassing.

I joined the Boys' Brigade when I was nine, and stayed in it until I was twelve. It meant going to Sunday School and reading the Bible and learning Christian values and all that kinda stuff, and dressing up in my uniform every Wednesday night and going down to the company to do things that I wouldn't have done otherwise. I didn't want to go in the beginning, but Andrea thought it would be good for me, so I did it to please her, more than anything else.

We had a yellow badge with '3rd Grimsby' on it – that was our section. Our motto was 'Sure & Steadfast' and I wore a blue polo neck with an armband that had the badges

I earned on it, like for sponsored walks and helping out the old people and doing other good deeds and stuff. I thought it was poncified and I took care not to let any of the bullies see me when I was all togged up like a treacle soldier, or my life would've been even more of a misery than it was already. But then I found out I was good at blowing the bugle, so the company captain gave me lessons and his own special mouthpiece, called a 'york'. Andrea bought me a bugle. I dunno where she got it but I think it might have been second-hand, because it came in a cloth bag and I dropped it once and put a dent in it. It gave me a new interest and I'd shove the bag into the bell so I wouldn't disturb the neighbours and practise for hours and polish it with Brasso. I could play the last post and reveille and mess-call and church-call and all kinds of stuff by the time I was finished.

We used to go away on annual camp to Swanage, with other Boys' Brigade sections from all over the country and I made friends with some older lads, who were about sixteen or seventeen. When we had a free day, we usually went into town and, once, these older lads gave me alcohol to drink. This was the first time I'd drunk alcohol since the Bass shandies outside the pub, waiting for Bob and Dave, so I wasn't used to it. I remember passing a restaurant and I was so merry from the booze I dropped my trousers and did a full moonie at the customers inside. I was in a right state when we got back to camp and they threw me into my tent to sleep it off. Next morning I was summoned to the officers' mess and I found out that four of them, the officers, were in the restaurant when I did the moonie. I had to peel potatoes for the rest of the day – with a stinking hangover.

But I did go on to win an award for the most improved bugle player and I was asked to play the last post in the officer's mess, which was an honour, apparently, as usually only a junior officer was allowed to play there. This was when my mother met George, one of the captains and they started going out together. It happened real quick and, after a few weeks, we were living with him on a private housing estate called Laceby Acres. Andrea kept up the rent on the old house on the Bradley Park estate, just in case, and I'd bike to school and back from our new home. As it turned out, George was all right. He was a proper laugh and he treated me well enough. He was separated from his wife and he had a young son called Richard. I was sleeping in Richard's bed and it felt strange, because the boy would come visit and stay over every now and then and it was awkward with the two of us in the room. But he was younger than me, so I didn't get any stick from him.

I liked George, he had a football team and he took me training and the men used to get me to fetch the footballs for them and stuff and it was like having a real, full-time father – like I always dreamed about having. George knew I loved football and he arranged a friendly with Grimsby Town and a senior Boys' Brigade side and he let me be ball-boy. At full time, all the ballboys came together for a penalty shoot-out and I was taking penalties against Nigel Batch, who played for Grimsby Town, and I loved it. I won the penalty shoot-out and got a pound note from Nigel and one from the referee and the two linesmen. I was also in the *Grimsby Evening Telegraph* and I had some big bragging rights there for everyone to see. And it was at times like that I really believed I was lucky – like, if something bad happened I expected it, but when something good happened, it was truly a moment to savour.

George had dark curly hair, like Kevin Keegan's, and he wanted it dyed blond. As Mam was a hairdresser, she put all the shit on it, like the foil and potion and all, then they waited to see how it turned out. When they took the stuff off, his hair was green – neither of them said nothing for, like, half a day, just stood there looking at it like they were dreaming or something. Then I started to laugh and George started to cry and Mam had to dye it again and turn it orange before it could be eventually turned blond.

It was summertime when we lived with George and I used to get up early to meet the milkman and go round with him on his float. I'd collect the empties and give him the notes for eggs and an extra pint and no milk for two weeks when they were on holidays. Sometimes they left the milk money under the empties and I'd have some of it for myself, not all of it mind you, because I wasn't a greedy bugger and the milkman would've twigged it. Just a little bit here and there and the people just thought it was kids from the area who nicked it. At the end of the week I got a quid wages and a bottle of silver top that I took home for my cornflakes. It didn't make them go soggy, like the bloody Five Pints stuff and it tasted absolutely lovely.

The Tearaway

Then I'd get hold of a newspaper and study the horses in the back pages like my grandfather used to do and I'd watch him when I was round there and got to know what it was all about. I'd sit outside the bookies until someone I knew came along and I'd give them my money and ask them to put the bet on for me. And if I won, I had to give the greedy buggers part of my winnings to get them to collect the money for me. But I was lucky and mostly won more than I lost and had to give away and I never bet everything, I always kept money back to play Space Invaders with a milkshake and a little container of Nutella in the cafe next door. It was a nice time, kinda free and easy.

After a few months with George, I sensed that something was going wrong. Maybe he was seeing his ex-wife or maybe Andrea was still seeing Mick the prick on the side, or maybe it was something to do with the green hair – I never knew. But the relationship didn't work out and I remember feeling heartbroken – sitting on the sofa with Mam on one side and George on the other and me crying, even though I said I never would again, and everything going dark again after being so bright for a while. The only way I can describe the feeling is like a real bad disappointment – a deep letdown. But, if I was honest with myself, I knew it was too good to be true and I was expecting it to end. I was just waiting for the thing to happen. Being fatherless again.

We went back to Bradley Park.

I always loved the Humberston Fitties, ever since Fred and Jessie used to take me there on holiday. When I got a bit older, I went back there with some of my mates during the six weeks summer holidays. We got our Multiriders renewed and wore our swimming trunks under our jeans and packed our bits of fishing gear and bussed it out past Cleethorpes and into the wilderness. There was a walkway down to the beach at the back of the chalets that took us to a creek – like a river in the sea if you get my meaning, where you could catch flatfish and eels. When the tide went out, I mean way out past Bull Fort, it left a deep ravine where the creek was and it was dangerous to mess about down there, because the sea could come back in and cut you off and then you'd be drowned for sure.

The Yachting Club was near this marshy sea-river and, in the middle, was a rickety old wooden platform that could hold about fifteen kids, like in *Jaws* the movie. We all got on it, pushing and shoving and pretending the sharks would get us if we fell in. Once we stopped mucking about, we cast our blob lines – orange twine with a lead weight and two hooks and bacon rind for bait. Looking for crabs that came up green and legs all tensed to make them look bigger and we dropped them down each other's shirts and screamed and danced around on the old platform like Michael Jackson on acid, trying to get the bloody things out. I've never liked crab all that much ever since.

Then we walked out to the old war forts, past the red and white lifebelts that were spaced out along the coastline. When we got to the edge of the creek we stripped to our swimming trunks and paced along the side, looking across a sixty-foot stretch of water and waiting to see who'd be the bravest or stupidest to go in first – ten-year-old boys, drifting on the day and in a kid's world with no adults to tell us what to do. We didn't know how deep the creek was, or how fast the flow, or if there was really sharks in there. The ripples of sand on either side stretched out for miles like little brown waves and it hurt our feet to walk over them, or when we caught our toes on razor clams. There was nobody else anywhere near us and it seemed like we were marooned in a desert. Then one kid jumped in, his arms spinning like the wheels on a bicycle. Someone else went after him, until all of us were in the creek, swimming for the other side, dragging at the water with our arms, to get through it as fast as we could.

We all made the opposite bank and pulled each other up out of the creek and everyone was out of breath and panting hard from the exertion – glad we made it and didn't drown and glad the sharks didn't get us either. I remember how small we were, running around this big old open space, with trawlers and tankers out on the horizon and Spurn Point in the distance and the old forts covered in barnacles and seaweed. It was like a boy's wonderland, where we could get away from the reality of our crappy lives and be whatever we wanted to be. We investigated the small lagoons all around us, some of them over eight feet deep and the water warm from the sun, like giant baths. We dived into them, each of us with his own private little salt-water tarn that was warmer and deeper and better than everyone else's. Mine had fish in it and I told the others that the fish could talk and they told me things about the sea.

Then we all piled together into one of the pools, raiding it like commandos, laughing and swallowing saltwater and getting sick – having fun and free for a while from whatever shit was waiting for us back at home. We went back to the creek after a while and tried to stay under water, see who could stay down the longest, who could beat the rip tide and undercurrent. I remember counting – one, two, three – getting to twenty and opening my eyes in the shitty brown water and the sun glimmering somewhere up above me. I tried to get to the surface, but I was being dragged all over the place. I knew something was seriously wrong and I wanted to cry, even though I swore I never would. Then I saw a hand coming down through the water, followed by an arm. The hand grabbed my hair and pulled me up until I was gasping for air, then a man hauled me out onto the side. The other kids had seen I was in trouble and called this bloke who was fishing some distance away and he came and saved me. He gave us a bollocking for being down in such a dangerous place on our own and told us to clear off out of it. We didn't go out there again.

McNamara's was a 7-Eleven shop on the estate that sold dried marrowfat peas in cardboard boxes. I'd nick a peashooter from Forwards Newsagents and a box of peas from McNamara's and go guying on Guy Fawkes and tricking on Halloween. I'd get the turnips from McNamara's on Halloween and scoop out the middle and stick a candle inside. Then I'd hang round outside the Bradley Inn pub until the drunk people came out all merry and I'd sing them a song.

The Tearaway

'Black is black, green is green
You got a penny for Halloween?
If not a penny, a pound will do
If not a pound, then god-damn you!'

Most of the drunks would toss me a few coins and, one year, I remember I made fourteen quid – a bloody fortune! But some of the buggers were tight as a duck's arse, and that's watertight, so I'd let them get a bit away from me, then shoot them in the back of the head or neck with the dried peas. Most of the time, they didn't know what was hitting them and thought it was some sort of night insect or something, and it would be hilarious to watch them swatting at the thin air.

On Guy Fawkes Night it would be the same. I'd make up a guy from a bunch of old rags and sticks and stuff and sit outside the pub and, if they didn't pay up, they got stung by the imaginary insects. It was easy money, and I didn't have to pull no bugger's popcorn to make it. So, you see, being a kid wasn't all bad. Especially when I could get out of town, out to Devil's Ditch or the mustard fields – that's what I called them, because of the yellow colour. I know they're rapeseed fields, but when I was a kid I called them mustard fields and that's what they'll always be to me. I'd go hunting through them with a catapult and the yellow stuff smelled like cat's piss and Mam would go mad when I came home stinking. There was another place I called the 'Red Barn' – it wasn't really red, just rusty and when it was late in the evening and the sun was going down, the sky behind it turned red too. There was a pond nearby that was all boggy round the edges and it had all kinds of little creatures, like frogspawn and newts and dragonflies and butterflies and magpies on the roof of the barn, shouting down with their croaky voices.

'Good morning, mister magpie, and how are you today?'

I'd go there sometimes on a Sunday, when I didn't have to go round Bob's.

I've got to tell you about the Army Cadets, which I joined just before I went to secondary school. I thought it would be cool because I'd get to wear a uniform, with a beret and a camo jacket and boots and I'd get to shoot real guns and all. I knew how to march and drill from the Boys' Brigade and it made sense for me to join. But I soon wished I hadn't. We had this sergeant called Jaycock and he was a right tosser. He organised an orientation night march and we had to pay money for food and stuff. It was supposed to take two days, through the coastal parts of Meggies, which is what we called Cleethorpes, and Pyewipe and the Humber Bank. Jaycock and his corporal took two female Air Cadets along for company and they were shooting darts from gat guns at us as we marched. One of them hit me in the shoulder and it hurt like bloody hell.

At about 1.00 a.m. we were ordered to make camp. Jaycock and the corporal had a tent and they were drinking lager and cider in there with the air cadets. That's where our food money went, to buy booze for those wankers. We built a big fire with bits of wood and hay and anything else we could find, but we had no food and no shelter, only sleeping bags and it started to rain. We got as warm as we could and as close as we could to the fire and fell asleep with the rain pissing on our faces. In my dream I could feel myself floating, like I was drifting through the sky, only it wasn't a dream. Jaycock and his drunken corporal thought they'd show off in front of the girls and they picked me up, in my sleeping bag, and threw me onto the bloody fire. I could feel the bag starting to burn but I couldn't get my hands out. The two dickheads were laughing like retarded seals but nobody else was. I started to roll and roll, until I was clear of the fire. The plastic parts of the bag had melted and my hair and face were singed and the two arseholes went back into their tent, still laughing. I couldn't get back to sleep after that.

Next morning Jaycock emerged from the tent, had a piss and started barking orders at us to assemble in two lines, ready to march. I felt exhausted and my clothes were damp from the rain and I looked like a scorched scarecrow. We marched across streams and through marshland and into bogs, until we came to an old brick war-defence building. Then Jaycock decided he was gonna have a survival exercise. We got a minute to run and hide, then him and his mate were coming after us with gat guns and pellet rifles. I ran like everyone else and hid in some reeds and bulrushes. We were told the brick building was safe and our objective was to get back there without getting shot. After waiting for half an hour, covered in ticks and fuck knows what else, I decided to stick my head up and see what was happening. I could see people making their way back to the building, but no shooting. Then, as soon as they reached the place, Jaycock and his mate were waiting inside and peppered them with pellets and darts. I saw kids running back out with holes in their faces, bleeding from their cheeks and chins. This weren't no game no more. This was bloody serious and I decided I'd had enough. I just walked away in the direction of some houses, wet, tired, hungry and stinking. I got to Great Coates and rang my grandma to come pick me up. That was the end of the Army Cadets for me. I heard later that Jaycock got discharged and was lucky not to go to prison.

When I was still at Crosby Juniors, there was kids who pissed themselves and kids who had nits and kids who were weird in this way and that, but the weirdest kid of all was Jamie, who used to pass out for no reason. There must be a medical term for it, but I dunno what it is. Jamie mostly used to faint in assembly and I found this was a way to make people laugh and, when you made the buggers laugh, they didn't pick on you so much. I mean, that wasn't so good for Jamie, but it was for me and, at junior school, it's every man for himself.

After hymn singing in assembly, we had to sit down on the parquet flooring and I'd try to sit next to Jamie whenever I could. Now, when you fart on parquet flooring, the wood vibrates and amplifies the sound. The head would be blah-blahing away about something or other and I'd time it just right to let one rip. The fart would echo round the hall and everybody would burst out laughing. I'd point at Jamie, as if to say 'He done it' and the div would faint and keel over. The teachers would come and take him to the medical room and this would divert their attention from the fart and I'd get away with it. I'd leave it a couple of weeks, then do it again.

I went to secondary school when I was twelve and the reason I mentioned Jamie in the first place is because, without me knowing it, Mam put me down for Hereford, which was a poncey, snobby secondary school and not one for a council estate kid. And I got in, by some sorta clerical error, it must've been, and I didn't want to go there because all my friends were going to Western or Chelmsford – all except Jamie. He got into Hereford with me. Trouble was we had to wear a blazer and tie and that was my worst nightmare. The harder schools were close by and poncey clobber made us a target for the tough kids who went there. So I started wearing the camo jacket from the Cadets over the blazer on the way to school. But that only made matters worse, because I stuck out like a sore bloody thumb and the buggers kept picking fights to prove I wasn't as hard as I thought I looked.

'Oi, you gyppo, fuck off back to your caravan!'

As well as that, the first day I was there some stupid fourth-year bollocks called me Bugs Bunny and another one called me Goofy and the name spread. It wasn't that I had buck teeth or anything, but it made me self-conscious about my mouth and I was afraid to talk to people and just kept my gob shut all the time. In a new school, that's massive and I was being picked on again.

Chapter Five

In the summer, Mam sometimes let me pitch a tent in the garden, as long as I was asleep by 10.00 p.m. Now, you might think this is for kids and not for twelve-year-old boys. But I'd pretend to be asleep, then about 11.00 p.m, I'd bugger off and go wandering round the streets. I'd try car doors and, if they opened, nick whatever was inside – tapes, sweets, whatever. If I found petrol, I'd go over to the playing fields and pour it out in a big cross and then set light to it. It was even reported in the local paper, people seeing this big burning cross in the playing fields every now and then and they couldn't figure out what it was, whether it was aliens or hooligans. When I got bored I'd come back to the tent, maybe about two or three in the morning, sleep for a bit until 5.00 a.m, then go out again. This time I'd raid the papers that were just delivered outside the newsagents, waiting for them to open up. I'd nick the magazines like *Playboy* and *Mayfair* and then go check out the milkman's round, looking under the bottles to see who'd left out the milk money, leaving notes with 'Three extra pints' or 'Eggs please'. Then I'd wait for the delivery and take the extra stuff home with me.

There was also this guy called Steve and he kept ferrets and sometimes he'd let me come with him hunting rabbits. We'd go out on the bikes, with the ferrets in a sack and head for fields far away – maybe ten miles or more. Steve knew where the warrens were and I'd help him set up his snares at the openings. Steve would put the ferret down one of the burrows and wait. Trouble was, there was always burrows Steve didn't know about and the bloody rabbits seemed to suss which ones to bolt out of. We'd see them running off into the distance, then the ferret would emerge and run off after them. I think it was Steve's way of releasing ferrets back into the wild. He never actually caught bugger all and maybe it was a good thing, because I don't think he would've had the balls to gut and skin them even if he did manage to catch one.

When I stayed at my dad's in town, there was this man called Trevor who Bob knew and he was into trainspotting. My father would give me money to go with him, and a packed lunch of cockles and tinned mackerel and liver pâté sandwiches, even though I didn't want to go because I thought it was something only stupid people who wore anoraks and black-rimmed glasses did. But I got to like it after a while and we'd go all over the place and sit on station platforms with notebooks, watching the trains come in and writing down the serial numbers. Trevor took me to York and to museums and we swapped numbers with other spotters and then he took me down to London once. After I saw London for the first time, I knew I'd want to see it again. I knew I'd be back.

It was round about this time I got into body-popping, which was all the rage back then. This film came out called *Beat Street* and I tried to do some of the moves. I got myself a square of lino and a cassette recorder and a few tapes and I polished the lino and put on the Adidas trackie George bought me, that was getting too small for me, and I thought I was the dog's bollocks. I wasn't really, because I should've had a real boogie box and a flash square of laminate and some proper threads, but I still busted all the moves – turtles and caterpillars and windmills and flares and head-spins and backspins and all the rest. There was a little green opposite my house and I'd place the lino there and polish it with Mr. Sheen. Some people would join in, but the wankers would take the piss and start trouble, especially if they were older. So I'd have to pack up and go back inside the house.

There was also a nightclub called Gullivers in town and, on a Saturday afternoon, it played hip-hop stuff and there used to be competitions. Or sometimes I'd go to another nightclub that had under-eighteens on Saturday. I had to look the part, so I went out and nicked a VW logo from a campervan and hung it round my neck on a piece of chain from Wilkinsons. I thought it made me look like one of the Beastie Boys but, in reality, I looked like a proper Charlie.

Even now, at twelve years old, I was still rocking myself to sleep at night – side to side, side to side, until the dizzy, soothing feeling set in and I'd nod off. Mam would wake me in the morning at the last minute and I'd bike it fast to school. She knew I loved to sleep, because I could be a footballer for Liverpool or an actor in a James Bond film or whatever I wanted while I was out for the count. So I was late a lot and it wasn't a good start at a new school. There was eight houses at Hereford and mine was Hillary, after Sir Edmund Hillary, which is where I went for registration and lessons and it also doubled up as a dining room. As I was a first year, I ended up as a 'runner', which meant I had to wait on a table of ten boys – get their stupid cutlery and food and take their stupid plates away – up and down, up and down to the serving hatch. By the time I got my own dinner, the food was cold. I didn't like that at all.

I also got a paper round when I was twelve, to help Andrea out – mornings and evenings in the Nunny. Now, I don't know if I told you this before, but it was bloody dangerous for boys of my age from the Bradley Park estate to be caught alone in the Nunny. The kids there didn't like us new estate boys and they were tough bastards and usually beat the crap out of us. What made it worse for me was I also went to Hereford School and most of the Nunny kids went to Chelmsford and the two schools were on the same piece of land and everybody knew who went to which. So, when I got a paper round delivering in the Nunny, you can see how detrimental to my health this was.

The morning round wasn't too bad, only about twenty papers and I'd get them delivered quick on my bike and be out of there before anyone was stirring. The afternoon round was the problem. I'd have to try and get about thirty papers delivered and get off the estate before the older lads got back from school. If I took too long, I'd get ambushed and beaten up. This happened so much that, in the end, I just went up to them and said:

'Let's get it over with, so I can deliver my bloody papers.'

They'd hold my arms while one or two of them punched me, then they'd empty out my papers and put the bag round my body so's I couldn't move and throw me into someone's garden. But I never cried, and that threw the bastards. They couldn't make me cry and they couldn't figure out the thing with me walking up to them and saying 'Get it over with.' Eventually, they got bored, because beating someone up who didn't care was no fun. So they left me alone.

Anyway, I got sacked from my paper round in the end, so it didn't matter. It was because I decided to do a burglary with this other kid at school and the opportunity came when one of my customers in the Nunny left their keys in the front door. I took the keys and thought they wouldn't notice and they'd just think they were in the house some-where. Me and the other kid planned to come back when they went on holiday and do over the house. I'd know when they were away, because they'd cancel their papers. Thing is, they knew they left the keys in the door and they knew I took them. I remember walking up the path with the paper a day or two later and the next thing the door flew open and this geezer came running out and grabbed me by the throat. He was screaming at me to give him back his keys. It was snowing and I managed to get away from him, but he reported me to the paper shop and I got the bullet. I never did go round to burgle the house, I just threw the keys away and I'm sure they would've had the locks changed – wouldn't they?

I got another paper round soon after, this time delivering the free sheet, which was called the *Target*. I had to deliver three hundred of them and it took me, like, ten bloody years to do it. They ran a competition every week to find 'Tommy Target', a little cartoon character hidden in the paper, and win a tenner. Every bollocks and his brother on the estate wanted to win, so the paper was popular. It was worse at Christmas, with all the promotional shit like catalogues for presents and flyers and dodgy loans and stuff – it all had to be hand-delivered and I couldn't even use my bike because the bag was too heavy and I was leaned over so far with the weight I couldn't steer it properly. If I missed someone, they'd ring up and I'd get a telling off. I only lasted six weeks, then I just got fed up with it and dumped all the papers in Devil's Ditch and they said I was 'unfit for the job'.

I got the usual bullying in secondary school, arseholes trying to flush my head down the toilets and punching me in the stomach and stuff. But, like I said, I didn't cry about it no more, and I never showed any pain. I used to remember Robert Powell on the TV as Jesus Christ, carrying his cross and all that scourging and thorns and stuff, and I figured if he could take all that and not complain, then I could take a bit of bullying. As well as that, I kept up the clowning around and playing the fool and making the stupid divs laugh so they'd leave me alone. But there was a watershed on the way and it came in the form of a fifth year called

Duggie. This bugger said he was gonna get me after school, don't ask me what for – probably because he didn't like my hairstyle or the shape of my feet or some bloody thing, they didn't need a reason. There was a crowd round the school gates at bell time, all chanting:

'You're gonna get your fuckin' head kicked in.'

I pulled on my fingerless gloves and waited for it to happen. Duggie was outside the gate, grinning with his mates. The chant changed.

'Fight! Fight! Fight!'

He hit me straight in the jaw and I saw little bits of white stars in front of my eyes. Then he hit me about four or five times more, before I could even get my hands up to defend myself. I remember feeling bloody angry, not normal angry, but raging like that day when I threw the spike through Andrew's head. Now, you must remember I was tall for my age and about level with Duggie, even though he was a lot older than me. He hit me again in the face and that was all I could take. I can only describe it like I was Bruce Banner turning into the Hulk. *Crack, crack, crack* – he didn't know what hit him and he staggered back away from me. I could see the look of surprise on his face and I went after him and hit him full force on the nose. Blood exploded all over his mush and he put up his hands to protect himself. I hit him hard in the stomach and he threw up, spewing blood and vomit all over the ground.

The other fifth years pulled me away from him and he ran off down the street, trying to wipe the blood and vomit from his clothes. I thought his mates would gang up and do me over but, instead, I suddenly found I'd earned respect. The other kids were looking at me differently now, people I didn't know and even the fifth years. The bullying stopped that day, except for one bastard called Adrian. I was to meet up with him at a later date.

With my new-found popularity, I made friends at Hereford and I'd hang around with these new kids after school and I started to take notice of girls for the first time. This one particular girl called Kathleen made it clear that she fancied me. Like I said, I was tall for my age and she was a couple of years older than me. We went for walks a few times, but didn't get up to much. I was coming into puberty and starting to get spots and stuff, but the worse thing of all was the fact that I wasn't growing any pubic hair. All the other blokes had bloody furze bushes in their underpants, but mine wasn't growing and this was a source of acute embarrassment for me in the showers after PE. It was round about this time I started to question my sexuality. I mean, I knew I liked girls and all that, but I wasn't sure if I was gay and, if I was gay, how would I know? The lack of pubes made me think I was different and I'd remember the stuff that happened with Peanut when I was younger. The more I thought about it, the more confused I got – it was like a battle going on inside my head.

If Kathleen wanted to go a bit far, I pulled back, not because I didn't fancy her, but because I didn't want her to know I had no pubic hair. She thought this was strange, because all the other wankers would've come their coco in their underpants before they even got them off and this started the rumours that I was an iron. Another thing was the tick – like, I'd repeat words, or say I was sorry over and over while punching myself in the chest, or say 'pardon me' for no reason. I did it for years and years, since before I can remember and there was no reason for it, except it must've been something to do with Bob and when I was very young. You'll probably say it was some sort of OCD and I suppose you'd be right, but it lasted until I was thirteen. I also heard voices in my head sometimes, since I was about eleven – like me arguing with another me, one nasty and the other nice – contradicting each other and confusing the hell outa me. Anyway, all this weird stuff made it difficult for me with the girls and it wasn't because I was gay or anything – not that there's anything wrong with gay – but I just didn't know what was what at the time.

I found out Kathleen had a boyfriend when he came after me, even though I never did nothing to her. I stayed out of his way, because he was older and too much for me to handle and I just hung round with a mate who had a girl called Helen. All three of us would go round her house and then they'd start getting serious and I'd have to leave and walk round in the rain for an hour or so, before I could go back inside. I got bored round this Helen's one night, while she and my mate were snogging and I stuck her goldfish into a little microwave she had in her room. It was the first time I'd seen a microwave and I wanted to see how it worked. The other two weren't taking any notice, until the little oven went *kerrrching* and the smell of cooking fish spread round the bedroom. I wasn't welcome back there no more after that.

You could say I wasn't really good at anything in secondary school, not like I was good at art in Crosby, even if my mam did do the drawing for me. Like, some kids are good at English and some are good at maths and some are good at geography – but I was good at bugger all. One thing I kept on doing was making people laugh and I was good at that. Like standing on a table and dropping my trousers while wearing a jockstrap with my arse cheeks sticking out, or lifting up the girls' skirts in the playground and making them scream, or like in chemistry I'd get a sulphuric acid beaker and empty it out down the sink and fill it with water, then I'd suck some up in a pipette and squirt it in one of the kid's faces, right in front of the teacher. I knew it was water, but the teacher and the kid thought it was acid and the kid would be squealing and screaming, thinking his face was melting and the teacher would be throwing water on him and the rest of the class would be rolling on the floor. We had a gas cooker in home economics and you pressed a button to send a spark to light the ring. I got a metal knife and pushed it in behind the button, then I got some kids to join hands and the one on the end touched Mrs Polly, the teacher. Then I pressed the button. The electricity went through me and through the other kids and they were all jumping like a mad Mexican wave and the shock nearly knocked poor old Mrs Polly off her feet. She was really ancient, like about fifty or something, and I'm sure the shock must've made her heartbeat do the bloody rumba.

This kind of behaviour got me into a lot of trouble and I was always being sent to old Brassneck, who was the head. He had a stiff neck that never moved and some people said he had metal rods put in there after an accident. I imitated the way he turned his whole body when he wanted to look round and my name was always being called over the tannoy:

'Dean Williams to Mr Pearce's office!'

But it was more than just a matter of acting the clown for the sake of the other kids; I was also bucking the system, trying to beat it. Some kids use violence to do this, others use defiance, some curse and swear and throw tantrums – I just questioned everything, and the teachers couldn't fault me for doing that. After all, that's what school's all about, ain't it, asking questions? I pushed their buttons and drove them crazy with 'why' and 'how' and 'what' and 'when' and 'where' and every time they answered my question, I came back with another one. You know, like a little kid of four or five asks questions all the time, that's what I was like, and asking in a really innocent way so they had to answer. It was like I was going out of my way to muck up the system and the teachers would eventually lose their rag and make me go sit somewhere on my own. This didn't bother me, it just proved to me even more that I was different. I knew I was.

One teacher I liked was Mr Freshney in metalwork. I had to stay in for school dinners because Andrea was so skint all the time and Mr Freshney would send me for his chocolate eclairs and let me keep one for running the errand. He was

a funny man, always being sarcastic and coming out with
stuff that was different from the other boring teachers. Like,
he'd hold up a file and say, 'This is a *bastard* file.' Then he'd
get us all to repeat what he said. Louder and louder, like he
found it hilarious to get thirty kids to shout out the word
'bastard' and there was nothing wrong with it. He was the
one I went to the first time I got suspended, and he
understood.

After I won the fight with Duggie, I wasn't worried
about nobody any more. It got me a reputation and I was in
lots of rucks after that and I very rarely lost. Anyway, this
big kid challenged me and he did this thing of swinging out
wide with his right fist and I'd be watching it and he'd hit
me with his left – straight in the jaw. He did it three or four
times before I wised up to what was happening – right fist
swinging out wide, nowhere near me, then the left coming
in and catching me square while I wasn't looking. There
was a big crowd round us and he was laughing every time
he landed a shot. It was like I was hypnotised by this fighting technique for a while, then I woke up. I didn't watch
the wide swing, just hit him before he could make a move
with the other fist. He stood looking at me like a copper
in a traffic jam, waving his arms all over the place. Before
he could recover, I caught him straight on the nose and I
heard it crack and saw the blood spurt out, all over me.
Then the teachers broke it up. The big kid was taken to
hospital and I got suspended for three days. Before I left, I
went to see Mr Freshney. He drove me home, all covered
in nose-blood.

'Dean, nobody died. Three days and you'll be back in school. It's not the end of the world.'

And it wasn't. The end of the world was yet to come.

I'd hang round town with my Hereford friends on Saturdays. We'd meet up with older lads and girls and just walk round in gangs. We'd go in the shops in fives and sixes and nick Gold Spot mouth freshener and computer watches – Tip-Top and Dixons and Binns. I'd wear a jacket with elasticated cuffs and I'd slip stuff up under the wrists and hold it in the sleeves till I got outside. I'd wear baggy trousers into the clothes departments of the big stores and take two or three pairs of jeans into the changing rooms and come back out carrying one and wearing the others. Woolworth's was handy for nicking chocolate and music singles and I stashed all the swag under my bed. It was the only way I could get decent clobber, like the kinda stuff the other kids had, the ones with fathers and older brothers. Mam couldn't afford brand names and the money I saved from the paper rounds and scams I pulled wasn't enough.

I did manage to buy a pair of Puma King trainers from Sports Supply once, and they made me feel bloody great, special like. And this gave me a taste for style. Back then perms were in fashion and I had a wedge done by Mam, but she didn't do it right, or maybe I didn't explain it right, but I looked like one of the stupid buggers out of the Human League. Everybody else at school had a proper wedge, so I told them mine was a more up-to-date version and I had to let it grow until I could get it done again – properly.

Like I said, I was getting more mouthy the older I got. I came in from school one day and Andrea asked me what all the stuff was under my bed.

'Never mind, you silly cow!'

I said it more out of embarrassment than brazenness, because I thought she meant the porn mags I'd nicked from the newsagents, but she was talking about the digital watches and the mouth fresheners. Then, out of nowhere, my head was smashed against the wall and I was knocked out cold. When I came to, Bob was standing over me. I didn't see him behind the door when I came in and gave Mam lip. He bent down and handed me a fiver while I was lying on the floor and told me to stop causing grief for my mother. Then he was gone.

I calmed down for a while after that, in case he came back. But it wasn't for long. I'd take the bus into the town centre and wander around People's Park and hang out at the Bandstand. Fridays would be Thunderbird night, drinking cheap fortified wine and smoking, girls hanging round and being pulled into the bushes by the older boys – and me one of the youngest there and watching everything that was going on. This is where I had my first experience of butane gas. The way you did it was to get a can of gas, spray it onto your scrunched-up sleeve and inhale it. I was on a kid's rocking horse at the time and the more I rocked it, the more it took off. I was hallucinating and thought I was riding Red Rum and I ended up putting my teeth through my bottom lip and my face was all frosted up and I had a headache for two days after it.

But once I did it the first time, I had to keep doing it and I was soon using a tin a night. It got so bad I was banned from buying the stuff in the local shops and I had to cycle miles to new shops that hadn't served me before. I told you about my green tackle box, well I kept it in the cupboard Bob used to lock me in when I was a kid and, after I used up a can, I'd crush it and throw it into the tackle box. Soon, I wasn't able to shut the lid, it was so full of crushed up cans. I got a name in school for being a 'druggie' and a 'solvent abuser' and I was losing my grip on reality a bit.

But the feeling was great, it made me light-headed and then I'd hallucinate, feeling all numb and tingly. It was in this fucked-up state I met Andrea's new husband-to-be. I was absolutely wasted on gas in the front room – I mean really gone. I'd done a full can after school and I was half-off and half-on the sofa when I heard Mam coming through the front door. I could hear her talking to someone.

'Come and meet Dean.'

My arms felt like heavy dumbbells and my feet were like they were set in concrete. I opened one eye and the gas can fell from my left hand and rolled across the floor and stopped at his feet. Andrea began to shout.

'What have you done? What have you done?'

It wasn't exactly the best introduction I could have to my new stepdad.

Chapter Six

By the time I got to fourteen, I was well ranked in school as one of the hard kids. I was even getting into fights with kids from other schools who wanted to take me on, just to build up their reputation – but I mostly beat the buggers and I only ever lost to kids who were bigger and older than me and, even then, not very often. Anyway, this kid called Woody came into school one day with a tattoo of Woody Woodpecker on his arm. I thought this was the proper dog's bollocks and it made him look right and hard – I knew I had to get one. Thing is, you had to be eighteen, but I was tall for my age, even if I was skinny, and I knew I could get away with it if I didn't say too much in a squeaky voice.

At this particular time, I was going over to the local college and getting sacks of sawdust from the woodwork department. I'd sift through it to make sure it was fine and re-bag it. Then I'd take it round the pet shops on my bike and sell the bags for £5 each. There was an old Polish guy with a mobile pet van doing the rounds on the Nunny and he used to take most of it and I knew the greedy old bugger would divvy it up into smaller bags and make ten times what he paid me for it, but it got me a bit of spare cash.

So I got £6.50 together and I brought a change of clothes into school with me, so's I wouldn't have to go into the tattoo shop in my uniform and I headed down to Freemo, which is what we called Freeman Street. I went in all casual-like and browsed the albums of pictures – there were ships and dragons and skulls and full-length arm sleeves and big buggers that would cover the whole of your back, but all my £6.50 would buy me was a swallow the size of a 50p piece. Anyway, I agreed to have it and told the tattoo guy I was eighteen and he believed me – maybe he didn't believe me and just wanted to take my money, but I didn't care, as long as he agreed to do it. He held my left arm straight to keep the skin taut and the needle started to go in and out a thousand times a second, but I never felt no pain or nothing like that. It was my first tattoo and the feeling was awesome.

The swallow itself was a fiver, so I had £1.50 left over and he offered to do three letters in a scroll underneath for 50p each. I should have said MAM, but all I could think of was BOB, so that's what the tattoo guy did – and now I was stuck with my father's name on my arm for all eternity.

'Dean Williams to Mr Pearce's office!'

The Tannoy rang out again as I was coming back into school from breaktime. It seemed to me like I was the only kid ever being called to the head on the bloody thing. I wondered what it could be this time. When I got round to his office, Andrea was sitting there with two men. I just slumped into a chair, not caring all that much. It turned out they were detectives that had been called in by my housemaster, Mr Webster, because he was worried about my welfare – whatever that meant. The detectives weren't impressed with my sulky scowl and they told me I was going into care. That sat me up straight! They said I'd become unteachable and unmanageable and I was so shitting myself I wanted to cry, for the first time in a long time. I looked at Andrea and I could see she was nearly crying too. The detectives asked me if I wanted another chance and I nodded real fast and kept nodding, like a stupid dog in the back of a car. They stood up and said, 'All right.' But if there was any more nonsense – that's how they put it – I knew where I'd be going. That's why Andrea decided I needed a man in my life and decided to marry Alan.

Before this, I met a lad called Nimbus – I know the name means a cloud or something, but he was cool enough. He was working and he had all the kind of clothes I liked and he knew people in town who hung round the phone boxes. They were called 'Dressers', because they wore the best gear, like Pringle and Kappa and Tacchini – they were the coolest kids in town. Nimbus had a car and was on a YTS and earned £29.50 a week. He introduced me to a lad called Geordie who was from the Willows estate and he was hard as nails. I saw him fight in town when his leg was broke from a kick and he was dancing round on one foot, but he still won the fight. That was my introduction to football hooliganism. I wanted to be involved in it. I was a teenager now and this was the scene for me, but I knew I'd never be able to afford the clothes or the kudos.

Anyway, Geordie told me Grimsby was playing Doncaster on the Saturday and, if I wanted to go, just turn up at the train station. Which I did. There was about three hundred people waiting for the train when I got there and they were all singing and drinking Skol lager and getting hammered. I didn't know anyone, but Geordie introduced me around to a few of them and someone handed me a can and I started singing too and it was like I was OK, I was one of them. We came out of the station at Doncaster shouting slogans and we marched through the town. Down the High Street, we were met by police on horses. Doncaster supporters began to assemble at the other side of the police line and we shouted at them and they shouted at us and things got thrown over the heads of the coppers. I was really buzzing and I loved it! Police were taking out the ringleaders and, all of a sudden, two plain-clothes bastards grabbed me. It was because I picked up a piece of concrete shaped like a tennis-ball outside the station and I was throwing it from one hand to the other and shouting insults and swearing and the coppers must've thought I was gonna smash someone with it. The other lads tried to pull me back, but uniformed reinforcements came in and truncheons began to swing and I was dragged to a van. I was fourteen years old, my first game – nicked under Section Four of the Public Order Act.

'What's your name?'

'Scott.'

'Scott who?'

'Scott fuckall to do with you!'

A punch in the ribs soon knocked the cockiness out of me. They took me to the station for 'processing'. I was charged with threatening behaviour and possession of an offensive weapon and was held until the game was over, along with about twenty others. Then we were taken back to the station and put on a train for Grimsby. But it was OK, because I was now initiated. I was in. So you can see how I was going from bad to worse, as they said, and why Andrea must've thought it was a good idea to get me a new father.

After that, I didn't want to go to school no more. I mean, I was a tough-guy now, knocking around with Nimbus and Geordie and hanging with the Willows and Wybers estate gangs. As well as that, it was coming up to the holidays and this lad called Les got me a job down on the docks. It was working in a place called Penguins, would you believe, that sorted out all the fish as they came in from the boats. My job was to put plaice and sole and other types of fish onto big square sheets of plastic on a tray. When the tray was full, it would go into a metal trolley with another maybe forty trays and I'd push the whole thing into a blaster freezer that was 35 degrees below. It was a five-day week, starting on Sunday at midnight, until 6.00 a.m. on Monday. I'd walk into town and then, once I got to the level crossing in the town centre, I'd traipse along the train tracks, all the way down to the docks. There was always trains coming and going from Meggies, so I'd have to keep a lookout for the white headlights and then jump off the tracks till they went past. I was getting paid £56 for thirty hours work.

I'd given my age as eighteen and no one was the wiser

until I was there for about four weeks. You see, there was this lad called Daz working in a factory across the road and he lived on my estate. He was one of the older kids who used to make my life a misery when I was younger. Well, I went over there one morning when I finished my shift and found out he was in the shatter-packing room. I walked in and took my jumper off and set about the bastard. He didn't know what was going on and I took him by surprise with four or five digs to the face and me shouting like a lunatic:

'It's my turn now. This is payback, you fucker!'

Then I put my jumper back on and walked out, same way as I walked in. A day or two later I was called into the office at Penguins and given my pay and my marching orders. Daz had packed in his job, but before he went he grassed me and told them I was only fourteen.

Spiteful, eh?

But, as it turned out, the manager of the place across the road where Daz used to work was now a man short in the shatter-packing room and he gave me the job, doing twelve-hour shifts. Now, I didn't know what shatter-packing was, but I soon found out. I turned up the following Sunday at 6.00 p.m. and was given a pair of wellies and a white coat. There was about twenty of us in the room on that first day, mostly grown men, along with a couple of eighteen-year-olds – and me. All I could see was boxes and boxes full of great blocks of frozen fish in blue plastic. These boxes were probably half my bodyweight and almost the full width of my outstretched arms. The job was to take a box, lift it as high as you could, then smash it down on the floor. The ice would shatter and the blue plastic would unravel and the frozen fish would then have to be picked up off the floor and thrown into baskets.

At the end of the week, after sixty hours, there was only three of us left – and I'd earned £130 pounds. This was a fortune to me and, along with nicking the milk and the fruit 'n'veg and the newspapers on my way home in the early hours, I thought I was on the pig's back at last. But the school holidays were coming to an end and I didn't want to go back there to the teachers and the kids, because I thought I was a real man now and didn't have time for all that juvenile shit. The school saw it a different way and so did Andrea.

My mother met Alan and we moved in with him on a nice estate in Grimsby called Waltham, which was out in the suburbs – it was like Mam moved in with these geezers as soon as she met them and she didn't think too much about my opinion of them or what could happen if we didn't get on. They used to pay a lot of attention to her in the beginning when they met her first and she never waited for the infatuation to wear off before she jumped in with both feet. Anyway, he had a semi-detached house and two sons. They didn't like me much and I didn't care all that much. They were older than me, one was in the army and the other was a hippie student. Alan was a model citizen. He was the manager of a Special Needs horticultural centre – a massive farm for men with Down's syndrome and other ailments. They were given private day-care at the centre and Alan was in charge. The other thing he did was breed prize budgies, which he sold for thousands of pounds all over the world. He was even on TV and in magazines and newspapers as an expert and I thought it was all a bit pukey because he thought he was so important, his shit didn't stink. Don't get me wrong, he was good to my mother and treated her well, but I'd got to the stage where I didn't give a shit about being loved or cared for and all I wanted was for my pubic fucking hair to grow.

I don't know what Alan thought about his new stepson, but our first meeting with me being smashed on the gas should have given him some idea of what might be to come. But he never said nothing to begin with and things just sorta deteriorated between us. I didn't have any respect for him and he had no respect for me. I don't know if he cared about it, but I didn't give a shit. Things came to a head one night when we were watching telly and he was taping a programme about budgies. I was watching *The A-Team* or something and he decided he wanted to watch the budgie programme as well as tape it. I had hold of the remote – when I say 'remote', it was a box with a twenty-foot flex on it, but I suppose you didn't have to get up to switch channels – and I wouldn't give it to him. I said it wasn't fair that he should tape a programme and watch it as well and he said it was his TV. But I still wouldn't hand over the remote and he tried to take it from me by force. Something snapped inside me and I smashed him three times in quick succession in the right eye. It ballooned up straight away and closed completely and I was made to go to my room by Andrea. Once I got there, I began to smash it up out of sheer frustration, just like Bob used to do to our house back when I was a little kid, and when my mam came up we had a fight and I pushed her down the stairs. Anyway, Alan had to go to hospital and when they X-rayed his eye they found out I'd fractured the socket.

Alan didn't press charges but, don't forget, I still had a court appearance pending for the Section Five and I was now told I'd end up in detention. I was still hanging round with Nimbus and he gave me some of his clothes so I fitted in with everyone else. Everyone was wearing the baggy look, white baggy cords and Kappa T-shirts and brown deck shoes. We'd go into town on Saturday and all the different groups would be there and sometimes it would kick off if a girl from one group made a move on a lad from a different group. I loved the sense of loyalty being part of a group – like all being brothers and looking out for each other. But as the court date got closer, I convinced myself I was gonna be locked up and the others decided I needed a good night out on the town, just in case it'd be my last for a while.

So I legged it home sharpish after school and got changed into the gear and met the lads at 7.00 p.m. We went to Pier 39 and got hammered. The next day in class I was hungover and drinking water out of a sink in the physics lab because of the dehydration.

I just turned fifteen when the Section Four finally came to court. We went up to Doncaster magistrates and I was surprised when I got off with a fine and a warning. They considered sending me away, but the magistrate said she wanted to give Andrea a break because she'd just got married to Alan. And I was now very lucky to have Alan for a father and they hoped he'd able to keep some sorta control over me – good job the stupid divs didn't know about the eye-socket. Anyway, they gave me a lecture that I wasn't listening to because I was so happy to be getting off so lightly and a bonus was that I was now in with Geordie and the Willows estate gang.

So, I didn't learn much from the experience and kept on doing what I'd been doing – hanging out with the gangs and drinking and doing the gas and stuff. Then one night I got arrested again, this time for being drunk and disorderly. They kept me in the cells overnight and I bit the letters 'GHS' into the wall-plaster with my teeth – 'GHS' stood for 'Grimsby Hit Squad', which was the hardest gang in town and I was making out I was one of them, which I wasn't. The coppers weren't impressed and just laughed at me in the morning because I was hungover and my mouth was full of plaster.

'Serves you right, you stupid bastard!'

I had to go to court again charged with criminal damage and I got six hours community service. They made me paint a youth club in town that was across the road from my dad's house – would you bloody well believe it? And the next time I went to the police station to report in, Bob was there with my mother. I wondered what the hell was going on, until Andrea shouted at him:

'You have him! I'm sick and tired of him!'

So I went back to live with my father.

It wasn't too bad to begin with, Bob was away at sea for three weeks at a time, so I was mostly left to fend for myself

– get myself to school, cook my food, do my washing, all that kinda stuff. I wasn't allowed to have anyone in the house and I knew the nosy neighbours would grass me up if I did. I mostly twagged school when Bob was away – go into town thieving or just go on the gas and get spaced. They sent letters from the school but I always intercepted them and I signed them and sent them back to the headmaster. But when Bob came back I had to toe the line and it wasn't long before I was called to Mr Pearce's office again. It turned out I'd signed the bloody letters 'D. Williams', not 'B. Williams' and they wanted Bob in to have a talk with him. I said he was at sea and I'd give him a message, but the secretary rang home and talked to him direct.

The thing about my father was, he wasn't a bad bloke when he was sober and he'd stick up for me sometimes and he didn't like toffee-noses talking down to him. So he told the secretary and Mr Pearce to go fuck themselves and that was the end of that. Except the head told me I was on report again and I was uncontrollable and a drain on the school's resources and he wanted me out – which was fine with me.

But, as you know, when Bob was drunk it was a different story altogether. I decided to do something to thank him for sticking up for me with the school, so when he went to the pub, I went out and bought him haddock and chips and mushy peas and onion rings. I thought it would be good for us to sit down and eat together when he came in, like have a good chat and be like mates or something. I was fifteen now and not a little kid no more and we could talk like men did and forget all about the stuff that happened in the past.

He came in bollocksed drunk, saw the oven was on and opened it. Then he bellowed at me to get into the kitchen. He started screaming at me about the onion rings, saying why the fuck had I wasted his money on something he could make himself. It was just an excuse to be a bastard, like he always was when he was drunk and he threw the whole plateful into the bin. Then he turned round and cracked me twice and I went down on the ground. I was raging inside and wanted to kick the shit out of him, but I knew he was too big for me.

He went back to sea again soon after – and I was glad!

When I did go to school, I got friendly with this girl called Sam. My pubes were beginning to grow and I wasn't so self-conscious, but I was still a bit wary with girls, because I still didn't really know if I was gay or not and I wasn't all that anxious to find out. Anyway, we'd hang round in People's Park together and sometimes I'd go back to her house and drink her parent's alcohol when they weren't there and play Ouija board and stuff. We weren't doing nothing sexual, just being friends and hanging out together. Anyway, Sam had a boyfriend three years older than me and it was just like when I was mates with Kathleen and these bastards must've been a bit insecure or something if they thought I was poking their girlfriends when I wasn't.

Anyway, this Sam's boyfriend was on steroids and into weightlifting. He must've heard something about us, because he started waiting for her outside the school gates with some Jock cousin of his. I was twagging again at the time because Bob was at sea and this bloke made it known he was gonna sort me out, good and proper. I used to meet up with the lads at the Market Hotel pub and hang out around there till about eleven or so, then get my fish 'n' chips and go home. This Thursday I got there early, before any of my mates, and Sam's boyfriend was standing with his dopey cousin, chests all puffed out and muscles bulging and I reckoned I had a choice, run and have to avoid the bollocks for the next fifty years, or face up to them. I knew the pair of them would batter me like a bloody haddock, but there really was no choice, was there? So I walked straight up to the mullet –

'Here I am.'

That's all I said. The people who were there stopped talking and waited to see what would happen. The bloke knew he had to do something before the gang turned up and I could see I'd taken him by surprise and he was thinking about it. Then his stupid cousin hit me and I just covered my head and let the punches rain down from the pair of them. I knew I'd get a shot at them eventually, but before I could this Jock arsehole saw I wasn't going down and he must've thought he was Bruce Lee or something, because he started hitting me with a set of nunchucks.

Before I knew anything, this paratrooper was passing and grabbed the Jock with the nunchucks and held him back away from me. That was the opening I was waiting for, I laid into the weightlifter boyfriend bloke and knocked seven colours of crap out of him and he put his hands up like he had enough. Then the para took the nunchucks from the Jock and pushed him in towards me.

'One at a time. It's your turn now, mate.'

But the Jock had seen what I'd done to his cousin and he didn't fancy it, so they both sloped off together and I never got no bother from them again. I was in town the following Saturday with Nimbus and feeling sore from the pasting I'd taken, when two GHS lads came up to us and asked if I was the kid who stood up to the weightlifter and his cousin. I thought for a minute they were friends of Sam's boyfriend and I was in for another going-over, but it turned out they saw what had happened and they were impressed and said I could hang out with them if I wanted. Now, the GHS boys were the toughest, they were hooligans and football thugs and everyone was scared of them. They travelled in packs and drank in packs and fought in packs and they were the fucking business as far as I was concerned when I was fifteen. It was a big deal to me to be allowed to hang with them. I was on the bottom rung of a very long ladder.

I don't want you to get the wrong impression – the lads from the GHS were just normal on most days, like when they weren't on the streets and that was all part of the culture and you had to be in with some gang or other or you had no protection. Otherwise we just played cricket on Ainslie Street in the summertime, or footy in People's Park. Or we'd go up to Corporation Bridge that was a lifting bridge in the old fish docks that used to have trams running over it and you could still see bits of the old tramlines. It had a great view over the whole River Humber where the old ferries would be moored and the names of lots of the workers who built it were engraved into the girders and it took ten men to drive the mechanism that raised it. The bridge was next to the bus depot on Victoria Street and we used to go in there and get old inner tubes from the bus tyres and the mechanics would blow them up for us and we'd spend the whole day jumping off the jetties and swimming or fishing for whiting and eels. So you can see, can't you, these lads weren't crazy psycho-killers like some of the newspapers made out – they were just lads like any others. Except that the gang culture was part of who they were at the time.

Then Bob came back from the sea and, when he went to the pub, someone told him who I was hanging round with – maybe it was the para or someone else, who knows – Bob had a way of finding things out. I think people told him things just to get on the good side of him. He started having a go at me again when he came home pissed, pushing me and asking me if I thought I was a tough guy now I was hanging round with football hooligans and arseholes. He asked if I thought I was hard enough now to take him on, but I knew I wasn't. I just walked away from him.

'One day, you fucker . . . I'm gonna bury you!'

I just said it under my breath, but he heard me all the same. Next thing I got smashed in the kidneys and fell down, winded. He started stamping on me and I was trying to get a puff out of an asthma inhaler, but he kicked it away from me and punched and punched and punched. When he stopped and left the room, I crawled to the front door and out into the street. I got to my feet and hobbled to the bus stop. I got on a bus to a place called Park View in Meggies. It was a kids' care home and I had a mate called Shaun who lived there. That's where I spent the next six months.

Chapter Seven

When I got to Park View, it was like a relief more than anything else. I told them what Bob had done and they took me in – it was better than going back to my mother and Alan and his poncey habits and his stupid budgies. It was as if I wanted to teach them all a lesson for not looking after me properly, if you can understand that. Going into care would be like they failed in their duty as proper parents and everyone would know and they'd feel guilty for fucking me up like they did. I only intended it to be for a week or so, then they'd come and get me and be all sorry and stuff and we'd go home and live happy ever after. But it didn't turn out like that. I waited to see who'd be the first to have me back – but no one came.

Park View was just a big terraced house, really. There was me and six other boys and the couple who ran it had their own kid called Darren. They had these weird rules and superstitions, like we couldn't say 'rabbit' and shoes on the table was a grounding and if anyone spilled salt, we had to throw it over someone's shoulder. The social workers came the day after I got there and they said they'd been round to see my dad and he told them it was just a misunderstanding, nothing to be worried about. They examined me for cuts and bruises and stuff and agreed I could be taken in under the Voluntary Care Rule, which meant they didn't see my case as being critical and it would be a temporary stay.

We all slept in bunk beds and, one night just after I got there, I was half awake and half asleep when I heard this tapping noise. It had a kinda rhythm and I started rocking my head to it, to make me drift off to sleep, which was something I still did. I woke again after a couple of hours and found that my bunk was wet. I thought I'd pissed it myself, maybe because of the reality of being in care or some other stupid psychological thing – or maybe I was dreaming I was swimming and decided to take a leak in the pool. I kicked the covers off and banged my head on the top bunk and water dripped down onto me. The bollocks above me had only pissed himself and it'd soaked through his thin mattress and saturated me. I dragged the bugger out of bed and he was screaming and the carers came in and shouted at us and pulled us apart and I nearly got thrown out. But they gave me another chance and we reversed the sleeping arrangements, with me on the top bunk and him on the bottom and it was all right after that.

I liked it at Park View in the beginning, once I got used to the rules. It was like a big family and I seemed to fit in with them. The carers were called Pete and Ann and she was a big Geordie woman with a good sense of humour. We had rotas for doing chores like washing up and garden-ing and hoovering the carpets and stuff and one day I decided to play a trick on Ann. It was my turn to do the carpets and I hid in the cupboard where they kept the hoover. I waited for ages, until Ann finally came, moaning that the carpets hadn't been done and she'd have to do them herself. Now, Ann was about sixteen stone and not a woman to be messed with. She pulled open the cupboard door and reached in for the hoover. I jumped out shouting 'Surprise!', but I barely had the word out of my mouth when she gave an unmerciful shriek and punched me straight in the face. I was unconscious for about ten minutes and she thought she'd killed me. She was relieved when I came to and she made me promise never to pull a trick like that again.

But pulling pranks and making people laugh was part of my persona by then, branded on my subconscious by the bullying at school. Fridays was always fish'n'chips for dinner, which I liked. It was a notch up from the shit done in dripping round Bob's and the healthy stuff I had to eat at Alan's house. On Saturdays, Pete got us a VHS video to watch and one time it was a slasher movie like *Halloween* or *Friday the 13th* or something, I can't remember now. Anyway, I'd seen this film before and I knew there was a part where an orange ball gets thrown onto a carpet by the crazy man before he kills all the kids and I pretended to go somewhere, for a piss or something, and hid behind the sofa. The room was dark and all the others were on the couch glued to the screen. Once the scene in the film came, I lobbed a ball over the sofa and it bounced on the carpet in front of them and they all nearly shit themselves, jumping up and screaming and running all over the place and I couldn't get off the floor for laughing.

The downside was I couldn't go out or, if I did, there was a 9.00 p.m. curfew. I also had to attend social courses and classes in English, maths and sports. The little pocket money I got went on rolling tobacco and fag-papers. I learned to roll the ciggies thin, like they do in prison, to make sure the tobacco lasted and, wherever I went, I'd raid ashtrays for butts, then split them for the tobacco which supplemented the rolling stuff. The other kids all had counsellors and sometimes they'd have to go to court if they re-offended – usually *twocing*, taking without consent, or joyriding or burglary. If they got sent to a detention centre, a replacement kid would come to Park View. I was the only one who wasn't in that system and who was temporarily permanent, if you get my meaning. I had two parents, but neither of them wanted me and I didn't want them. That's not strictly true, I wanted my mother back, but I didn't want her with a boyfriend or a stepfather. I wanted her to myself, like it used to be when I was a little kid and Bob would be away at sea. Like when we had each other and there was only the two of us. But I wasn't a little kid no more and I knew I wouldn't get those rare times back again – ever.

After liking the place to begin with, the longer I stayed at Park View, the more restless I got. Like I said, it was all right in the beginning. It was a novelty being part of a family, even if it wasn't a real family. But I started getting into trouble, sneaking out through a window when Ann and Pete weren't there and staying out late and getting grounded and having my pocket money confiscated and getting lectures from the house guv'nors. I thought, sod all this and, as I was under a Voluntary Care Rule, I asked if I could be allowed to try and make things up with my mother and Alan. They came to the home and we all sat down with social workers over a period of a few weeks and things seemed to be going well. They let me go to them for weekend visits at first and they took me to youth clubs to make friends with proper kids, not the hooligans I was associating with, and I had to learn how to cook for myself and take lessons in social behaviour. It was like I was being programmed to live on my own, rather than to go back into a family.

They also let me go stay with my father. He took me out with his brother, Dave, on a tugboat over the weekend. It was a two-day short-haul job and I got to steer the boat and was up on deck with them while they towed a ship into the docks at Immingham. They called it a pleasure trip and I had my own bunk and they let me wander about the boat with the crew. It rained most of the time we were out at sea, but it was an adventure and I saw for the first time what life was like for my father – going out onto the wet deck and seeing the massive ropes thrown over to the bow of the ship. They showed me the radar, how it went round and collected all the ships' positions and they told me their tug was the latest thing and it could turn 360 degrees on a two-inch washer. All the rudders and stuff were under the centre of the boat and when they let me steer it I thought I was Captain bloody Kidd the pirate. It wasn't easy, I had markers to follow, but as soon as I turned the wheel the boat seemed to lag by a few seconds, so I was forever steering to port to correct the veer to starboard – they're the seaman words for left and right – 'port' and 'starboard', in case you don't know.

When we got back to shore, we washed up and went to the pub. We played pool and darts and the jukebox and it felt like they were treating me like a man instead of a boy – like I was equal to them, even if I wasn't. The place had no carpet, just lino floor covering and we waited there until they got called for the next job. Bob and Dave didn't seem to be affected by the amount of beer they drank while they were waiting, but I think the few pints of Guinness they bought for me did the job. I remember going to my bunk and sleeping like a baby while everyone else worked through the night.

That trip is a good memory for me. I was part of my real family, with my uncle and my dad. At the time I thought I wouldn't mind following in their footsteps and working on the boats. They told me there was an unwritten rule that boys could automatically follow their fathers onto the tugs and they'd put my name down for it if I really wanted. This made my father smile and it was one of the few times he ever showed that he might actually be proud of me. I'd disappointed him before when he tried to get me into the merchant navy, but I forgot to tell you about that – he made me go for an interview at a maritime school but I didn't get in and he was disappointed. Me wanting now to go on the tugs seemed like it made up for that and it made me happy to make him happy. But it was only for the time that I was on them, for the weekend. I never did go back to sea.

When the weekend was over they put me in a taxi and sent me back to the care home. My head was buzzing with what happened. I was telling all the other kids I was driving ships and all kinds of stuff and I remember being asked to pipe down a bit, because the other kids were mostly orphans and they didn't need to hear what it was like being out with your dad and your uncle because it was never gonna happen to them. But for me it was one of those rare times I was made to feel special and I wanted everyone to know about it. Looking back on it now, I think it was just a matter of both Dad and me being on our best behaviour. I wanted to get out of the home and he didn't want social workers coming round and sticking their noses into his life. So the thing worked out OK for both of us. Soon after, I was reunited with my mother and Alan in Waltham.

The school had given up on me by now and agreed I could see out my final year by doing just two days a week, on condition that I went to the horticultural centre with Alan on the other three schooldays. He saw it like this was me saying I was sorry for what I did to him and asking him to give me another chance. I saw it like it was better than bloody school. I was getting on for sixteen now and Alan decided to move to a different house. This was a semi-detached, just round the corner from my grandparents, Fred and Jessie, and it meant I was out of reach of the gangs on the Bradley Park and the Nunny and the Willows and the Wybers.

I had to do manual stuff at the horticultural centre, like knocking up cement for making concrete paving slabs and mowing the grass and cleaning up the shit from the animals and ploughing the farm patch. I did this with the inmates, who all had learning difficulties to some degree or other and most had the mental age of a twelve-year-old. I didn't mind like I thought I would and, in a way, it gave me a sense of achievement and it made me feel good about something other than the gangs and that. It was like I could feel free and still be told what to do, if you get my meaning. It was like I was independent in a weird sorta way and what I was doing had a purpose to it. I still thought Alan was a bloody tithead, but I liked the special needs people. It made me mad when we all went out places for the day and kids shouted things like 'spazzos' and 'windalickers' and 'dilly-mongs' and I wanted to punch the fuckers' lights out, but I had to restrain myself because it would've upset the inmates. I found it strange, because they're the words I would've been shouting myself before I went to work at the centre.

There was one particular guy called Malcolm and he kept trying to set me alight. My overalls would be smouldering and I wouldn't know nothing about it until my arse got hot and I'd be running round trying to put the flames out and he'd be standing there laughing and clapping his hands and shouting 'Fire!', 'Fire!', 'Fire!'. Only thing about Malcolm was, it weren't just me he tried to set light to, it was the centre itself and, in the end, he had to be moved to some-where more secure. The only time I had any trouble was with this other bloke who's name I can't remember now. He was a big guy and he would only do what he wanted to do. If I was working with him, I'd try to make him dig or something and he wouldn't do it. He had this pink purse that he loved like life itself and I got so frustrated with him one day that I grabbed it from him. Well, he picked up a spade and I knew he weren't gonna dig with it and he chased me round the place until he finally got close enough to whack me across the head. I collapsed onto the ground and he just dropped the shovel and took his purse back and walked away.

But life at the horticultural centre ended when I did the English and maths exams I had to take by law and then I was out of the system – finally. I was sixteen.

I got a job in an electrical shop that sold washing machines and tumble dryers and TVs and video recorders and radios and all that kinda stuff. It was a six-and-a-half-day week for £35 and I had to wear a smart shirt and trousers and I only lasted six weeks. But I liked it when I had to go out with the delivery man. That's also where I began to learn how to drive. Other than that, I was just stood around in the shop dusting the bloody TV screens. But when we went out in the clapped-out Transit van with all rainbow colours on the side, the delivery bloke would pull into a car park and let me drive it round for a while. Any time I was left in the van alone, I'd jump into the driver's seat and take the handbrake off and let it coast down the street with me steering. The delivery man would be getting the customer to sign the paperwork for the goods and the van would drift past him and he'd come running after it, shouting and waving his arms. So he decided it would be better if I knew how to drive the thing and that's why he let me drive around car parks.

The Tearaway

The other times I got out of the shop was with this bloke called Peter who came in on Thursdays to do collections and repossessions. He was about twenty-one and tall and well-spoken and he had a military look about him that was definitely wrong, because he was bloody crazier than I was and he'd drive the van with his feet on the steering wheel while he was rolling a cigarette. Collections involved us going round all the council estates – anything electrical on HP would have a meter attached and you put fifty pence into the box, which was locked. When the money ran out, it cut the electricity and the thing wouldn't work. Our job was to empty the boxes. What I didn't know was this Peter bloke liked older women – and when I say older, I mean a lot older. After a week or so, he started letting me do it on my own – collecting. He sent me to this house once while he done the one next door, but he must've forgot who it was. I'm standing there in my shirt and chinos and the door opens.

'I'm here to empty your meter, madam.'

Well, I nearly turned and ran because there was this woman behind it in a pink chiffon see-through dressing gown and pink slippers with fluffy things on the fronts – and she was about a hundred and fifty.

'Where's Peter?'

'Next door.'

'Come in.'

I edged past her with my back to the wall and she showed me where the box was and I had to bend round this wooden cabinet thing to get to it. So, I'm trying to unlock the box when she grabbed me by the arse and I nearly jumped out through the bloody window. I dropped the box on the floor and it was empty. She just looked at me and said:

'Usual rules?'

'What?'

'Reset the meter and wash your cock in the sink.'

'I'll get Peter.'

But there was no need, he was already at the front door apologising to her for the mistake and saying that I should go wait in the van. Which I was glad to do.

The repossessions was another thing. We'd have a list of people who were behind with their payments and these were usually on the roughest estates. We'd have to go in and remove the appliance, whatever it was – twin-tub washers with the clothes still in them, gas cookers swimming in grease that had to be disconnected by a plumber, televisions with the kids crying because we were taking them, things that were still hot and things with lard and bacon rind all over them and things with mice behind them and things on carpets that looked like the hoover should have mudguards and places where you wiped your feet on the way out. I never liked doing this work because they were all poor people, or single mothers, or junkies, or foreigners. But it didn't bother Peter, he'd just go in and take it, whatever it was. Women and kids crying didn't influence him and he wasn't open to negotiations, unless it was a grandmother or some tart over seventy at least. I remember snatching a washing machine back once and the house stunk and the mother looked a state with red greasy hair, shouting and screaming and calling us all the bastards under the sun and the poor kids running around everywhere. It was bloody horrible!

The only time it got dangerous was if there was a husband or a boyfriend and he was home. If that was the case, Peter would send me to the front door to pretend I was selling fire extinguishers or lucky pegs or dusters or something and he'd go round the back to try to get in that way. If it all went tits up, Peter carried a baseball bat and he wasn't afraid to use it. But it was a totally shit job and I eventually got sacked when I refused to work Saturdays any more.

Then I went for a YTS placement in plastering at Lincoln College. It wasn't that I particularly wanted to be a plasterer, I just wanted a job where I could earn some decent money for a change. Anyway, there was only one plastering placement available and two of us were up for it. The other kid had better school grades than me and he got it and I was offered a placement in mechanics at Grimsby College instead. So I took that, it was better than nothing. While I was at the college, I met this girl called Julie. She was a couple of years older than me and her dad was a teacher there. Now, as well as police, one thing I always had an adverse reaction to was teachers. I couldn't stomach the bollocks and this put me off her too for a while. But my pubic hair had grown and it was about time I did some proper screwing. Apart from Paula, back in People's Park, I hadn't had much sex because of the problem with my pubes and my sexual doubts and I thought it was time for that to change.

But I forgot to tell you about Paula, so I'd better do it now.

I was fifteen and she was four years older – I always seemed to attract older girls and don't ask me why. Maybe it was because I had a name for being a bit of a strange one, a bit of a queer one, at school and they thought they could find out for sure. Who knows? I never was much for figuring out what women think. Anyway, I met her at a party in the park where the cider 'n' black was flowing. I was still doing the gas, but not so much now, as I heard about this kid who died from brain damage and it put me off. The only thing with drink was it made me stupid and made the whole bastard earth spin round quicker than it was supposed to and it was like I was gonna fly off into space at any minute. Then I'd puke up and it'd get a bit better. It was like the old saying – 'You're never drunk if you can lie on the floor without holding on.' Paula was training to be a professional tennis player and she was fit as a butcher's dog. It started out with just kissing and I was still worried about my pubes and whether I was an iron or not. But it soon became more serious.

I was still celibate, if you don't count wanking, and I didn't have a clue about the female fanny and I wasn't sure whether I wanted to either. I seen stuff in magazines, and I knew the basic position, like. But I was worried about how to get it in the right place and what to do once it was in there and what if I wanted to have a piss or something? Paula wouldn't take no for an answer, she was determined to pop my cherry and she dragged me back into the school after it was closed. This was it, the time was up, it was shit or get off the pot. Before I could get it into her, however, she insisted I put my head between her legs and this was a major crisis for me – if I was gay I'd bloody-well know it now, wouldn't I?

Anyway, I was kissing her belly and her knees and her hips, anywhere except the important part, then she grabbed me by the hair and rammed my face right into the middle. I could hardly breathe and her pubes were up my nose and on my tongue and she was screaming:

'Bite my bacon! Bite my bacon!'

'Oi, you two . . .'

The caretaker came out of nowhere and I tried to make a run for it, but my trousers were down round my bloody ankles and I fell over on my face. Paula passed me and I could see she was limping for some reason and the caretaker was closing on me with his broom handle. I pulled up my strides and just made it out the door in time and away down the street.

My mother had started to see Alan at that time, but we hadn't moved in with him yet. She figured out what I was up to when I asked her questions, like:

'If you asked Alan to bite your bacon, what would you want him to do?'

'You're having sex with that girl, you dirty little up-all-night! You're too young. She's too old for you.'

So I stopped asking. Anyway, the relationship ended, if you could call it that, when we were walking along Weelsby Road and she said her auntie was away and we could go to her house. We went round the back and she told me if I tapped the window gently, the metal handle inside the old frame would fall down. It did and the window opened. She then told me to climb through and I was wondering why the hell we couldn't just go in the front door like anyone else.

Once we were inside, she was straightaway upstairs and within five minutes she was suffocating me and I'm thinking not the bloody bacon-biting again. Then I heard a commotion outside and people shouting and, when I peered through the curtains, there were cops everywhere. Here we go again! I pulled up my trousers and tried to make a run for it, down the stairs and out the back door. I could hear the front door being smashed open, just as I was clearing the back gate and I could hear the shouts:

'He's gone out the back!'

Before I could get very far, the police were on top of me and I was dragged to the ground, kicked a few times and cuffed. I was taken back inside the house and saw Paula being led down the stairs. We spent the day in the cells until they were convinced it wasn't a burglary, then Mam and Alan were allowed to bail me out. We had one more go at it after that in a church, but the sight of Jesus staring down at me from the cross put me off and I just couldn't do it. Paula got fed up with me and went on to screw my mate Nimbus who I told you about earlier.

Anyway, back to Julie. Her dad liked the fact that I was gonna be a mechanic and, even though I couldn't stand the arsehole, he still got me an application form for the fire brigade, to be an apprentice diesel fitter. Over a hundred people applied for the apprenticeship, but I got it after two interviews. He must've pulled some strings. Before that I was doing my YTS at Mazda and I had this trick I used to do at school with a couple of matches wrapped in foil and when they were heated up they took off like a rocket. Except this time I hit the boss in the eye and the dopey bastard wanted to throw me out for nearly setting fire to the storeroom. I knew I was never gonna last there – £29.50 for a forty-hour week and the buggers thought they were doing you a favour.

I had my leg in plaster when I met Julie. I played football a lot, and I had a slight tear in the cartilage of my left knee. We went ice skating the first night, would you believe, even though my leg was wrapped up and I bought her a Slush Puppie and a Marathon bar. I had crutches and all the birds were asking if they could sign my leg. The thing about it was, there wasn't all that much sex between me and Julie and it was more like we were mates than lovers and that kinda suited me after my experience with Paula. Thinking back now, I can't remember much of what happened between us, except that we were together for a year or so. She had a car, a red Metro, I remember that. We used to drive out of Grimsby to maybe Tetney or Marshchapel or somewhere like that in the country and we'd have a bite to eat and talk and stuff. We'd sometimes go to nightclubs if I could get in – Pier 39 or McCartney's and we'd smoke a bit of weed together and get laid-back. It was pretty cool for me, because she used to drive me to footy on a Saturday or

Sunday and stay to watch the match. Then we'd go to the pub afterwards and just generally hang out. She'd do her stuff with her mates and I'd do mine and we'd meet up as and when.

Like I said, her dad was a college tutor and his brother was into mechanics. By the time me and Julie drifted apart, I'd managed to get the job at the fire station and if that hadn't happened, I might never have had a career or went on to build my business in London. You might be saying, why am I telling you about Julie when nothing of much significance happened with her, but it's one of those little things in life that might seem like nothing much at the time, but later you realise that it was really life-changing. No Julie, no father – no father, no job at the fire station – no job at the fire station, no career – no career, no London – no London, I wouldn't be writing this now.

But I did get the job and my grandad got me a blue canti-lever toolbox, with spanners and screwdrivers that were made in China and my mother was relieved that I was gonna straighten myself out at last. I was thinking, four bloody years as an apprentice – four years of £72 a week. I'd be twenty for God's sake and I wanted to be earning some real money so I could be one of the boys. Since moving to this new area, I'd begun drinking with some local lads who knew I sometimes knocked around with the GHS crew and they reckoned they got a good scrapper for their gang. So they arranged a set-to with the Willows/Wybers lot, many of who were still good mates of mine. What could I do? I was in a no-win situation. We all met up in the dark on some playing fields and I tried not to get too close to the lads I knew – just punched a couple of divs I didn't recognise and made sure I was seen doing it, then I backed off. Afterwards we all went to a pub and boasted about who did what and someone said I had to be initiated. I asked what that was and they said I got to take a full-on punch in the face. So they grabbed my arms and pinned 'em behind my back and this bloke who was the leader smacked me right on the jaw. Now, I'd been with tougher gangs than this and I'd been with the football firms and when they let me go I gave this wanker a few back.

So, despite having a bit of a career mapped out for me, I was still tearing it up on the streets and I wasn't ready to become a regular member of society just yet. A little while later I was in town with my new mates and the leader guy who smacked me in the face got into a fight with one of the town topmen. I knew a couple of them, the ones who used to hang round by the phone boxes, dressed of the best and with all the girls dripping off their arms. The leader guy was called Shelley, which is a girl's name and you had to be half decent to be able to go through life being called that. Shelley was tall, but gangly and thin like me, and this other bloke was built. After a while, Shelley was losing badly, so I decided to step in. I mean, I wasn't a stupid bloody hero type or anything like that, but when you're in a gang you got to stick up for the others. Anyway, me and this bloke fought and fought, up and down the street, with groups of people watching – lads calling other lads over all the time to see. I was sixteen and he was about twenty or so and the fight went on and on for fucking ever. Then, he just stopped. He wasn't down or anything, he just stopped. I won. It was as big a surprise to me as it was to everyone else.

After that, everyone in town seemed to know what happened, everyone was talking about the fight and I felt like a bloody Grimsby A-lister. I only found out later that the bloke I beat was not only a Dresser and a town topman, but he was also hated by the GHS. I was shitting myself for a while, in case his crew came after me. Although I knew some of them and they liked me, I reckoned they wouldn't like someone getting involved in their business, even if I didn't really know what I was doing, and wouldn't let it pass without some kinda reprisal. A couple of days later a few of them came up to me and I thought this is it, I'm in for it now.

'You want to join the GHS?'

That's all they said. I'd already been convicted of being a hooligan the previous year and I had a bit of form, so they reckoned I'd fit right in. Before this I was just on the edge, on the outside of it all. Now I was right in the middle.

Chapter Eight

OK, I'm sixteen, living with my mother and Alan in a decent semi-detached house on a quiet side road and going for an interview with the Humberside Fire Brigade. You'd think that would've been enough for any kid my age, wouldn't you? Thing is, I didn't really want to be a mechanic. I wanted to be a plasterer, or something else in the building trade. I heard people on the buildings were earning £200 or maybe £300 a week and that was a lot of money in 1988. Here I was, a YTS mechanic, earning £29.50 for a forty-hour week at Mazda and going for a job that paid £72 for a thirty-nine-hour week. All I could think about was how much more I could do with £300 a week on a building site – considering a pint of Tennent's Extra was less than a pound and haddock'n'chips was £1.50 and a quid for twenty Embassy, I'd have loads left over for nights out and for some proper gear like C17 baggies and Matinique shirts or maybe Gabicci, instead of the rubbish I was getting from the Sunday market at Wonderland.

But apprenticeships were drying up, not like it was in the old days, and my mother saw this as a fantastic opportunity

– a new start. A gift to us all. It would take me into a trade that was thriving throughout the world, according to Alan, and it would give me a skill – I'd be a craftsman, I'd be qualified to do something worthwhile, I'd be able to gain employment. So I went for the interview in my best Farah trousers and Le Shark shirt. They asked me questions on diesels, which I knew nothing about – and stuff like: 'What was my understanding of the air braking system on a fire engine?' I gave them a blank look and I thought 'That's that', and I kept on walking after the interview was over, back to Mazda and my £29.50 a week. As a punishment for taking the morning off without telling anyone, I was ordered to go clean out the boot of a car that had been involved in a crash. What they didn't tell me was, the car was carrying trays of eggs in the boot when it crashed and the omelette was still in there.

Don't forget, it had taken the insurers a long time to give the go-ahead for the repairs and as soon as I opened the boot, millions and millions of horrible bluebottles swarmed out onto me. I could hardly see, it was like it suddenly became night or something and the smell was like I'd opened up a stinking grave. Putrid. So I said to myself, 'I don't deserve this shit – I'm not doing it, not for £29.50 a week!' I went into the stockroom and sat there and had a cigarette. That's when I made the rocket with the two matches head to head in foil, just as the boss walked in. Hit him in the eye and set fire to the carpet. Anyway, after that I had to go out and clean the stinking boot or get the sack – and I didn't want the sack. Twenty-nine pounds fifty was better than nothing.

The thing that made all this shit bearable was football. I still played on Saturdays and Sundays and I looked forward to it all week. Everything was put on hold for that ninety minutes while you were on the pitch, all the stupid opinions and the arguments and the abuse and the fear and the fighting and having to be a tough guy – it all stopped while the game was going. I won some trophies and was player of the match a couple of times and I loved it. I loved the ritual of it – the cleaning of the boots and the packing of the sports bag and the smell of horse liniment and eucalyptus oil. Salad or pasta before a game and trying to chill out watching Big Daddy and Giant Haystacks wrestling on the telly and then being picked up with the rest of the team and the excitement in the back of the van, the anticipation and the energy. Getting the praise for a decent pass or scoring a goal, like pats on the back from your team-mates and the spectators shouting:

'Well done, Dean!'

It's like the way sixteen-year-old kids should be living, not having to go to court with a Section Four, or worrying about whether they're gay or not, or having to fight this bully or that bully, or cleaning stinking bluebottle-infested eggs out of the boot of a Mazda car. Life should be simpler, like a game of football. Shouldn't it?

Anyway, I thought I was the dog's bollocks of a footballer and I was always showing off to the younger kids in the street – you know, like flicks and spins and headers and knee-ups and stuff. Playing 'kerbsie' for points and the little kids thinking I'm a premiership player or something because

I'm so skilled. Then this neighbour bloke who was working on his car shouted over at me:

'You think you're a clever bastard, don't ya!'

I went across to see what his problem was and the tosser took a swipe at me with a hammer. I pulled back just in time and he missed me by a millimetre. He was about to swing again, but I threw the ball at his face and punched him twice and he fell back against the railings at the side of the road. His legs went bandy, but he came at me again. This time he brought me to the ground with a rugby tackle, trying to hit me with his fists. But he was a bit punch-drunk and couldn't do any damage. Luckily for me, the little kids had gone and called some people who pulled him off me. Alan told me not to do my football tricks outside on the road any more, because it was provoking people.

After that I used to go get cans of lager and walk about five miles to the Astro Turf area at King George playing fields, drinking the booze on the way. It would be getting dark and I'd be half pissed by the time I got there. Then I'd do all my tricks on the empty football court – running up and down, twisting, turning, passing, smashing my ball into the back of the net. I'd imagine I was playing for Liverpool in the FA Cup final and I'd be commentating the match as well, merry on the lager:

'Williams takes on Graeme Sharp, nutmegs him . . . he's on the edge of the box. Williams gets past Southall . . . puts the ball back to Dalglish. Dalglish shoots. Gooooaallllll.'

This was my theatre of dreams. This was where I could be what I dreamed I was – even if I was half-pissed and there was no one else there. And if my life was shit and lonely sometimes, I always had myself to keep me company.

Anyway, getting back to the fire brigade, a couple of weeks after the crap interview, I came home from the Mazda garage and there was a letter waiting for me. It had the HFB frank on the envelope, saying 'Fire Kills'. I'd forgotten about the thing because I reckoned I didn't have a chance of getting the job and this would just be them putting the rubber stamp on my failure. The envelope was bulky and I thought they must be sending me a consolation diesel air-braking manual, just to rub it in and take the piss. But, when I opened it, there was a contract of employment and a welcoming letter inside. Andrea and Alan were over the moon. I was no longer on YTS, neither was I on the dole or on the docks, I was a bona-fide apprentice with the emergency services. Julie's father must've pulled some heavy-duty strings.

I started my apprenticeship at Peaks Lane fire station in 1988. The boss was called Ken and he'd been there nearly for ever. The head fitter was Alan and it was his job to train me. College was also part of my training and Julie's father and her uncle were my teachers. The college hours were 9.00 a.m. to 9.00 p.m. – twelve hours of looking at projectors and writing notes and learning about the workings of diesel engines. It was a struggle for me. I hated the feeling of being back in school and the restrictions it put on my free time. My social life consisted of hanging round with either Julie or Nimbus, but the GHS didn't like Nimbus. I mean, they'd asked me to be one of them and that was a dream come true, but we were close mates and I didn't want to throw him to one side, just like that. So things were a bit stagnant and the long college hours didn't help much.

Being at the fire station was good though. There was another senior fitter there called Dennis and he was a big man – he looked like the geezer out of *Clockwork Orange* and I was still the joker in the pack, just as I was in school. I couldn't stop being a prankster, I'd been doing it for so long and I did things that weren't even funny, just for a cheap laugh, maybe you'd say to get attention. I dunno. Anyway, I used to play jokes on this Dennis and I knew he was getting a bit fed up with me. On this one day, he told me to go make him a cup of tea. So, I filled the cup with boiling water to make it hot on the outside, then I filled it with cold tea on the inside. When he took a mouthful he spat it back out shouting:

'You fucking little bastard, I'll fucking kill you!'

And he grabbed me by the throat and tried to strangle me. I was lying on the floor and he was on top of me and my eyes were bulging and my face was turning blue. Alan and Ken finally managed to pull him off before he killed me and we were both suspended, pending a disciplinary inquiry.

I had to pay a year's subscription fee to get the union to represent me and it took two weeks to get all the statements and make the case for my defence that I was just a stupid kid, making a stupid joke and I didn't deserve to be strangled for it. It came out during the inquiry that Dennis's wife had just left him and he was on the edge and my prank with the tea was the last straw for him – the one that broke the camel's back, so to speak. Anyway, I was given a verbal warning and Dennis was given a written warning, but he left soon after. It was the first of three disciplinaries I was to face.

Ken, the boss, was old school. He ran the workshop with an iron fist and he didn't like my jokes and he didn't like the fact that I'd lost him a senior fitter. After the disciplinary, he said he didn't want me there no more and I should leave. What I didn't know was his wife was dying and he was maybe grieving inside or something and he didn't need a wanker like me causing problems round the fire station. I said I wouldn't go. I said I was there to learn and, love me or hate me, I was staying. But he had his hooks into me, no mistake. My official start time was 8.00 a.m., but Ken's rule was that we should be on site for 7.45 a.m., that way we'd have a cup of tea at 7.55 a.m. and be ready to work at 8.00 a.m. I had to bike it to work and if I got there after 7.45 a.m., he'd tell me to go home, even though I was officially five or ten minutes early. When it was hot outside, he made me work inside while the others would be out taking in the sun. And when it was pissing down with rain, I'd be outside, stripping down a water pump. He'd fish out a bucket of rusty nuts and bolts from under the work benches and make me stand all day at the wire-wheel cleaning every bloody thread. But I made myself believe I could learn something, even from this soul-destroying job, and I used the time spent standing there at the wheel to learn about the pitch of threads and about the head sizes of the bolts.

Anyway, just round the corner from where we had our

tea break, there was a wall-mounted spark-plug tester and cleaner. You pressed one button to send electricity through the plug to check the gap, and another button sent grit through to clean the electrode. We sat on metal chairs and I figured if I could wire Ken's chair up to the mains of the tester, I could teach the bugger a lesson in common decency. So I got a piece of wire and attached it to the seat of Ken's chair and another wire from the chair to earth it. When we were at tea break, I pretended it was my turn to go get the rock cakes and I went round the corner. Alan saw what I was doing and he gestured to me to stop, but I wouldn't. I turned the spark-plug cleaner on and pressed the button to the wire going to Ken's chair. All I heard was:

'Alan . . . I've been fucking bitten!'

And I could see Ken's tea being chucked across the floor. When I came back round the corner, he was standing up and holding his arse and Alan was choking himself trying not to laugh. Ken never found out what really happened.

Ken's wife eventually died but, a short time later, he remarried. He was a changed man after that. He didn't hate me no more and life got better at the fire station. I even set up a windscreen-washer jet above his chair – the washer bottle was where he couldn't see it and the switch was rigged up to the wooden panel my chair backed onto and the power came from a fire-engine battery round the corner. Now, Ken always wore a flat cap and, for about a week or so, every time he joined us for tea I'd flick the switch and a jet of water would hit him on the cap. I'd just keep a poker face and Alan would be contorted trying not to burst out laughing. But Ken never noticed, his bloody cap must've been waterproof with age or oil or something. I had to get the cap off and I did this by fixing a fishing hook to a line and pulley. I stuck the hook into his cap without him noticing when I passed behind him and I simultaneously pulled on the line and flicked the switch. Well, his cap flew off and the jet of water hit him straight on his grey-haired, Brylcreemed bonce. This was too much for Alan, who collapsed in a fit of laughter. Ken jumped up saying the sprinkler system must be faulty, while I retrieved his cap and extracted the hook. But a faulty sprinkler system in a fire station ain't a good thing and Ken went to the main office to report it. I had to run round and dismantle my little set-up before the officers came to do the inspection.

My second disciplinary was bloody unfair. This bloke's name was Dean, just like me, and he had a wooden leg. Well, it might not have been wooden, it might have been plastic or something, but it was false, like a prosthetic limb they call it. Anyway, this Dean was a fire hydrant inspector and he was also a real pain in the arse. Maybe it was because my name was Dean too, but if I had a bike with ten gears, he had a bike with sixty gears, if I had three GCSEs, he had forty GCSEs, if I had a tenner, he had a monkey – and if you counted up all the jobs he'd had, it'd make the bugger about eighty-four, instead of twenty-seven. The first part of the disciplinary centred round his leg. He came in one day and said it was giving him a bit of gyp, because there was a bolt poking through the top bit, where he put the stump of his real leg. Anyway, he took it off and told me to grind it down a bit, while he hobbled off doing his rounds on crutches. After I'd sorted the leg out, I took the trainer off and screwed it to the concrete floor, then put the leg back in. When Dean came back, he plonked his stump into the false leg, which was standing upright and he strapped himself in. But when he tried to walk away, one leg went with him and the other one didn't. He ended up in a weird position where he fell on the floor, but the leg was still standing upright.

That was the first part of the disciplinary. The second part was about his automatic Austin Allegro. I jacked up the front wheel just enough for it to spin and left it on bricks – I mean, you wouldn't see it unless you were looking for it. Dean got in and tried to drive off, but nothing happened. It took him half the day to figure out what was wrong. After looking at the engine and the transmission and this and that and the other, he finally looked at the front wheel and he had to take his leg back off to jack the car up and sort it out. Anyway, that was enough. Everybody knew it was me who did it and I got a written warning and a three-day suspension. The problem with this was, the apprenticeship now had a guaranteed, full-time job attached to it and I was jeopardising this with my stupid pranks.

I was still knocking about with Julie, but there was really not much to the relationship, as I already told you. I was also beginning to get back into the town scene again, like with the gangs and stuff. My mam used to have a bucket next to the front door with washing powder and water in it and, when I came home after being fighting, my clothes were always covered with blood – either my own or someone else's. So I had to get undressed by the door and soak the bloody clothes in the bucket before going to my bedroom. The bedroom itself had a cupboard that was built into the wall and I kept clippings from the papers and photos people used to take of the rumbles we had with rival firms pasted up in there. One night I came home and they were all gone. Alan had gone into my room and took them down and binned them. I said nothing, but I knew my days in that house were numbered.

And I was right. I was biking home from work this day and I met my gran and she told me I shouldn't bother to go home. I took no notice of her but, when I got to the house, the doors were all locked and I couldn't get in. I waited outside for about an hour or so, then the next thing I knew, my mother and grandmother were behind me and they said I didn't live there no more. They took me to a house near where I worked in Hainton Avenue. It was a bedsit and Andrea had paid a month's rent and she'd packed all my stuff in a bag and it was already there in the room. I was supposed to live in this fleapit on my own from now on. The room itself was a depressing place and I had to share a bathroom and kitchen with a load of other tossers I didn't even know. I hated the bloody place and it wasn't too long until the room got burgled and they took everything I had. The coppers came and took fingerprints, but nothing ever came of it and then I got sick. I was vomiting all over the place and blocked up the sink with the puke and I was feverish and hallucinating and everything. This bloke, whose name I never knew, came in from one of the other rooms and stayed with me through the night and I was raving and asking him if I was gay. He didn't know me much, but he was reassuring me I was straight but I didn't believe him and I was saying I knew I was gay. It was like all the images from the past were flashing through my head, but I was older now and they weren't innocent no more. They were dark and dirty.

I was sick for a while, in a shit-hole place with shit-hole thoughts going through and through my mind. The voices were back too, arguing and contradicting each other and one saying one thing and the other saying the exact opposite. I thought I was going crazy and nobody came to see me except the neighbour bloke and he called in to the fire brigade for me and I still never found out his name. I was sick with some virus and confused about where my life had been and where it was going from here. I kept asking myself questions that I didn't have answers for and I wasn't sure if I was physically sick or mentally sick or what the difference was between the two. Then it went away, just as quick as it came – the sickness.

I got up and went back to work.

I met this girl called Jo from the town crowd one night when I was out with Nimbus. She let me stay round her house sometimes to get away from the bedsit and her mother was fond of me. Not in a sexual way or anything, but she just thought I was funny or something. Anyway, she must've got fed up with me hanging around there because she sorted me out a house-share with two other girls called Joanne and Frances in Cleethorpes. It was such a relief to be out of the bedsit and with people who were my age and on my wavelength. We got on great and I kept on being the funny man and playing jokes and making people laugh. But one night I went too far.

Frances had a big date lined up with a new bloke and she told us she'd be bringing him back to the house. Joanne decided to stay at her boyfriend's house and they both asked me if I could put some clothes on and not walk around the house naked. I said I would and, when they went out, I took off down to the fag-and-paper shop on the corner and bought some *Men Only* porn mags. I hung the pictures up all over the walls and then I cracked a couple of stink bombs into an old black plastic 35mm film case. I stuck a few pinpricks into the top of the case, to slowly release the smell of rotten eggs. When Frances came home with the bloke, he nearly shit himself when he saw the pictures and neither of them could make out where the smell was coming from. The last straw was when I walked through the room wearing one of Joanne's frilly nighties and flashed a seductive smile at the bloke. That was it, he was out the door like a cat with a can tied to its tail and Frances after him, trying to say it was all just a joke and he shouldn't take no notice.

The girls got even with me one night when I came in plastered drunk. When I woke up next morning, I found a hamster in a cage beside me in the bed. You can imagine my surprise when the hamster said:

'Hello, Dean.'

At first I thought I was still asleep and dreaming.

'Thank you for bringing me home last night, Dean.'

The hamster spoke again, in a male voice with a Welsh accent. I jumped back away from it, then out of the bed and looked around the room to see if someone was there. Nobody behind the door or in the cupboard or under the bed. I tried to think what I'd been on the night before – acid, gas? I couldn't remember.

'We had a good time, didn't we?'

I really freaked when the hamster said that. I ran out of the room, looking for Joanne and Frances. They weren't in the house. My clothes were in the bedroom and I was afraid to go back in there and the hamster was calling to me:

'Dean . . . where are you?'

Joanne's boyfriend, James, was in the electronics game and he was into all that state-of-the-art stuff and he planted a little remote transmitter thing in the cage, don't ask me how, and sat outside the house in his car with the girls. It was him speaking and they kept it going for about fifteen minutes with the hamster calling me from the room:

'Dean . . . Dean . . .'

I was just about to call my mother and tell her I'd finally gone crazy when they came back in, laughing. I never fooled about with Frances after that.

Anyway, I'm a year into my apprenticeship and I'm seventeen and it's 1989 and my world was about to change for ever. There was this firemans' fete in the summer and Ken gave us the afternoon off. I saw this girl wandering through the stalls and the rides and the other attractions and she seemed to stand out from everybody else. She was dark-haired and beautiful and had a look of class about her. She wasn't like your typical northern bird, at least not like any I knew. Her hair was shining and her clothes were real stylish and, when I came up and said something to her, she spoke with an accent – not French and not English, but something in between. I can't remember what I said to her, but I kept talking and talking because I didn't want her to go. Her name was Nicole and we ended up swapping phone numbers.

We didn't have mobiles in them days and nobody liked me using the landlines in their houses to talk to my mates or to girls, but I managed to ring Nicole anyway. We arranged to meet at the Wellow pub in Cleethorpes and I found out she was living very close to the fire station where I worked. After that, we started to meet regularly at the Horseshoe pub and she was just great to be with, a class above anyone else I knew. She made me feel special and all the demons I had in my head didn't seem to be there any more when I was with her. There was no conflict and no voices and everything seemed clear and normal. For the first time since I was a little kid with my mother, I felt like I was in love with a woman.

Chapter Nine

I got myself a Honda 90 moped when I was living with Joanne and Frances. I went everywhere on it and back again and it was like when I was a kid and riding off to places on my bike. It was unrestricted, like the top speed was about 50 mph, but that was fast enough to get me from Grimsby to Cleethorpes and back again. Flat out on a good road, I could get it up to 60 mph and I loved the freedom it gave me. But I wasn't a kid no more and sometimes I'd try to get on the thing after drinking and I'd just fall over the other side. Sometimes people passing by would help me to get on the bike and I know that wouldn't be heard of nowadays, but it was like how things were at that time. I was in that state one time when the cops started following me. I wasn't zigzagging or anything, or at least I didn't think I was and I couldn't understand why they were staying behind me. So I thought I better pull up and see what the buggers wanted. That was a mistake. You see, I might've been able to ride the moped without swerving, but I wasn't able to speak. They pulled up behind me and approached slowly like they do in the films.

'What you been up to, then?'

'Nothing.'

'Where have you come from?'

'Maggies.'

'Who's Maggie?'

'Meggies . . .'

'You been drinking?'

'No, sir, I bin swimmin'.'

'Swimming?'

'With women . . . swimmin'.'

There was two coppers and they were grinning all over their chops by now. Smirking at each other like they knew I didn't get off the bike because I wasn't able to stand, as well as not able to speak.

'Let me get this straight, you've been swimming in Cleethorpes with some women?'

'Yesh.'

'And who might these women be?'

'My housemaids.'

'Housemaids?'

'Mates . . . mates . . . housemates.'

'Where's your helmet?'

'On me 'ead.'

I tapped on my head with my finger, but there was no helmet, it was still in the helmet lock. That's why the bastards were following me.

'Come with us!'

That was it, fun over. They put their pig heads back on and handcuffed me and put me into the back of the police car. On the way to the station, they got a call that a fight was kicking off somewhere close by and they decided to go there, and take me with them. They left the car to go break up the fight and the keys in the ignition – and I was seriously thinking if it would be a good time to nick a police car while handcuffed, you know how you get crazy ideas in your head when you're pissed. Anyway, before I could do it, they came back with this young bloke and threw him into the back of the car with me.

'Grassing bastard!'

The kid shouted at me and tried to headbutt me. Luckily, he was handcuffed behind his back and I managed to keep out of the way of his forehead. I dunno what he thought I grassed him about; I didn't even know the tosser. Maybe it was a case of mistaken identity, or maybe the coppers said something to him. But all the way to the police station he was trying to butt me and the two bastards in the front were laughing their arses off.

At the cop station I told them I was unemployed. I mean, I couldn't tell them I worked for the fire brigade, could I? That would've been the end of my apprenticeship for sure. But it took so long to get there I blew under the limit when they breathalysed me and they just left me in the cells to stew for a bit and I was hoping they wouldn't put the head-butter from the back of the car in with me. But they didn't and, after a few hours, they gave me a caution and let me go. I had that old moped until the engine blew up from me hammering it. I'd ride it all over, down to Mablethorpe to the shitty amusement park – anywhere to get away from

The Tearaway

Grimsby, like I used to do with my mother when we'd go off on our bikes and I'd take my fishing net and jam-jar to catch butterflies and caterpillars and frogspawn and stuff.

But I was telling you about Nicole, wasn't I? The more I saw of her, the more I fell in love with her. She was everything my dream woman should be. Her father was a professional photographer and her mother was an accountant – very posh sorts altogether. Nicole was studying for her A levels and she was gonna have a career as a doctor, not a job – a career. But the thing is, I was an apprentice diesel fitter, not the brain surgeon her parents had hoped for her and that didn't go down too well with them. But we were in love, at least I was. It was like I felt proud when I was with her, around her – she gave me a tingle and butterflies in my stomach and a dry mouth when we talked. It was a big, big buzz. Even though I never passed no driving test, we'd borrow her dad's Volvo without him knowing and go for days out and the old fart would've haemorrhaged from the eyeballs if he found out – maybe that's what she liked about me, that I was, like, a bit edgy and unpredictable. But she did and that's all that mattered to me and I didn't care why. It wasn't like before, with Julie, this was different. It was like we were adults, not kids.

Hubbard's Hills is a place for family picnics and school outings and stuff. A river runs through it, with stepping stones and a handrail to help you cross. Me and Nicole liked to drive out there and we just seemed to blend into the happiness of the place – like it was a romantic movie or something, with kids throwing frisbees and playing ball and slipping into the stream. It was hot and beautiful and we were holding hands and she was talking about something intelligent and I was talking crap and we just flowed on the day, kinda with the day, if you know what I mean, like we fitted into all this sunny stuff naturally. Like it was that painting on the wall by some French Impressionist, you've probably seen it, and everyone was relaxed and we were part of it – the painting, holding hands and talking and walking. It was what I always wanted. To be loved. Don't get me wrong, I don't mean that in any mushy, crappy way – it's just how it seemed.

Then we decided to go on a holiday, like a proper holi-day, abroad, for a couple of weeks. My mother paid for it because she was sorry for throwing me out of Alan's, into that mangy bedsit and not coming to see me when I was sick. We chose Benalmádena, near Málaga in Spain, because it was cheap and it was over the Christmas holidays and I'd never been on an aeroplane before. Nicole had been all over Europe with her family and I'd only been to Humberston, five miles away – and Scotland a few times with Fred and Jessie. That's why she fascinated me so much, she was rather sophisticated for her age, like she was older and she knew about art and history and politics and stuff. All I knew was how to fix diesel engines and drink and sniff gas and knock people about. Like I said already, maybe that's why she liked me, because I was different to her. She was confident and I was edgy, she was sure of herself and I was sure of nothing. She knew what she wanted and knew how to get it, I didn't know what I wanted and, even if I did, I wouldn't know how to get it. Maybe that's what it was, that crazy conflict between us. Maybe that's what made it as good as it was.

Anyway, we flew out to Málaga, just the two of us, with me not knowing what to expect. It was a self-catering apartment and the place was quiet at that time of year. The weather was warm, not too hot, like summer in Grimsby I suppose and we soon found this good place to eat. It was a Geordie pub called The Fog on the Tyne, would you believe, and it had all memorabilia stuff on the walls from Newcastle and Paul Gascoigne's stupid record playing in the background. Now, you'd think the first time I was out of the country I'd want to go explore the local cuisine and sample the atmosphere of Spain, like Nicole wanted me to, instead of spending time in a bloody English pub eating burgers and chips and drinking pints of Tennent's lager. But the place came alive at night for the karaoke and they had a pool competition that I won and made myself twenty quid and I was nervous being in a strange place, away from the only things I'd known all my life. But the novelty wore off after a couple of days.

So I did what Nicole wanted me to do and we hired a couple of mopeds and went off to explore Mijas, which was a small town on the side of a mountain. We had to go up a long, windy road, right up to the top of the hills, looking back down on Benalmádena. When we got up there, we went into the local church and it was cool and quiet in there and not like I thought it would be and we lit candles and I felt like I was at peace or something, like the world wasn't outside no more, it was gone somewhere else. That was the same way Nicole made me feel, peaceful and relaxed and kinda spiritual – even when she pissed me off by always stopping me in mid-sentence if I said a word wrong and correcting me like I was back at bloody school. But I didn't mind really, that's how much in love I was then.

One night when we were out and I had a bit too much to drink, we met a Scottish couple who had a disabled son. They were staying in the hotel next to us and we walked back together, even though they didn't want us to. I offered to push the young lad's wheelchair and I was messing around with him, tipping it backwards and sprinting along the path. The kid was laughing his head off and telling me to go faster and the mother was having a cow in case I pushed him out into the road and a car ran over him. I kept shouting to the kid:

'How fast will we go?'

'As fast as we can!'

So I started revving up the wheelchair, pretending it was a drag-race car, then I took off down this hill with the kid's parents and Nicole screaming behind me. There was a junction at the bottom and I couldn't find any brakes on the bloody wheelchair, so we just kept going, right across the road. Luckily, there weren't no cars coming, but we hit the kerb on the opposite side at about 150 mph and the kid flew out of the wheelchair like a rag doll and did a triple somersault in the air, before sailing over a fence and landing in a field.

Everybody stopped stock still. Nicole had her face in her hands, afraid to look. The kid's mother was standing there with her mouth open, but no sound was coming out. The father just walked slowly down the hill towards me. Then we heard laughing coming from the other side of the fence and everybody rushed and looked over. The kid was just lying there in the grass, laughing his head off. His mother and father rushed to him and picked him up and checked all his bones for breakages, but he was OK. I tried to help them get him back into the wheelchair, but they just pushed me away and took off down the road, looking back to make sure we weren't behind them and leaving me to take the flack from Nicole. Needless to say, the Scottish couple avoided us for the rest of the holiday, even though their son waved to me like mad whenever he saw me.

Two days later and it was Christmas Day and Nicole and I were still in love, despite my stupidity with the wheelchair kid. Only trouble was, nobody told us the whole place closed down and we couldn't get food anywhere, except for bar snacks in the hotel. I looked in the fridge-freezer in the apartment and all that was in it was four eggs, half a pack of bacon and a box of frozen hake. I dunno where the hake came from, maybe from the people who were in the apartment before us and they forgot to take it out, but it was all we had and we were starving. So I cooked the rotten stuff, along with the eggs and bacon. The hake stank like the way fish stinks. The whole apartment reeked of it and it reminded me of when I had to stay with Bob, even though Bob never cooked hake. Nicole got sick first, like violently vomiting in the toilet. I tried to help her, like pulling the hair out of her eyes while she puked and telling her it'd be OK. Then

I got sick as well and it ended up with the two of us kneeling on the floor and calling up Hughie Green on the big white telephone.

We stayed in for a couple of days after that, until New Year. Nicole just lay in bed and I wandered round the hotel complex, throwing cats into the swimming pool. The manager hated that, but there was hundreds of the buggers all over the area and anyway I used to blame the local kids.

'They just scarpered off that way, mate.'

The first night we did go back out was New Year's Eve and the first thing we saw was this woman curled up in a ball, sobbing. She only had a blouse and knickers on and Nicole asked her what was the matter. She said her boyfriend had beaten her up and thrown her out and I thought about Andrea back in the bad old days. But the woman was drunk and I didn't want to get involved, just in case her boyfriend turned out to be Bob. Nicole, on the other hand, wanted to play the Good Samaritan and she took the woman back up to our apartment. So, while Nicole was busy trying to calm her down, I went downstairs to the reception to let the hotel manager know what was going on. Trouble was, the receptionist spoke Spanish and I spoke Grimsby and he couldn't make head or tail of what I was saying. When I made a punching gesture, to indicate that the woman had been hit, he pulled a baseball bat out from under the counter and waved it at me. I didn't want no trouble, so I decided to go back to the apartment. On the way, I met this bloke who asked me if I've seen a woman in her underwear and, when I told him she was in my room, he went bloody wild.

Now, it seemed clear to me straight away that this bugger was the jealous type and that's why he hit the woman in the first place. Also, he was definitely out of it on something, I didn't know what, but I wasn't taking any chances. So I headbutted him. Next thing I knew, the Spanish twat from the reception was behind me and he swung the bat and just missed me by a millimetre – I could feel the thing whistling past my head. I ran up the stairs and into the apartment, but the crazy boyfriend followed me. He began smashing up everything on the floor we were on and banging doors, trying to find me and his woman. She was scared and she told Nicole that they were both heroin addicts and the fight was over methadone, not another man at all. I rang down to reception, but all I could hear on the phone was the receptionist shouting: '*Policía!, Policía!, Policía!*' Next thing, six Spanish coppers burst into the apartment and wrestled me to the floor and handcuffed me behind my back. They dragged me downstairs to the lobby, but then the bollocks behind the desk told them about the nutcase smashing the place up, so they left me sitting on the stairs and went up after him. They must've missed him somewhere between floors because, in the meantime, he came back down and saw me sitting there handcuffed. Well, he booted me straight in the head and I was taking a right old kicking from him before the *policía* came back down and restrained the bastard.

The upshot of this Good Samaritan act was that me and Nicole were taken to Málaga police station and kept in the cells overnight. It was New Year's Eve, for God's sake! They threw us out at 5.00 a.m. the next morning and we had to walk all the way back to the hotel. On the way, we just sat down arm-in-arm on the beach and watched the beautiful sunrise. It was a new day – and a new year – and a new decade. We spent the rest of the holiday waiting to go home.

My relationship with Nicole wasn't like a normal romance. We were different as catfish and caviar and nobody gave it a worm's chance in an aviary. When we got back from Spain, her father had been making enquiries about me and found out about school and how I had a criminal record and I was banned from her house. Like I said, he wanted her to become a doctor and marry one as well and give him a load of little paediatricians. He definitely didn't want her hanging round with a felon grease monkey. I went back to the fire station and I'm two-and-a-half years into my apprenticeship by now. I was sneaking round to see Nicole every chance I got, when her parents weren't there and when she could get out without them thinking she was seeing me. I remember taking her to a beer festival at the Winter Gardens in Cleethorpes and they were serving up this real ale stuff. Now it looked like something that came out the arse-end of a dog with diarrhoea, but I thought I'd give it a try. I started sampling stuff that was about 3 per cent and that wasn't too bad. The next lot was about 5 per cent and I was feeling a bit merry after a few plastic glasses of that shit. The stuff that finally laid me to rest was about 10 per cent and I walked into a door, so they tell me, and split my top lip open and had to go to hospital.

After that, Nicole was sent away to study medicine in Cambridge. Our relationship was relegated to writing letters, or me going down there on weekends, or waiting for her to come home on term breaks. I bought a car to get down there – but I should tell you more about learning to drive, shouldn't I? Well, it was back when I was seventeen and I was still hanging about with Nimbus at the time, just before I met Nicole. One of the firemen was selling a Datsun 120Y for £50. I bought it from him and decided to teach myself how to drive it. Nimbus told me the basics and he decided to go in front of me in his Ford Escort, made to look like an XR3i with skirts on. There was something wrong with the Datsun to begin with, I mean, there must've been – it bounced backwards and forwards, almost smashing into Nimbus. So he got out and told me the technical term for what was wrong with my new car was 'kangarooing', caused by 'clutch control' or, in my case 'no clutch control'.

The next lesson came later, courtesy of a policeman. I was hiding the car all over the place because I had no licence yet and nobody told me I couldn't park it facing into oncoming traffic on a one-way street. As well as that, the exhaust was smashed because I drove it out to Keelby when it was snowing and had to do a handbrake turn and hit the kerb and fractured the exhaust. Anyway, I parked it in that street because it was close to the college and I was learning welding and wanted to get the car in there to fix the exhaust. When I went to move it into the college, a stupid copper heard the noise it was making and issued me with a parking fine and warned me I better not to drive it in such an unfit state, or I'd be prosecuted. I said 'Yes, sir, no, sir, three bags full, sir' because I didn't want him to ask me for my driving licence. He didn't and, when he buggered off, I drove it into the college anyway and fixed the exhaust. I had that car for a good while, until it started falling apart and the police kept pulling me over in it. In the end, it wasn't worth the trouble it was causing me, so I just dumped it.

Anyway, back to Nicole. Someone at college was selling an Escort Ghia 1.3 and I went to the bank and asked them to loan me £1000. Now, don't forget, this was 1990 and the banks were flinging money at everybody, people on the dole and in mental hospitals and people who were dead and even people who weren't the people they said they were. Anybody could get a loan, even a third-year apprentice diesel fitter, earning £72 a week. The loan was to last for three years, the car lasted three days.

Before going down to Cambridge, I went with the GHS boys for a night out. The only way I can explain this is if you've ever seen the movie *Fear and Loathing in Las Vegas*. We went to a football match first and there was the usual cans of lager and rucking and stuff, then I drove some of them into town, showing off my new car and being the big bollocks. The pubs didn't open till 7.00 p.m. on a Saturday back then, so I ended up at someone's house popping Anadins and drinking Mad Dog 20/20 through a straw. I then drove to Grinders nightclub and, after loads of Tennent's and another punch-up, I decided to go home – via Cambridge. You probably won't believe this, but how I managed to navigate down through Boston and Spalding to Peterborough, I'll never know. One minute I was awake, trying to keep one eye on the road, and the next minute I was asleep, going over the catseyes and the bumping waking me back up. Just as well it was so late and there was no traffic on the roads to speak of. I remember arriving in Peterborough and looking at the speedometer – it was reading 90 mph and all I could see in front of me was this massive roundabout. The road was on a steep decline and all I could do was take my foot off the accelerator and stamp it down hard on the bloody brake pedal. I know what you're saying, that this kinda thing ain't funny and it's criminal and I could've hurt innocent people – and I agree with you. If I could go back and meet myself on that night, I'd give myself a few kicks up the arse and take the car keys away. But I didn't think about things like that back then – you know, things like consequences.

Anyway, the brakes were too late and I hit the roundabout at speed, smashing into the black-and-white chevron sign thing. The car vaulted up into the air, then crashed back down again, shattering the windscreen and cutting out the engine. It slid along the road for about an hour and then came to a stop. I was wearing my seat belt, but I was still thrown around like a dummy in a crash-test car. Then everything went quiet and silent, like – except for the steam shooting up from the bonnet. And dark, black dark, like there was no street lights and the car headlights had gone out, caved in I think. Then, after a minute or two I could hear the crackle of a police radio and a voice:

'I think he's dead.'

But I wasn't. I only had some superficial cuts and bruises, so I climbed out through the smashed windscreen and they arrested me for drunk driving.

Dean Williams

I had to go back to Peterborough magistrate's court and they gave me a one-year ban and a £70 fine. The car was taken to a breaker's yard and they took me round to see if there was anything I wanted from it before they crushed it. I froze inside when I saw it, the front end was all crushed in and the doors were bent beyond recognition. The breaker guy just shook his head:

'You should be dead.'

That's all he said and I dunno if he meant that I was lucky to be alive or that I should be dead because I was such a bloody danger to other road users.

Chapter Ten

But you probably want me to get back to telling you a bit more about the hooliganism and not all this love stuff with Nicole. Like I said before, the hooligans in Grimsby had two main names – the 'Dressers' and the 'GHS'. They were the town centre lads, the kings of the telephone kiosks. There were other, like, minor groups that hung round the shopping parades on the estates. But if they came into the centre of town, there was bound to be trouble with the Dressers or the GHS. The girls would all gather round these guys, wanting to be seen with the top lads in town. There would be up to a hundred teenagers kicking around on any given night and people like me who were called 'footsoldiers' but we were really just dogsbodies, running round on the rob for the older lads. These top men stood out from the rest, with their smart haircuts and loafers and designer threads. If you stood up close to them you could hear the kind of conversations they had, like:

'My shoes cost more than your fucking suit.'

'Oh yeah? You look like a fucking tracker.'

'What? You two-bob Adidas two-striper!'

Then there'd be a bit of pushing and shoving and it was cool and crazy for a kid like me to be part of the scene.

I was there because they saw me fight and that kinda thing carried kudos with them. I began hanging around in the town centre when I was still at school and, no matter where I moved to, I always came back there, even when I was with Nicole. Like I said earlier, I started out on the bottom rung of the ladder, then I took a step up through Nimbus and again through Geordie. The dynamics of how any gang works depends in the long run on the people it brings up through the ranks. I started out in the Grimsby Under Fives, which was the junior section of the Grimsby Hit Squad, not because the kids in it were under five years old or anything, but that's just what it was called. You have to understand that, in the beginning, I didn't do much, just exchanged nods and kept quiet and listened to the senior guys discussing the upcoming matches and which mobs were attached to which teams. There was a pecking order in the groups and a lot of it revolved round big families. Like, families would have uncles and brothers and cousins and nephews in a gang and if you fucked around with one of them, the others would all come after you. I had no brothers or uncles or cousins to look out for me, so I had to be careful.

There was also a set of rules – and a code of punishments if you fell out of line. In the evenings, when the shops were closed, we'd just sit around outside McDonald's or roam the streets and sometimes meet up with the older lads. On match days, blokes in their twenties and thirties would join up with us, men who had jobs and businesses and families and respectable lives outside the football thing. These were the organisers, the generals, who made sure we were where we were supposed to be for prearranged fights. The older lads at the front and the U5s supporting them and the generals screaming at us to stand our ground. And then it would come on, the enemy surge, like a bloody medieval battle. The ICF, or Inter City Firm, as the West Ham were known, or the Wolves' Subway Army, or the Tranmere Stanley Boys, or the Villa Hardcore, or The Derby Lunatic Fringe, or the Preston Para Squad, or the Hull City Psychos – they all had names, all the hooligan gangs. And it would be fists and feet and sticks and chains and Stanley knives and iron bars and blood and screams and fucking chaos. The first time I saw this I was rooted to the spot where I stood, like I wasn't able to move for fear and disbelief and a sick feeling in my stomach. Then the adrenalin rushed in and it was like nothing I'd ever experienced before – no drink or drug had ever giving me the same feeling, better than the best roller coaster in Alton Towers, crazier than a skydive, more G force than a jet aeroplane.

It was sickening, when you think about it, to see people being headbutted and kicked like rag dolls and stabbed and noses split and ears bitten off and heads cut open. I was in the thick of it once when someone shouted to me:

'Remember the rule!'

'What rule?'

'Always protect your tool.'

Next thing I got a whack in the bollocks and I went

down, coughing and spluttering to the ground. Only to be pulled back up again by someone close by. It wouldn't last long, maybe five minutes or so, then it would be over as quick as it began. They'd leave calling cards, the gangs, it was a trend that was started by the southern firms, but the northern crews soon took it up and you'd leave a card whether you won or lost or ran or whatever. Then afterwards in the pub there'd be all the talk, all the bragging and the boasting and the piss-taking and God help whoever walked into it – strayed into it. It didn't matter if they were out for trouble or not, or if they were with a bird, or their mother, or their little cousin Annie. They'd soon be surrounded and beaten shitless. It was mindless and sickening and I didn't like it at first, but I soon got used to it, like you can get used to anything. Can't you? You can come to accept anything, if you see it often enough.

Then we'd all disperse to different parts of the town, going in groups of eight or ten and one night I knew of a party going on somewhere on the way home. So I said so long to the others and went there on my own. I was a centre of attraction at the party, because some of them knew I was with the GHS and I really thought I was somebody. Then a knock came to the door and somebody said it was for me. I made my way out and saw it was the people I'd left earlier.

'Hey lads . . . you coming in?'

'No. Why don't you come out?'

So I did and they walked away and I followed behind them.

'Where we going?'

But they didn't answer and I traipsed after them because I got the feeling things weren't right for some reason and I didn't want to be kicked out of the group. We walked for about five or ten minutes, cutting into cobbled alleyways like rat runs.

'Hey, lads, what's up? Don't blank me.'

We were in an alley that was a cul-de-sac at one end and it was dark, except for a street lamp at the other end. Then they came at me without warning, no shouts or nothing, just jumped me like I'd strayed into their pub after a footy-fight. My jumper was pulled over my head and I could feel the kicks going into my ribs and my head flying back every time it was punched. They were swinging me from side to side, trying to kick my legs away. But I didn't go down. I daren't go down, because I knew what'd happen if I did.

Then they stopped and walked away, out of the alley. I was in bloody bits – clothes torn, eyes cut, nose bleeding, lip swollen and body bruised. But I went after them and pleaded with them because I didn't want to lose their favour. I mean, it wasn't just the group, I'd lose a lot more if they kicked me out and I'd be a target for everyone with a grief against me. I'd have to go and try to get back in with the Bradley or the Wybers or the Willows lot and they'd take it out on me for going with the GHS in the first place. After a while they talked to me and told me never to leave the group again – never! We all go to a party or none of us go. This was the punishment I mentioned earlier if you done something they didn't like and it was a heavy lesson to learn.

Being involved in football violence wasn't something I ever thought was wrong – at least not at the time. It was like an organised testosterone-reduction valve for youths and men – a safety valve for them to let off steam in the absence of a good war to cull some of the buggers. The general public didn't care too much as long as we beat the crap out of each other instead of taking it home to our wives and children. I mean, nobody complains about the violence and killing in a war, as long as it ain't on their doorstep – like, as long as someone else is suffering the violence and killing. And that's what it was like, a tribal thing that replaced the battles of the olden days and your football team was your flag – it represented what you were and where you came from and it gave people like me an identity that we never had before. Like something to care about that cared about you in return. Or so it seemed at the time.

My amateur football career was also on the up as well and I was playing for Barton Town. But the fighting came first, before the sport. The police and government erected high fences at the grounds to keep the firms apart and they issued ID cards for the generals and banned people from the games, but it didn't matter. We found ways round all the regulations. I'd wake up knowing what was on for that day, wondering if the coppers had sussed it or would the ruck be uninterrupted. It was rife up and down the country and I loved it – at least, that's what I told myself. We'd congregate in town and listen to the whispers and work ourselves up until the older lads and the generals got us organised. If we were away, we'd be drinking on the trains and we'd have to march into the enemy town and sometimes we'd be ambushed on the way.

I remember one time it all kicked off early with the Scunthorpe True-Iron firm, when they smashed up part of Grimsby town centre after getting off the train. We were at Lucky Las Vegas Amusement Park and my heart raced when we were told it was gonna be a big battle. It was something I was addicted to in some weird way, it was me getting back for all the things that happened that I couldn't do nothing about. I decided this, not someone else. I decided whether to fight or run or who I'd take on or who I'd avoid – who I was gonna face, the size of them and how old they were and what they were carrying –

'Man up, you little prick!'

Sure, I'd manned up all right. But I still felt the terror, deep down. The waiting was the worst, the anticipation, like when I was young and me and Andrea would be waiting for Bob to come through the door from the pub. Once the waiting was over it was all right, once the fist-swinging started. But the waiting was like wanting to throw up, like you didn't know whether to piss or shit or shout out:

'I don't want to be doing this, but I don't know what else to do.'

Anyway, we met up with the Scunny firm and they ran us ragged. We were on the back foot and running when the meat wagons turned up. We were caught between the two and I knew I had to somehow get through the police line. I was in the fire brigade by then and if I got arrested and convicted I'd be out on my ear. Then a copper dragged me to the ground and he was reaching for his handcuffs when the retreating GHS crowd ran straight over him like a herd of stampeding wildebeest and by the time he knew what had happened, I'd got back to my feet and scarpered.

We were to meet the Scunny True-Iron again, at Isaac's Hill and that's where I was to make a name for myself, even though I didn't do it deliberately. Four-hundred hooligans from Scunny converged on the roundabout between Clee Road and Prince's Road, all bouncing up and down. We were about twenty yards away, all lined along the A180-Grimsby Road, bouncing and chanting. I was right at the front and so close I could smell the stale beer off the bastards' breath. There was no police and it was at boiling point, with the generals shouting at us to stand:

'No fucker runs!'

'Stand your ground!'

There were between two and three hundred of us and the commands were being yelled up and down the ranks. I wasn't sure what I was supposed to do and the waiting was doing my bloody head in. Then something snapped and I made a run towards the heart of the enemy front line – on my own. I was screaming like a lunatic:

'I'm gonna bury you! I'm gonna bury you!'

My fists were swinging wildly, trying to connect with someone – anyone. Then I got smashed in the face a few times and someone kicked me in the kidneys and I fell down, winded. Feet started stamping on me and I was trying to get a puff out of an asthma inhaler, but they kicked it away from me and punched and punched and punched. Then about twenty GHS were around me and I managed to crawl away from the front line and back down the street. Police vans were turning up and I was lifted to my feet and dragged away through the alleys of Cleethorpes.

Then Hillsborough happened. You probably know all this anyway, but the stadium in Sheffield was segregated like most football grounds in the country at the time and the coppers put the Notts Forest fans in the Kop end, which was bigger than the Leppings Lane end, so that the routes of the supporters wouldn't cross. Some Liverpool fans were delayed and, just before kick-off, they all congregated outside the turnstiles at Leppings Lane. A bottleneck developed and there was more LFC supporters than could fit into the cages in the middle of the terrace. The match kicked off and the fans outside could hear the cheering inside. The coppers opened a gate with no turnstiles to let the 5,000 fans in and this caused a rush through the gates. The cages were already overcrowded and the rush of supporters crushed the people at the front up against the high wire fences. It was some time before anyone realised what was happening, until fans began climbing over the fences to escape and others were pulled to safety by people in the West Stand, directly above the Leppings Lane terrace. The fans were packed in so tightly that many of them died standing up. Eyewitnesses said the police were too busy making a cordon to keep the Notts Forest and Liverpool fans apart and when people tried to get through to take the injured to ambulances, the coppers forced them back. Forty-four ambulances arrived at the stadium, but the cops only let one in. It was all in the inquiry that came out afterwards and the Taylor Report and questions asked in the House of Commons and everything. Ninety-six people died and only fourteen of them ever got to hospital. A further seven hundred and sixty-six fans were injured. Seventy-nine of the people killed were under thirty, the youngest was only ten.

It was all on the news, like I said, and you've probably seen it a thousand times. The television cameras were there to show the match, but instead they showed the disaster. Every football fan and hooligan in the country watched in silence. And you might think we were heartless tossers, but we all felt the despair of the families involved. We all felt the hatred for the police and the government cover-up that followed. There was no fighting that Saturday, no rucking and no drunkenness. It was the saddest day in British football.

We were away to Wimbledon once in the fifth round of the FA Cup. Now, some people we knew from Grimsby had moved down to Heathrow to work as caterers or something in a hotel and told us they could put us up in the staff quarters for a night. So, instead of going on the regular fans coaches on the Saturday, a group of about ten of us decided to buy one-way tickets to Victoria, London, and go down the previous night. We met up outside the town hall at 8.00 a.m. and got on a National Express coach. There was no lager on the coach, but that was cool, we just played cards all the way down for pennies and smoked baccy and were looking forward to the night in London, where I'd been once before with Trevor the trainspotter. So I was giving it big about how I knew my way around down there and I'd soon find the way to the hotel. Anyway, when we arrived at Victoria Coach Station, the place was massive and all I could see was different colour lines running in all directions along the bloody floor – red lines and blue lines and yellow lines and green lines and purple lines and I didn't even know how to get out of the place, never mind find my way to bloody Heathrow.

Eventually someone told us our best bet was to take a tube, so we asked our way to the Underground and got on the first tube-train we saw. Now, none of us knew how to read a tube map and I think we were down there for about six months, going north, south, east and west and not knowing how to find an escalator to get back above ground. Some bloke from Hindustan eventually told us to get on the Piccadilly line going west and not to get off until the train stopped.

We called our friends at the hotel when we finally arrived at Heathrow and they came and took us to the local pub and we stuck out like a sore thumb – ten northern lads in a London pub, even if it wasn't really London. But it went all right and there was no aggro for some strange reason and it might have been because the people out in Heathrow were used to all sorts coming in off the planes and didn't worry too much about a few Grimbos. Anyway, we only had one room between us in the staff quarters back at the hotel. We were fairly merry by the time we got there and we ended up smoking ganja and nicking the food from the kitchen and, when we were stoned, we pretended to be Harry Carpenter, interviewing each other for the telly. We drew straws for the bed and I ended up with a pillow on the floor. There was some other lad asleep beside me on another pillow and I must've chucked up in the night all over him and neither of us woke up. But, next morning, I opened my eyes and saw him sitting up bleary-eyed, with the pillow congealed to the back of his head. The vomit had solidified during the night and stuck his hair to the pillow and he didn't even realise it until he looked in the mirror.

Once we'd cleaned ourselves up and robbed everything in the hotel we could carry out in sports bags, we got back on the Piccadilly line and headed east for Wimbledon, via Hammersmith and Earls Court. The Grimsby coaches had arrived and the GHS were all in the Swan pub, drinking and singing and chanting. Then we marched to the stadium with a police escort, and the coppers rushing in and snatching any likely troublemakers, all the way down to Plough Lane. Grimsby were beat fair and square and it never kicked off like we hoped it would. The only thing we did was introduce Harry the Haddock to the world, which was a big inflatable fish and it was the Grimsby Town mascot for a while, before the Mighty Mariner. Getting home proved to be a bit of a problem, as we only bought one-way tickets and we had no money left. We tried to cadge a ride on the supporters' buses, but there was no room, so we ended up hitchhiking, which took us two days of starvation and dehydration and sleeping in bloody fields.

The Tearaway

I left the house-share with Joanne and Frances because they had boyfriends and I was like a spare prick at a wedding. I couldn't move in with Nicole, because her father would've had a bloody apoplectic fit, so I was just drifting from one mate's house to another for a while, staying until I wore out my welcome and then moving on somewhere else. I was well into my apprenticeship by now and looking forward to finishing it and getting a real job. Anyway, I was living with this GHS bloke called Moby, which was a reference to his penis, and he had loads of brothers who were all GHS as well. He was a nasty bugger and he'd always be punching at me or trying to give me a dead-leg or something and I put up with it because we both knew his brothers would kick the crap out of me if I sorted him. One of his older brothers in particular was a real vicious bastard and he used to burst into the bedroom with a copper's truncheon when he was pissed up and smack us across the shins when we'd be lying top 'n' tail in bed.

'Riot police. Wake up, you slags!'

'Fuck off!'

'It's been reported you're a pair of irons in bed doing nasty things to each other.'

'Leave us alone!'

One night he was so drunk he came in with a machete and cut me across the leg so bad I had to have stitches.

Anyway, this particular night I was out with Moby and I had a bad dose of the shits for some reason. We'd done a half-bottle of vodka and the Anadins before going into JDs night-club, but I had to get in the bog fast. I was sitting there, biting the back of the door, with what resembled a gallon of double-strength Turkish coffee coming out of my arse, when Moby kicked the door and it smashed me right on the bridge of the nose and there was claret and scutter everywhere. I didn't know whether to wipe my arse or my nose first and Moby was pissing on himself laughing – that was the kind of warped sense of humour the tosser had. I don't know whether this was the last straw or whether it was the argument we were having on the way home about some bloody stupid thing or other that I can't remember now, but he headbutted me on my already busted-up nose. Well, I didn't hold back, I leathered the clown. All the little digs and jabs came back to me and I wouldn't let him fall down, I held him up and kept on hitting him and it was like he was dead on his feet. When I stopped, he just collapsed on the ground like a rag doll.

I ran back to his house and climbed up the drainpipe and in through the bedroom window. I wanted to get my stuff and get out of there before Moby got back and his brothers saw what I done to him. I was just heading back out onto the landing when I heard his older brother letting Moby in and he looked like the Elephant Man's cousin. Next thing I know this big tattooed bastard is rushing up the stairs at me. I bolted back into the bedroom and out through the window, throwing my bag down ahead of me, then sailing down the pipe and away up the street before the bugger could lay hands on me. But I knew I'd have to face the music sooner or later. I went back to Joanne and Fran's house in Meggies and they let me stay a couple of nights until I found somewhere else.

Next night I went into town, it was either that or try to
hide – which wasn't an option. I went to the Bull Ring and
they were all there, except for Moby and his brothers. One
of the leaders called Lobo came over to me and said if Moby
was out of order and I did what I had to do, then I'd be safe.
But if he wasn't, then it would be bad for me. He told me
to keep out of the brothers' way until it could be sorted out
and I did and it was. I never heard nothing more about it.
That's how things worked in the gangs, you could get
stamped on when you didn't expect it and, when you did
expect a hiding, you got off free. That's how unpredictable
it was.

I can't remember where I dossed down after that, but I
moved around a bit, so it could be any one of a few places.
Wherever it was, I was going back there one night after
being to a pub or club and I was fairly mashed on the booze
and the weed. Well, you know how I like to play pranks
sometimes and there was this bike parked on the street – a
racing bike, like with the curved handlebars and it had a
chain in blue plastic and a combination lock on it. I thought
for some reason it would be a giggle to move it up the road
a bit, but I couldn't open the lock. So I just picked it up and
started carrying it, which wasn't easy with the curved
handlebars. I managed to get it about ten houses along
before I fell over, so I just left it there and walked on. About
five minutes later, this car crawled up alongside me and the
window wound down.

'Did you take a bike back there?'

'No.'

'We saw you.'

'You must be seeing things, mate.'

'We *saw* you!'

Then the car pulled up in front of me and this big bastard got out.

'Get in the car.'

'Fuck off.'

'Get in the car!'

The bastard grabbed me by the arm and forced me towards the car. There was another bloke inside behind the steering wheel. I thought they might be plain clothes and I was too mashed to either run or fight.

'You can show me where my bike is.'

I thought I might as well, then I could bugger off and get some sleep. I didn't want no grief with the law in case it got back to the fire brigade and it wasn't far back, maybe about two hundred yards or so. So I got in the back seat. The car drove back, past the racing bike and kept going for another half mile or so, turning left and right every so often as we went. Then it stopped outside this house and the two big buggers dragged me out and bundled me through a porch door and into a hallway. I didn't know what the hell was going on – maybe they were friends of Moby and they were gonna sort me out proper for beating him up. As they frog-marched me through the hallway, there were doors on either side and one of them was open as we passed and, inside, I could clearly see a grown man buggering a young boy of about thirteen. My stomach churned and my legs turned to jelly. They threw me out into a small yard with no gate, just high brick walls and a concrete floor. I don't know how long I was out there – it seemed like hours, but it was probably just minutes. Then a different bloke came through the back door, being all nice and telling me not to worry. Then he said he'd give me £50 for sex. He said it would be quick and it wouldn't hurt. I was still half-mashed and I didn't know what to say.

'No thanks, I'm not like that, mister.'

'I'll make it £70.'

'Eh . . . all right, but I want the cash now.'

He smiled and went back inside, maybe to get the money – I dunno why. The minute the door closed, I launched myself at the wall, trying to scale it. But it was too high. I crashed back down and landed on my back. There was frosted glass in the back door and I could see someone coming towards the yard, so I launched myself at the wall again, this time clinging on by my fingers and ripping my nails and digging my trainers into the joints between the bricks. Then I was up, falling down on the other side and staggering through the alleys and out onto a main road. I made it back to where I was staying, keeping in the shadows and out of sight as much as I could. And when I finally crashed into bed I couldn't sleep. All I could think about was that young kid – and what they were doing to him.

Chapter Eleven

I tried to find that house several times after, but I just couldn't remember where it was. I was mashed on lager and locoweed and it was dark and I was disoriented and intimidated and I just couldn't bloody remember. Even if I had been able to find it, I dunno what I'd have done about it – tell the police? They might have *been* police for all I know. The thing about it is, abuse was widespread in Grimsby during the time I was growing up. I wasn't the only one. I found that out when I got to be a teenager and most of my mates had been abused just like me – some far worse. One of my close friends, Matty McCourt, told me there was abuse on every street and in every house on the Nunny – and he don't mind me telling you this – husbands abusing wives, families abusing other families, kids abusing other kids – it was all over the bloody place, like a disease.

Matty was an only kid, with no brothers or sisters and there was just him and his mam, just like me. She was seeing this Glaswegian hard-man tosser who was always battering her and she had nobody to protect her except Matty, a ten-year-old boy at the time. Matty used to spit in the bugger's tea and rob his wallet when he was drunk and do little things like that, to get back at the bastard for all the times he slammed his mam's head into the wall and all the black eyes and kicks in the stomach with steel-toecapped boots on. When Matty got older, he took up karate and boxing and was fighting with the drunks outside the Nunny Tavern and carrying a blade and fucking up anyone who messed with his mam – and I helped him kick shit out of the bastards whenever he needed me to.

Another mate of mine called Fazza had to leg it all the way home from school every day because his mam's boyfriend ordered him to and if he was a minute late he got a bad beating. His younger brother, who was only five years old, had to be kept off school for three months due to his injuries and Fazza was told to lie to the teachers if they asked about him. At night, this boyfriend of his mam's would make Fazza and his brother get into the bath with him and sexually abuse them. After the bath, he'd beat them on their arses until they bled and then make them do things to each other and then sexually abuse them again. Fazza's dad found out what was going on when the boys went for a visit with him. He took the kids to the police station to have their bodies photographed as evidence, then he went looking for their mam's boyfriend with a sawn-off shotgun. However, the man wasn't there and the coppers took the gun away from him. The man was prosecuted for the horrible things he done to those little kids, but he only got a fifty-quid fine for GBH, because the kids' own mother testified that no abuse happened. Fazza later found out she received death threats to make the thing go away. Makes you wonder, don't it?

Anyway, I knew all these stories about the widespread abuse that went on in Grimsby when I was a young boy and that was still going on when I was a teenager. So who would I go to, even if I did find that house? Who could I trust? Nobody. The only people I could trust were the lads on the streets and in the gangs who'd went through the same and worse abuse as me. They were the only ones who understood what it was like and how it was all over the place, in every house and on every street – like a fucking epidemic. Like a horrible, stinking, sewer-hole plague. So I forgot about the kid who was getting buggered in that house by those big men and I went on my way.

As far as the gangs were concerned, I was getting a reputation for being a bit of a liability. You see, every now and then I'd come across one of the bastards who used to knock me about on the Bradley Park estate, or terrorise me when I had my paper round – the ones who were ten when I was seven and who were thirteen when I was ten. In the space of a year I must've kicked shit out of about a dozen of them, the people who'd wronged me in the past, and I didn't care what family they came from or what gang they belonged to. This went against all the rules. I was angry all the time and I didn't care how I got even and I always let the buggers know who was beating them up, whether they remembered me or not. It was round about this time I met Adrian again. Remember I told you about the bullying stopping that day – except for one bastard? Well, this Adrian kept it up because he was a lot bigger than me and he was a fifth year and I was a second year and he did it because he was a mean, vindictive fucker. Every morning – a punch here, a dig there, a neck hold, a trip, a dead leg. Anyway, I was at the back of the Yarborough Vaults in the train station car park in the town centre. I was pissing up against a wall, seeing how high I could get the stream to go. It was dark and I sensed someone behind me. As I turned round, this voice I remembered spoke to me.

'You Dean Williams?'

'Yer.'

'I'm Adrian, from Hillary. Remember me?'

'I remember you alright.'

'I hear you're settling old scores?'

I could make out two other shapes standing behind him, so I figured best to get the first shot in first. The pub opposite the Vaults was being refurbished and the skips outside were full of broken scaffold planks. The fight spilled out into the light of the street lamps and I'd been waiting a long time to lay into this fucker. This wasn't the school playground and I was a lot bigger now than I was then. It only took a couple of minutes to put him down and I hit one of his mates with a piece of scaffold board from the skips and knocked him out cold. The third one came at me with a length of lead pipe, but I grabbed a dustbin lid and used it as a shield. He made a wild swing and I smashed the lid into his face and he went down on top of the other two. I didn't normally kick people when they were on the ground, but I figured these fuckers deserved it and I gave them a few boots before I went on my way.

Revenge was sweet – I knew it would be. But the senior guys in the gangs didn't like this; it drew too much heat and made targets of everybody. Things were getting difficult.

One day in the Bull Ring pub playing pool, the inevitable happened. It's a wonder it hadn't happened before then, but I suppose that's just the way life is – when you're least expecting it. Who walked in the pub but my father and his brother, Dave. Now, my old man and my uncle had more of a reputation than all the gang leaders put together. They even looked hard, if you know what I mean. They looked like men who weren't to be messed with and all my mates knew it. Bob nodded in my direction and I nodded back, but he didn't speak or come over near me. He and Dave went to the bar where a lot of older people were drinking. I was nervous. There was an atmosphere in the place the minute they came in and I knew something was gonna happen, but what would I do if it did?

It didn't take long – an argument broke out at the bar, where Bob had been talking to some bloke's missus. The man rushed over to where we were playing pool and grabbed a cue and I didn't know whether I should clout him before he got back to the bar or not, but I did nothing, just stood there rooted to the spot. Maybe this guy would give it to my dad; maybe he'd be able to sort him. But Bob had seen too many things being swung at him in pubs over the years. He launched his left fist, just as the man came into range and it hit the bloke square on his jaw. He went down like a chimney collapsing in on itself.

Bob and Dave drank up and walked towards the exit,

slowly, making sure everybody knew they weren't worried about anyone in there. On the way out, my dad stopped at the pool table and gave me a look again; this time there was a question on his face, as if to say 'Here I am, Dean. Here I am if you want me. I gave you more grief than all those kids you're beating up. Come and take me on.' But I did nothing. I just stood there looking at him. Then he smirked at me and I knew he was saying 'You're not ready yet, boy.' He walked out and the bloke he hit had to go to hospital to have his jaw wired.

I don't know why my father came into that pub on that night. Was it a coincidence, or was it deliberate? Did he hear from someone that I was hanging out around there and I was getting a bit of a reputation as a hard kid and he wanted to see what I was made of? I dunno – what d'you think? Anyway, to finish off about all the football hooligan stuff, we went to a lot of games, home and away. Not just Grimsby Town games, but Liverpool as well. Although Town were my first team, I always liked the Reds and they played in the top division and this attracted all the big firms, especially from down south. Like the Chelsea Headhunters and the Millwall Bushwackers and the Yid Army from Tottenham and Section Five from West Brom and all the others as well. But we all ganged up together when we went to the England matches, where we fought with crews from Germany and Holland and Spain and Turkey and all over Europe.

One of the last memories that stands out in my mind from the days when I was a hooligan and a thug was Barnsley at home, pre-season. As you know, I was obsessed with the media images of the fights and I kept them all pinned up in my cupboard until Alan found them and threw them out. My face was always blurry and unrecognisable in them and I decided to take some pictures of myself in the next ruck. As a kid, I loved *The Professionals*, Bodie and Doyle; remember I told you earlier about my jumble-sale jacket? Well, I didn't have a camera, not like nowadays when there's one in every mobile phone, and I saw this MI5 Professionals spy kit in a toyshop in town – badge and cap gun and walkie-talkie and spy camera. So I nicked the camera from the kit and all it was, was a small cube-shaped thing like an imitation micro 110, with a flip-up plastic square for a viewfinder. But it took real pictures and that's all I wanted.

Anyway, we were told there was a mob of Barnsley supporters down the seafront and we were walking up from the ground towards Cleethorpes. The idea was to start at the top end of the seafront where all the pubs were and hunt them down. As I had a camera, I decided to go the other way and walk up from the Sunday Market end, or Wonderland as it was known. My idea was to catch the action from behind and then get someone to take a few snaps of me in the middle of it. I walked along the seafront area where the ramp-like sea-defences slope down on the left and there's a concrete wall running along on the right, until I came to the popular area with the beach and the black metal railings – sometimes it was a four-foot drop on the other side to the sand and sometimes it could be six foot, all depends on the wind. On this day it was quiet – just passers-by. No mobs causing havoc and smashing up the candyfloss stalls and the arcades and ripping the ornamental wooden belaying pins off the walls of the seafront shops and using them as clubs. I stood next to the railings and a young bum-picker – which is what we called the Cleethorpes Beach Patrol firm – ran past me. I shouted to him:

'What's happening? You seen Barnsley?'

'Nah. I'm told they're down here, like.'

I had this stupid kid's camera in my hand, with one foot on the railings and one on the ground. Then I felt a tap on the sole of my shoe. I looked down at the sand and saw about thirty Barnsley Riot Squad all stood tight up against the promenade tide-barrier thing. The CBP lad bolted, and I wasn't far behind. But we were running away from the action and only two of the Barnsley decided to give chase. When we got too far away for any backup, me and the kid turned round. They were close to us and beckoning.

'Eh up, flower, does thee want a smack?'

'Is your mam an' dad brother and sister?'

This riled them a bit and they started coming at me. I started snapping with the camera and that confused them, they didn't know what the hell I was doing. Then I threw the camera to the kid and told him to take my picture, as I waded into the pair of them. Before they knew what was happening, I'd given them both a couple of whacks and they were stunned a bit. Then they started to fight back and I took a few clouts and kicks, before a commotion down the other end of the seafront caught their attention. The main ruck was kicking off down there, so they ran back in that direction. But, before they did, one of them grabbed the camera from the CBP kid.

I went after the buggers, into the mayhem – sixty or seventy lads all going at it with the batons ripped from the walls and fighting running battles through the arcades, but I couldn't get hold of the one who took my camera. A few weeks later, I was watching television somewhere when a local news programme came on and there was me, rucking with the two Barnsley hooligans and the police were wanting to know if anybody recognised these men? Apparently, the Barnsley mob got stopped and searched on the way back to their train and the toy camera got confiscated and the bloody coppers had the pictures developed, would you believe? Luckily enough, I wasn't living with me mam or dad at the time or I'd have been in big bloody trouble. All the same, I wore a cap and a scarf round my face for a few weeks after and I just had to hope nobody at the fire brigade had seen the report. But luck was with me – for a change.

As they got older, all the football hooligans began to settle down. Some of them got married and others moved away and the rave scene was in full swing and the government was clamping down big time on the violence. The fighting was dying out. I wanted it to keep going for ever, but the groups in the town centre dwindled, until there was only us lads with nowhere left to go. Everybody was getting into acid and E; the scene had exploded from nowhere and was taking over Grimsby. OK, I'd been doing the booze and the weed and the gas and stuff, but I'd never done any acid before and I heard stories about people jumping out through windows and thinking they could fly and killing themselves. They said you had to have someone with you when you took an acid tab to stop you doing crazy things and there would be flashbacks later, after you came down from the trip. Anyway, a few of us decided to see what all the talking was about and we bought eight purple oms between four of us and went out for the night.

We started off on Meggies seafront – I can't remember if it was in McCartney's or the Casablanca, but the music was 'Pump Up the Jam' and we all went into the toilets and took half a tab each and waited for something to happen. Every minute we were asking each other:

'What d'you feel like?'

'Dunno. What d'you feel like?'

'Normal.'

Then someone remembered that alcohol was supposed to ruin the trip, so we all went on orange juice.

'What's happening?'

'Nothing.'

And then I realised I was laughing. And everyone else was laughing too. My face was going numb and my head felt like it was someone else's. My heart-rate was fast and there was a lump in my throat. We decided to make our way over to the Winter Gardens and maybe listen to more acid music, but just getting there was an experience. By now it felt like I wasn't in my own body, I was in the elastic man's instead. In the Winter Gardens, I was dancing like I was having an epileptic fit and, when I wasn't dancing, I was staring at the patterns on the wallpaper. Thoughts of fighting or violence never even entered my mind, even when some bugger barged into me and half his pint went down my new shirt. Anyway, it would've been like trying to punch Medusa and Bugs Bunny and Elmer Fudd all at the same time – that's what he looked like to me. And when he glared at me and I lifted my fist, my arm was Popeye's, with an anvil on the end and, before I could use it, Bugs Bunny poked me in the eye with a carrot.

One of my mates was licking the wallpaper and the other two were behaving so weirdly they attracted the attention of the bouncers and we got kicked out. It was dark by now and the cars were whizzing past and all I could see was a drizzle of lights, white and red, in perfect lines – like you see it sometimes in the movies when the camera is speeded up. I could have sat on the wall all night, just watching stuff morph into strange things. For the next six or eight hours, we wandered the streets of Cleethorpes like zombies. Crossing the roads was a nightmare, even at 3.00 a.m. The roads themselves looked like rufty-tufty roads and I could just step across them with one stride. The Belisha beacons looked like orange lollipops on liquorish sticks and if I wanted I could step across and eat a Chupa Chups. The pavement looked like the sea, like it was breathing, and my black shirt had little white animals running all over it. One of my mates freaked out and ran off, screaming that I was the Devil and one of the dogs had bit him – he must've been having a bad trip.

We were all starving, but by now there was nowhere open for us to get any grub. And, as well as that, there was this grown-up doll waving to me from a top bedroom window. I waved back and she started dancing. By 5.00 a.m. we were back on the seafront again and there was this castle and we scaled the outside wall like Spiderman. But I was slipping back down and the others pulled me up to safety by my boxer shorts. Then we rolled down the sand dunes in the desert and came across a funfair. I wanted to sit in the topmost bucket on the big wheel and I began to climb up the steel ropes to get to it. But halfway up I started to come down off the acid trip and my fear of heights kicked in. I was stuck, afraid to go up and afraid to climb back down. The other two had to climb up and get me, prise my fingers off the steel rope and help me down and I didn't know whether they were still tripping or not. When we did get down, we found we were surrounded by cops. Not because we climbed up the big wheel, but because McCartney's nightclub was broken into and the burglars left footprints that led our way. We were ID-checked and one of the others was arrested for non-payment of fines and taken away. Me and the other guy were told to go home. Weird night or what?

Chapter Twelve

But I suppose I should get back to Nicole, shouldn't I? Because I really ought to explain a bit better what it was like. There was this film out in 1990 called *Truly, Madly, Deeply*, with Alan Rickman and Juliet Stevenson, about these two people called Nina and Jamie and he dies and she can't accept he's gone. Nicole wanted to see it, so she got the tape and we stayed in my place one Sunday afternoon with the rain pouring down outside and watched it. Now, I wasn't really one for watching mushy films on the weekend and, if I had to be in, I'd rather be watching *Grandstand* or something and sitting there having to be quiet and concentrate was too much like being back in school for me. It didn't feel right for some reason, like it was uncomfortable and it was safer for me to joke about it, to take the piss and stuff, the way I always did to get me by when I felt threatened by something. The truth was, deep down, I could feel Nina's pain. The film was beautiful and I thought to myself this must be how people appreciate art and classical music and stuff like that – stuff I never understood much about. It was like Nicole opened a door slightly and let me have a little peep through.

The Tearaway

When the film was over, Nicole asked me what I thought – like, she asked for my opinion. Well, I didn't want to give her no opinion, because I didn't want to leave myself open to being ridiculed or rejected or laughed at. I think it was because I thought people like me weren't supposed to have opinions. I mean, I never had no one around me who I could have an opinion with – except the gangs. We could talk about football firms and how many lads would be turning up to a ruck, or the ins and outs of a diesel engine at the fire station, or about clothes and chart hits and trivial stuff with some of the girls I knew. But if I mentioned the subplot of an art-house movie, I might as well have just come out and said I was bloody gay. No, people like me weren't meant to comment on intellectual stuff. We were meant to follow in our fathers' footsteps and beat shit out of our wives and kids and not go places we understood sod all about and not share opinions with people like Nicole.

I didn't know about art, or about subtle, emotional films. Nicole knew about that stuff and sometimes it seemed like I was more of a project than a person to her – you know, like the geezer in *My Fair Lady* who bets he can make the Cockney bird talk proper. All I knew about was what life had taught me, like how to survive and stuff, even though I knew there had to be more to it. Like sometimes when it seemed there was something inside me that was struggling to get out but I didn't know what it was – except that it might be I was gay or bisexual or something crazy like that. A physical thing, not a mental thing or a brainbox thing or a thing that was studious in any way. Anyway, Nicole wouldn't let me off the hook, she kept asking for my opinion – like, it was more provoking me to say what I thought rather than asking me, if you know what I mean. Like she knew I had an opinion inside me and she was determined to find the bugger. It took a lot, but eventually I said I didn't know if Jamie really died, or if it was all inside Nina's head. I waited for her to laugh, but she didn't. And I was surprised when we started to have a real conversation about what we'd just seen and I listened to her and the things she said stayed in my canister and I began to think about other things, stuff I didn't even know was in the world – not exactly like kindness and gentleness and warmth, but something similar.

We adopted the phrase 'Truly, Madly, Deeply' after that, me and Nicole. We used it when she was away. We whispered it to each other – not 'I love you' or anything like that, just those three words 'Truly, Madly, Deeply'. When she went back to university after term break, I made a tape of all her favourite songs and I said them words at the end of it, just to surprise her. And once I rang the local radio station to play a request for her and the message I sent with the request asked her to marry me. But I forgot it was local radio and she wouldn't hear it down in Cambridge, but it made me feel good and I pretended she had heard it and that it made her feel good as well. The strange thing about it – or maybe it wasn't so strange – was that being with Nicole gave me a taste for stuff – like I wanted some of that sophistication she had. I wanted it to rub off on me, but I knew it never would. Not much of it anyway. I wanted to know more about Nicole's world. I liked the mystery of it, the challenge of it, like on a snowy winter's night when you see a light in the distance through the blizzard and you think it might be an angel or something and you go towards it, but the more you follow it, the further away it gets and you can never get near enough to see what it really is.

Nicole was studying medicine and she knew what she wanted in life. I was just a street-philosopher, always trying to keep one step ahead and not get caught by the inevitability of it all. Now there was something new. But then the unthinkable happened. We'd spent most of the summer together, on and off, when she could get away from her lousy parents, with me doing my own stuff in between. But we were getting closer all the time and the thing between us was beginning to move in on everything else – like everything else was being pushed away. I was living in a shared house near my work and Nicole spent the last few days there, before going back down to university.

We said goodbye and 'Truly, Madly, Deeply' and all and I never thought any more about it – until one night I got in from work and there was an envelope addressed to me on the side. The only letters I got were either threatening ones or from Nicole, so I opened it, looking forward to reading her posh ramblings and laughing to myself at her forty words where one would've done. But this time it was short and to the point. It was a 'Dear Dean' letter and it was like I'd been kicked in the stomach by a bloody ostrich. It was like the house was falling in on top of me and the sky was falling in on top of the house.

I read the letter again, because the first time I didn't see any of the words after 'It's over'. She was saying things like how she'd lost her identity and how she needed some space and I thought, if you need space why don't you become an astronaut and how can someone lose their identity? Why didn't she keep it somewhere safe? It was like this world of hers that I was getting used to had turned on me like a dog and was trying to bite my balls off and I didn't know why – I didn't know what I'd done to it to make it hate me. We didn't have mobile phones nor Facebook and I knew if I rang her house number in Cambridge, I'd be told she wasn't available. I could write a letter back and wait a week for a reply, if there was a reply – so I knew there was only one thing for it, I had to get down there. I was skint, as usual, still paying for the car I'd smashed up and I'd just paid up the rent. So I decided to hitchhike.

I never packed or nothing; just stuck the letter into my pocket and headed out onto the A16 and started walking. It was getting into November and the nights were cold and I was glad I was wearing my work coat with 'Fire' written across the back. It kept me warm and it made it easier for me to get lifts. We weren't supposed to wear the fire coats outside of work hours, but I didn't care right then, I just had one thing on my mind. My first lift was an articulated lorry that took me as far as Lincoln, then a van to Grantham and a farmer's pick-up that smelled of pigs the rest of the way down to Cambridge. I'd never been to Nicole's house, because I crashed before I got there the last time, if you remember, and all I had was an address. All I knew was that she was sharing and it was close to the campus. It was late by the time I found the place and all the lights were out and I guessed they were all probably in the student union bar. So I posted Nicole's letter through the door and went round the back. There was a concrete cupboard where the bin was kept and I thought about waiting in there out of the cold. But every time I tried to go in, I imagined the door closing behind me and being locked from the outside and a man's voice shouting.

I don't know how much later it was when I heard them coming in. A female voice with a Birmingham accent said:

'Durs a letta here for yew, but it says Dean on eet.'

'That's my letter. That's what I sent to Dean.'

The second voice was Nicole's, so at least I knew I was at the right house. Other voices were piping up now and I could imagine them all looking at the letter.

'How did it end up here?'

'Has it been redirected?'

'Has it been opened?'

And while they all chattered amongst themselves, I knocked on the back door. Everything went quiet. Then I heard a whisper:

'He's here.'

Nicole finally came and opened the back door. I could see the straining faces of the other girls inside the house.

'You shouldn't have come, Dean.'

'It's cold out here.'

'What's that smell?'

'What smell?'

'Like pigs or something.'

'Must be the silage from the farms round here.'

Anyway, she let me in and took me upstairs, where we could have some privacy to sort out the thing about her finding her identity out in space. The problem was, people had heard the local radio song request and proposal, even though she hadn't and they were talking about her and me in the same breath and her parents were shitting in their pants to hear she was getting married, especially as she didn't know about it herself. You see, Nicole was a modern woman, even back then. She didn't like people making decisions for her and that included me. I managed to convince her it was a spur-of-the-moment thing, like a moment of madness or something – a 'Truly, Madly, Deeply' thing and she understood and we were back on again.

Next day, I rang in sick to work and Ken was OK about it, saying he couldn't cope with me moping around and I should stay home till I got better. It took three days for me to get well and I hung round campus while Nicole was in lectures. I felt a bit like Dustin Hoffman in that film *The Graduate* when he goes up to Berkeley to talk Elaine into being with him. I should tell you this, because it was on my mind at the time, curiously enough – shortly after I first met Nicole, I got a tattoo with a rose and a heart and a scroll with both our names on it. She didn't like it because it was something I'd done without asking her and, all the way down in the artic and the van and the farmer's pick-up, the thought was going through my head that, if we didn't make up, I'd be stuck with her name on my arm, just like I was stuck with Bob's.

Curious, ain't it?

Anyway, after that, I thought I'd better get transport again, so I bought this MZ 150cc motorbike. It was winter now and after testing it out on a trial run down to Cambridge, I decided to take it further afield – to Swindon, where a couple of my mates from Grimsby had moved, to escape the town. I had my 'Fire' jacket on and my Head bag packed with three days' clothes, but I kept having to stop because it was pissing down and the electrics got wet and the engine kept cutting out. Then, after I'd only travelled about forty miles, I lost control of the bike on a double-S-bend. I was going too fast and I clipped the kerb and ended up being catapulted onto a ditch bank. It hurt so much when I tried to pick up my gear and push the bike to the nearest petrol station, I thought I'd broken my shoulder. I sat in the forecourt and lit up a cigarette in an effort to relieve the pain. Then the Tannoy system went off, screaming at me:

'Please extinguish your cigarette!'

I was right next to a 4-star petrol pump.

I was in agony. I couldn't move my right arm and, if I was gonna make the 200 miles to Swindon, I needed to sort something out. Really I should have turned back, but I'm obstinate like that; once I get it into my head to do something or go somewhere, I have to do it. Anyway, the throttle was on the right of the handlebars and I wasn't able to keep it open with my right hand. So, I gritted my teeth and managed to get a matchstick into it to keep it open, meaning my arm could just rest without having to do any work. But, by the time I got to Rugby, the pain was too bad. I had to stop off at a hospital that didn't have an A&E and they told me I had a broken collarbone. But there was nothing they could do except put my arm in a sling, which was bloody useless, as I had to ride the bike. So they gave me some painkillers and I kept moving.

I eventually made it to Swindon, but it took ten hours altogether and it was dark when I got there and I pulled up outside a telephone box and rang my friend, Mark. He came and met me in the town centre and took me to his sister's place to stay. I had a few quid on me, nothing much, but enough for a few beers and petrol for the bike. I said nothing about the broken collarbone, because they'd only want me to go to hospital and I'd be stuck there for the whole bloody weekend.

Later that night, Mark took me to the local pub, where I met another Grimsby mate called Andy and the three of us got steaming drunk and upset the locals. One of them started giving me the evil eye when I was coming back from the bog and I heard him say something under his breath about goat-shaggers and gudgeon-eaters. Then the same bloke goes past me and bumps my bad arm, just as I'm trying to lift a pint with my left hand and spills half of it all over my bloody legs. When we were leaving, him and his mates barged past us, pushing us to one side and, as we were going down the street, they started shouting abuse at us and calling us inbreeds and strumming air-banjos and humming that tune the little kid with the big head was playing in the film *Deliverance*. That was too much to wear. We went at them and they took out to run and thought we were too pissed to catch them, but I managed to clip the mouthy one's ankle and he fell down and Andy jumped on top of him. The others all ran off and left their mate, that'll tell you how good they were, and Mark and Andy battered him proper and, while they were at it, I went through his pockets with my good arm.

I was surprised when I found a big wad of money and a load of drugs. He was obviously a dealer and, while he might've been a useless scrapper, the people who were supplying him might be more dangerous. The bloke was out cold by now, laid out like a starfish and we took the money but left the gear, because we didn't want the aggro of being caught with it, either by the coppers or the dealers. Just as we were leaving, I went back and booted the bastard square in the bollocks, just because I wasn't able to clout him a few times like the other lads, but there wasn't so much as a groan out of him. I mean, he'd just taken the full size ten in the nads and he didn't even whimper and I thought then we might have bloody killed him. That sobered us up a bit and we made off sharpish back to Mark's sister's house, where we divvied up the cash – over £300 apiece. But it was on my mind that the guy was dead and I decided to go back and see if he was breathing and get an ambulance or something. The others wouldn't come with me and it was the early hours and I was stumbling round in the dark trying to find him, but I couldn't. I finally convinced myself that he'd come to and buggered off, so I went back. But it was an uneasy night.

Next day was Saturday, and me and Mark decided to go into town and spend some of the money we nicked from the geezer. But we were no sooner in the shopping centre when we see him, his face all black and blue and he's with these blokes who looked like they just stepped out of the bad side of the Bronx – they could even have been carrying guns because their jackets looked a bit bulgy to me. Then the bugger saw us and pointed and the grease-heads started coming our way. We bolted through the crowd and, after about fifteen minutes of dodging down this street and that, we seemed to have lost them. I thought my weekend was well and truly bollocksed now, but just as we were walking past the Army & Navy store, I saw they had a wig shop inside and the sun shined on me again. Now the syrup I chose cost £35 and it was a proper, long, permed thing and when I tried it on I looked like the buck-toothed one out of the bloody Bee Gees. But I reckoned it would keep me safe from the drug-killers, if they happened to spot us again and I could get on with enjoying my weekend, for the sake of which I'd broken my bloody collarbone.

That night, Mark's cousin invited us to a car party – which is where they all go somewhere in a load of cars and they pull the motors round in a circle, like the covered wagons in the cowboy films I used to watch when I was a boy. Then everybody goes from one car to another to see what's there – booze or weed or tabs or whatever – like a game of freaked-out musical cars. Anyway, I wore the wig and nobody knew any better, because none of the buggers had seen me before except Mark, and he didn't give a bollocks what I looked like. We got to some loch and all the cars formed up and the music went on and the beer came out. Everyone's jumping from one car to another and I did the same – lager in one, a joint in the next, a slug of vodka in the next, and so on, until we started scoring acid tabs. People were tripping all over the place and I got into one car and this bloke said he liked my hair. I was starting to rush and I moved the wig back and forth so it was covering my eyes one minute, then back straight the next. The bloke was fascinated and he said my hair was dancing. Then I just whipped the wig off completely and he fucking freaked out, screaming and jumping out of the car and running off into the night. I couldn't understand what the hell was the matter with him.

Mark found me a bit later and he said we should go for a walk and see what we could make happen – like getting the trees to talk to us or the grass to wave at us. The loch or lake or whatever it was, was built up on both sides and we climbed the bank and found a grass verge down to the water. The water was like a dark carpet, with a streak of moonlight ripping it across the middle. Mark stood admiring his reflection in the glass surface and it was getting difficult to tell which was the water and which was the grass.

'I'm gonna walk to the other side.'

'It's water, Mark.'

'Yer . . . I'm Jesus.'

'But you ain't Moses.'

He walked forward and, for a minute, it seemed like he really was standing on the water. Then he was gone. You see, seconds are like minutes when you're tripping and I was trying to figure out what had just happened, whether it was a hallucination or whether it was real. Then I saw him clambering out through the looking-glass like bloody Alice, minus his shoes. It was getting cold and nobody would let him into their cars because he was dripping and tripping and then someone threw out a tartan travel rug and he sat in the middle of the ring of motors like a big shivering shaking smileyface.

Things didn't go too well on the way home either. The engine seized up on the bike and I had to let it cool down for an hour before I could crack on – and my bloody arm was killing me. I'd just turned nineteen.

Chapter Thirteen

Andrea married Alan in 1987 and they divorced in 1992. It meant the house had to be sold, but I didn't care much because I wasn't living there. I met her a few months later and she was already seeing a new bloke called Sandy. As well as being a Jock, Sandy was an optician and he had a nice house in Humberston, just south of Cleethorpes. I met them a few times and me and him seemed to get on all right. He was a bit of a piss-head, always with a bottle of whisky on the go, and he said I could move in with him and Mam if I liked. I'm not sure if Andrea was too pleased, but it was his house and I was serving out my final year as an apprentice, so the saving on rent and rates appealed to me. Nicole persuaded me to buy a dog as a moving-in present – a golden retriever called George and me and Sandy used to go shooting with it and everything was good. Sandy was a decent bloke and he was on my wavelength and I wasn't as rebellious as I used to be, thanks to Nicole.

I remember she got invited to a ball one time at the Earl of Colchester's place and she asked me to come with her. Sandy went out and hired me a Rover Metro Sport and a tuxedo and cummerbund and dicky bow and everything I needed. The ball was a five-course meal, with a dance afterwards and all the high-flyers from the university were there. I was mixing with people studying to be lawyers and politicians and doctors and, when they asked what I was reading, I told them the riot act for a joke but they didn't laugh, just nodded like a bunch of pigeons who knew exactly what I was talking about.

I was watching what I was saying and trying not to stick my bloody size tens in my mouth. I didn't want to change my accent, because it would sound like I was a right poncey trimmer, but I didn't want to let Nicole down either. I'd never even heard of a champagne reception before, never mind be invited to one, and I never imagined I'd be mixing with these people or wearing a penguin suit. It was like I was Nicole's prince glass-slipper for one night only and it was an occasion to remember – drinking wine and smoking cigars and talking bollocks to people who couldn't tell that what I was saying was a load of shite.

It was the end of year so, the next day, we crammed all Nicole's stuff into the motor and drove back to Grimsby and, on the way, she told me she was pregnant. I nearly crashed the bloody hire car. She said she wanted an abortion – there was no alternative. I knew in my heart she was right, because it would ruin her career and I was still in my final apprenticeship year and we'd never survive on my wages, but I felt strange about it. This kid inside her was mine, like it was part of me. Neither of us were ready for a child but, in a way, I wanted her to keep it, to have it, and I'd work something out. We'd be happy together, me and her and the little kid and I'd bring it up better than I'd been brought up. I tried to get her to talk about it – like, to at least discuss it. How we could survive on my wages until I finished my apprenticeship and the fire brigade gave me a real job and how we could get a flat and she could finish her degree at the Open University and how I'd look after the kid while she was studying and this and that and the other.

But we both knew it was just bullshit.

We borrowed Sandy's Ford Escort to go to Hull for the termination. She wouldn't let me drive in case I did something stupid and crashed the car and, when we got to Hull, we had to go to a little clinic above a shop that was like some nasty secret place. Even though abortion was legal since the sixties, people still frowned on you if they found out – that old head-shaking and nose-snorting and mouth-shouting –

'Man up, you pair of pricks!'

There was loads of young girls there, younger than me and Nicole and I'm thinking it was more of it buggering up their schooling rather than their career for them. Anyway, they wouldn't do it in Hull because it was only a consultation place and they referred us to Leeds for the actual termination. On the way over, we had an argument about our last cigarette – Nicole wanted it, but I told her it was bad for the baby and she called me a bloody fool and said the abortion was bad for the baby and that made me angry, for her to make a joke of it. We were shouting at each other and Nicole wasn't paying attention when she overtook a car on a dual carriageway and she didn't signal or see what was coming in the outside lane. The car spun sideways when a lorry hit us and we were dragged along the central railings, facing the wrong way, while the truck's brakes screeched and tried to stop. Then it was like everything went quiet. The inside of the car was smoky and there was a smell of petrol and my ankle was twisted up under the passenger seat. Nicole grabbed the last cigarette and tried to light it. Her hands were shaking and she couldn't manage it. I took the lighter off her, in case the bloody car exploded and we waited for an ambulance to take us to hospital.

Luckily, we escaped with minor injuries and my ankle was swollen for a while. I mean, Nicole didn't even have a bloody miscarriage, so we still had to go through with the abortion. Sandy's car was a write-off and neither of us was insured to drive it. But he didn't go mad or nothing, just opened another bottle of whisky and poured a big glassful. We got another appointment after about a week or so and travelled over to Leeds the night before and stayed with one of Nicole's friends from university. I couldn't sleep, knowing that the next day what was made by me would no longer be. But it was inside her, not inside me, so she got to make the choice – all I could do was remember the day for the rest of my life and try to tell myself it wasn't a real kid, not a fully developed kid or, on bad days, to read about what a foetus can or can't do at sixteen weeks. We went down to the clinic the next morning and I sloped off to the pub while Nicole was inside and when I came back she was ready to leave. We didn't say nothing on the way back

– and we didn't tell nobody either, so it was just the two of us to cope with it. Simple as that.

It wasn't long after when we decided we needed a break from each other. Well, actually, Nicole decided she needed a break. I wasn't surprised. And the last thing I did was play 'Stars' by Simply Red for her as she was leaving, so she'd think of me every time she heard that song. But I didn't make a fuss like before. I didn't let her see how much I was hurting and she went and I spent my time going to work and coming home and walking for miles and miles with the dog and wandering round the places we liked and listening to our favourite songs on the Walkman. All my old mates had either settled down or moved away or were into drugs in a big way and I kinda slumped into a bit of a depression. My routine was to get a dozen bottles of Newcastle Brown and twenty cigarettes and just sit there drinking and smoking and playing music like the world had ended or something. And it had – at least the world I knew for a while with Nicole, like, the one-way mirror on a better life and culture and stuff. Now it was just me again and it looked like nothing would change. I'd finish my apprenticeship and get a job and go drinking and that would be my life. I'm not complaining or anything, that's a good enough life – it would've been a good enough life, if Nicole hadn't shown me a better one and then buggered off with it.

Anyway, after a while I met this nurse called Christine and she was so fantastically stunning she snapped me out of my self-pity. I went to a club for a drink and there she was, sitting up at the bar and surrounded by all these dickheads who looked like they just jumped out of a John Lewis catalogue. I thought, what the hell have I got to lose, so I said:

'Would you like to buy me a beer?'

'No. But you can buy me a Cleethorpes cocktail.'

'What's that? Half a brown ale with a pickled onion in it?'

She laughed and I knew I was there.

'No. A Cinzano with bitter lemon and a just a dash of grenadine.'

'Ice?'

'Of course.'

She worked in the local A&E and I used to ride over there on Andrea's shopping bike, stopping off to buy her a bottle of Cinzano or Martini or some other shit like that. But it wasn't long before I realised this would be a high-maintenance relationship. She was so sexy-looking that all the blokes would just turn their heads and gawp at her, or would blatantly disregard the fact that I was with her and chat her up in front of me and she loved all the attention and it would be just one fight after another. So I stopped seeing her, but by then she'd got me out of my depression.

Things weren't going well at home, though. Sandy was seeing some slapper at the opticians and Mam packed her bags and left, without saying a word to me, just leaving me and Sandy to live and drink together. I didn't like this woman much because she made my mother leave me again, just when we got back together. She was twenty-five years younger than Sandy and he was always bringing the tramp home and expecting me to drink with her and she swanned around the house like she owned the place. Don't get me wrong, I liked Sandy better than any other of Mam's boyfriends, except maybe George, and he earned great money, but I didn't like her and she didn't like me and we never missed an excuse to have an argument.

I'd turned twenty and come to the end of my apprenticeship and was expecting to be given a job by the fire brigade. But, after a third disciplinary and a court hearing in front of my station divisional officer, who was also a magistrate, they decided not to keep me on. It was the first time ever that an apprentice wasn't given a permanent job with the fire brigade and, even though I hated the fire station when I first went there, I'd got used to the routine of the place and it was a bit of a kick in the teeth. After four years' work, I had nothing much to show for it.

I had a bit of money, but didn't have enough to survive on for long. The weekends would be football and the rest of the time I'd be in the pub. I became friends with the assistant manager of the Horseshoe, due to the amount of time me and Sandy spent in there. The bloke started giving me free drinks and free meals and we had lock-ins till two and three in the morning. Then something happened to Sandy that he never told me about and he was declared bankrupt. He had to go to Hull to meet with the receivers and he took me with him for company. After the meeting, we drove into town and started drinking. We had about eight or nine pints and then Sandy decided to drive back to Humberston. I didn't argue, because everyone was drunk-driving in them days, nobody gave a bollocks – it wasn't like it is now. Anyway, as we pulled out of the pub car park Sandy nearly hit a police car. It was going in the opposite direction to us, so he thought it'd be OK and carried on driving. But we'd only gone about half a mile when the cop car was behind us with lights flashing and siren blaring. Sandy needed the car for work the next day, so he floored the accelerator and away we went, with the cops at high speed in pursuit. We drove down byroads and side roads and lanes and one-way streets, just missing other vehicles and making them swerve out of our way and it was like something out of *Bullitt* and I noticed he was heading straight for the fire station. That's when I yanked on the handbrake and we screeched to a sliding halt, before he could drive into the workshop and try to hide the car. The police were still behind us and we both got arrested. Sandy lost his licence and, because the case was in the papers, his job as well. So now we were both unemployed and bankrupt.

All we did after that was drink the whole time. Sandy couldn't afford the heating bills, so he just sat in the front room in a sleeping bag drinking cheap whisky and I was worried about him because I think I told you we used to go shooting now and then and he had a shotgun. When we got our dole money, we'd go down to Netto and work out how much food we'd need for the fortnight, until we got our giros again. Sandy's menu was eggs and mash – poached, boiled, fried or omeletted, and the rest was fags and cut-price whisky. I needed to eat a bit more than eggs and mash, so I bought bolognaise and bubble and potatoes for chipping and mashing and cheap chicken.

The financial pressure meant that I spent even more time

drinking in the Horseshoe with Dan the assistant manager and his freebies. Even though Sandy lost his licence and I didn't have one, we still drove the car to the pub and, one night when I went there, Sandy's tramp girlfriend took it from the car park, which I thought was both inconsiderate and inconvenient. She only lived up the road, so I went round there and, when she opened the door, I grabbed hold of her and warned her to stay away from the house and Sandy. I drove the car back to the Horseshoe and Dan was giving me free bottles of Newcastle Brown.

At closing time, I was walking towards the car to drive it home, when I was approached by a couple of policemen.

'You Dean Williams?'

'Why no, officer . . . never heard of him.'

So I gave the car the bodyswerve and carried on walking before the bastards could question me further. The silly bitch had only phoned the coppers and told them I was drinking and driving and they were waiting for me to come out. Anyway, I was a bit mashed and not thinking straight and what I should've done was go home and come back for the car in the morning. Instead, I went back into the pub, where I'd been drinking with a mate called Michael and I gave him the keys and asked him to take the motor home for me after the coppers buggered off. Dan called me a cab and I went off in it.

What I didn't know was Michael couldn't drive and he was too pissed to remember that he couldn't. It was about 3.00 a.m. and I was in bed, when I heard someone knocking on the front door. I went down and opened it and

Michael was standing there covered in blood with the car keys held out in his hand. There was a great bald patch on his head where his hair used to be and no car, only the keys. I brought him in and up to my room, hoping that Sandy wouldn't hear us and I found out he'd managed to drive the car out onto the main road, before ramming it into a lamp post in the town centre. Next thing, there was all these flashing lights and sirens outside in the driveway and the police were at the door. I was arrested on suspicion of drunk-driving and failing to stop and taken away to the police station to be questioned. They soon realised it wasn't me driving the car, when they found half of Michael's scalp on the shattered windscreen, where he'd gone through it, and they had to let me go. But I still had to go back and tell Sandy that another one of his cars had been written off. This time he wasn't so understanding.

Then Nicole came home for two weeks on term break and we met and she said she was going away to Paris to study for a year. She said she missed me and I said I missed her and we started up again from where we left off before the abortion and she invited me to go to France with her. I'd had enough of Grimsby, what with not having no job and the prospect of not having anywhere to live as well, so it sounded like a good idea. I packed my sports bag and got on the coach and twenty-four hours later I was in Paris.

It was weird and wonderful. Nicole lived in a dorm with eight rooms on her floor and they all shared a kitchen and showers and stuff and you could see Montmartre and the Basilica from her window in the morning. She took me on

a tour of Paris to see the museums and the art exhibitions
and the cathedrals and the culture and the food and I got the
shits from something I ate or maybe from drinking the
water, I dunno. We were in this restaurant with a group of
her friends and I whispered to her:

'Where's the toilets?'

'Can't you read?'

'It's in French.'

'Ask the waiter.'

'Excuse . . . un bog, monsieur?'

I sounded like something off *'Allo, 'Allo!*, and all Nicole's
friends were laughing and I was desperate because my stomach was churning now and I had to run down the stairs
where the waiter pointed.

Well, in England we have urinals for pissing into and a
toilet to sit on for a shit. But this place didn't have either of
them. It had a half-door and behind it was a hole in the
floor and a cushion stuck to the wall to lean against. It took
me a few minutes to figure out what I was supposed to do
and my stomach was telling me that this would be like
giving birth to a Porsche at high speed. So I dropped my
jeans and boxers and crouched down, leaning my back
against the wall, but I didn't have time to position myself
right because it was like I could've shat through the eye of
a needle and I soon knew I'd got it wrong. I hadn't slouched
down far enough and I was half standing and I had to bin
the boxers and clean the top of the jeans with water and
wear them wet back into the restaurant.

But, over the next few weeks, my English stomach

adjusted itself to the French food and, although I never tried the snails or frogs' legs or bulls' balls or any other crap like that, I got used to having red wine sauce on my well-done horse-steak and chips. Nicole's parents were sending her a generous weekly allowance which would've stopped if they knew I was living off it as well as their daughter – but they didn't, did they? She went to her lectures during the day and I'd chill out in the room, or play chess with the people I met and smoke weed and drink Pernod. It was real laid-back and I loved it. Booze was cheap and so were meals away from the main tourist areas of Paris.

We travelled back together for the Christmas holidays and I went back to Sandy's. He wasn't too pleased to see me and neither was his slaggy girlfriend, but he let me in. I hadn't heard anything from my mother, so I could hardly go round to her place and Bob was definitely a no-go. I was losing touch with my gang mates and didn't have many girlfriends after meeting Nicole. So Sandy's house was the only place I could go. I told him it was only temporary, because I'd be going back to Paris and he wasn't a bad bloke, so he said I could stay. But it all came to a head when I found out his bird was only using him. She was seeing someone else and taking money from Sandy that he couldn't afford. So I went round her house again and, when she opened the door, I grabbed her by the throat and told her that I'd hurt her really bad if she took another penny from Sandy or came near him again. I threw her on the sofa and walked out. But, within an hour, two detectives were round banging my door down. She'd grassed me to the police again, this time for assault. For once, the buggers weren't aggressive and it was like a domestic and they didn't want the hassle of it once I gave them my story about two-timing and money and stuff.

As they were about to go, one of them said he'd have to radio through to see if I had any warrants outstanding. I had fines for violence and driving offences and assault that I never paid and the bastard cops only had a warrant out for my arrest. That was that. I was taken to the police station and kept in the cells overnight. Then I was sent to a youth offenders prison in Doncaster called Moorlands the next day. On the way up, the coppers told me to stock up on fags and tobacco, but I only had a tenner on me, so all I could get was forty Embassy and a bit of baccy. When I got there I had to strip naked and two bastards checked me for drugs and stuff, like up my arse and everywhere. After the strip search, I had to go to this hatch, where I was given a second-hand crappy uniform to wear, like a navy trousers that was too short and a jumper that was too big and Y-fronts that looked like some clown from the circus had been wearing and a pair of plastic slip-on shoes. I looked like a bloody refugee from Boratistan. Then the guard took me to my cell and banged the door shut and I could hear other prisoners shouting out:

'New boy!'

The cell had a sink and a toilet and a bunk with an itchy grey blanket and I never got back out for the rest of that day. Next morning, the newcomers were herded to a doctor on another wing. We lined up outside and, while I was waiting,

I was able to size up who was who and who'd done what and how long they were in for. I was only in for non-payment of fines, so I wasn't the main attraction and it was usually one day for every £100 you owed. I owed £500, so I figured five days. I'd be out before I got to really know any of these lads. Anyway, I was called in to see the doctor and he told me to drop my trousers and then the bugger cupped my balls.

'Cough.'

'You fucking what?'

'Language, Williams!'

The guard growled at me and I was wondering why the doctor needed to feel my balls and why I had to cough. Was it something to do with me not knowing whether or not I was gay when I was younger? But that wasn't the worst of it. Then I had to bend over while he looked at my starfish, but at least he didn't stick his finger up there like the bastards checking for drugs. I was glad to get back outside.

Next I was taken to a counsellor who went on about why I was inside and what my fines were for and how I should stop re-offending and what I was gonna do when I got out in twenty-one days. Hang on!

'Twenty-one days? That should be five, shouldn't it?'

'No, twenty-one is what I have here. But you won't have to serve it all if you behave yourself.'

How the hell did that happen? Twenty-one days – even if I didn't have to serve it all? Thing is, nobody knew where I was. Sandy was still in bed when I got arrested and he probably hadn't even missed me, and I'm sure the tart never said nothing to him.

The Tearaway

As well as that, when I say a youth offenders prison, Moorlands wasn't a hostel with a room and a TV set where kids get sent when they've been unruly. This was a proper lock-up, banged in a cell for twenty-three hours and only let out for an hour to walk round the filthy shit-strewn yard, so I was a bit put out with having to stay there for twenty-one bloody days.

Anyway, last stop was the library and I could have three books. Then I was marched back to my cell. Now, being from Grimsby and in prison in Doncaster wasn't all that great, if you get my drift. There was plenty from around Leeds and Barnsley and Huddersfield and other places that I might've belted back in my gang days and some of the bastards might even be in here. Association varied, some days you'd only get yard exercise and other days you could play pool or table tennis or use your phone card. Association toilets didn't have doors or walls and they were just right for an ambush. So, if you wanted a bit of privacy and self-preservation, it was better to take a dump in your cell.

In the mornings I was let out to go for breakfast – porridge or cornflakes or Weetabix and tea or coffee. No sugar, sugar was a luxury and it had to be paid for, one way or another. I went back to my cell to eat and followed the same routine for dinner and tea. Cell doors would be locked outside of association and all the inmates would be shouting to each other through the hatches. It was like a bloody madhouse. After a few days, they gave me a job cleaning the floors and the stairs on my hands and knees, but I got a couple of quid for it to buy sugar and a bit of baccy. At night-time, the bastards would be banging the pipes and shouting to each other through the windows across the exercise yard and one bollocks had a tape player and he was constantly playing Whitney Houston singing 'I Will Always Love You' and it reminded me that, eight weeks earlier, I was watching the film *The Bodyguard* with Nicole on the Champs-Elysées.

As the days went by, I kept my head down and tried to stay out of trouble – maybe I'd only have to serve half the twenty-one days. But there's always some stupid div. Ain't there?

Chapter Fourteen

The number one lad on my landing was a Scouser. His cushy job was to serve up the food and, for some reason known only to himself, he decided to give me small portions every time I held out my plate – and they got smaller and smaller as the days went by. I never said a word to the bugger and I couldn't figure out why he had it in for me, except that he was in for a good stretch and waiting to be sent to the big man's prison, whereas I only had three weeks to do. Maybe he was thinking to himself that he'd make my life as miserable as possible while he could – some people are like that, ain't they? Anyway, we had our first set-to on association. I'd run out of matches and couldn't smoke. I knew I'd have to give a fag away to get a light and I didn't want to do that. There was this younger kid, maybe fifteen or sixteen who was in for serial burglary and he had a home-made Clipper with a mop string for a wick and a flint that sparked enough to make it glow. I asked the kid for a light but, just like I knew, he wanted one of my ready-mades for it. Just then, this Scouser prick came up and snatched the kid's packet of baccy out of his hand and walked away.

Now, I don't like bullies, because I had enough of it myself when I was younger. As well as that, I had it in for Scouser for giving me short measures of grub, so I went after him. I also knew he was one of the officers' arse-lickers and I didn't want to be in this place any longer than I had to.

But fair is fair, ain't it? There was a blind spot next to the stairs and I dragged the arsehole in there.

'Give me the baccy.'

'Fuck off!'

This Scouser knew I didn't want to risk an extension to my sentence and he was being stubborn and wouldn't give me the kid's tobacco. Earlier, I'd met this huge lad who was in for twocing and burglary. He knew a pal of mine from the old days and I was seen talking to him a couple of times.

'You see that big guy over there?'

'I see him.'

'Give me the baccy, or I'll call him over here to play mammies and daddies with you and you'll end up with an arsehole the size of a clown's pocket.'

It was a bluff, but it worked. The tosser handed over the baccy and I traded it back to the kid for his makeshift lighter. I got full portions of grub from then on as well.

The days went by and I just tried to keep my head down as much as I could. The bastards never took no time off for my good behaviour and I reckon they just told me that so I wouldn't cause them no hassle and I ended up doing the full twenty-one days. Maybe the Scouser grassed me, I dunno but, if he did, I couldn't prove nothing. And the bugger got the last laugh on me. On release day, you got a knock at

6.00 a.m., then you got dressed and made your bed and sorted out your cell and stood to attention by the bed, waiting for the screws to open the door and let you out. When it was my turn, I got everything sorted and stood to attention, waiting for the footsteps to come. They came – then walked right past my cell door. I didn't know what the hell had happened. Maybe they'd found some other warrants or something, or maybe I'd counted wrong. I kept standing there, smiling to myself like a divvy, for what seemed like hours. Finally, the lights went on in the cell and they opened the door. It was a wind-up. The Scouser put them up to it, to get one over on me. He knew I'd be leaving and wouldn't be able to get him back for it. That was the end of my one-and-only stint in prison. I collected my little bag of possessions and a rail warrant back to Grimsby and the £14 I'd earned while I was in there.

The first place I went was the Horseshoe pub. Dan was there and he gave me a Newcastle Brown and a dinner on the house. Now I'm sure you've already guessed that Dan was gay and that all this free stuff would have to be paid for, sooner or later. But I never thought like that at the time. The man was funny, he was sharp in a bitchy way and sarcastic and he made me laugh when there wasn't much to laugh about. He gave me free booze and food and I trusted him and told him stuff I didn't tell anyone else and I liked him. As well as that, I was curious. Because of my own sexual doubts, I wanted to find out how he knew he was gay, how he was so sure about it. Like, was he born gay or did he get gay when he found out about sex and stuff? When did he get an inkling? Did he try women and didn't like it? Was it a disease or a lurgy and was there a cure? I know now all that is complete bollocks, but I wasn't sure then. I had Nicole, but she wasn't all about sex or anything like that, she was about love and that was different.

Tell the truth of Dan, he answered my questions as best he could, always with a funny remark or two and it made me feel at ease about myself. But then I'd have the dreams again about being in the den with Peanut and the house where the kid was being molested and the things that happened at school and all the rest of it. I couldn't work out in my head if that stuff was me and I was making it happen, or if I should just resign myself to the fact that I was gonna be gay. The voices would argue inside my head and I'd be drawing conclusions walking down the street, like if there was ten lamp posts I was gay and if there was only nine, I wasn't. Or if the car in front of me turned right, I was gay, and if it turned left, I wasn't. Crazy stuff like that. I'd be betting against myself and beating myself up with this crap and there was always a dull droning noise inside my skull.

I went back to Sandy's and the bugger didn't even know I'd been gone – sat there in his sleeping bag, drinking himself stupid on cheap rotgut. He woke up the next evening and looked at me like I'd been there all the time.

'Hey, Dean . . . why don't we go for a drink down the Horseshoe?'

'OK.'

'Who'll drive?'

'Me.'

Dan was giving me the free booze as usual and you remember I told you about Paula who played tennis? Well, she was there with her family and it was four or five years since I'd seen her and she'd asked me to bite her bacon. She was sitting in a corner with a long dress on and her brother was in a wheelchair, because he had this muscle-wasting disease called muscular dystrophy. I went over to say hello, but her family started getting all agitated and I didn't know why, so I left them alone and went back to sit with Sandy. It was quiz night in the pub and Sandy liked to think he was the cleverest Scotsman in the universe, answering all the questions about who invented penicillin and what was the capital of Kaboobooland and why some shit floated and some sank. Anyway, it took my mind off Paula and I never noticed her again until closing time.

Dan was giving us a few afters and I realised Paula's family were all gone, but she was still sitting there. So I went back over to her.

'Where's the family?'

'Gone. I told them you'd help me home.'

'They don't like me.'

'I know.'

I was a bit pissed from the free Nuclear Brown and I never noticed that she said 'help' instead of 'see' her home. When Sandy ordered a taxi I said she could share it and we'd drop her off and she asked me if I could get her chair. It turned out that she had the muscular dystrophy thing as well and she had to give up tennis and everything and I felt really, really sorry for her because she was such a fit girl when I knew her before. Anyway, when we got to her place, she asked if I'd come in for a coffee and I didn't want to, but Sandy was drunk and slobbering in the front of the cab and I thought it would be better than listening to him all bloody night.

I helped Paula into her chair again and pushed her inside the house and it was all geared up for a disabled person, I mean the toilet and everything and she was able to do that for herself without my help, thank fuck, and she could make the coffee and everything, even though I offered to make it for her. We talked about the stuff that happened to us since we knew each other before and I found out she got married and had two kids, but they lived with their father now and she lived here alone, even though her family were very good to her and helped her a lot. I told her about Nicole and how I was leaving to go back to Paris in the morning and she said she was glad for me and hoped I'd be very happy. The ground floor of the house was hers and she didn't have to go up any stairs or nothing and the booze was wearing off me with the coffee. Then it was time for bed. She said we should do it for old time's sake, because we were always getting interrupted and we never really got it on − did we? I was kinda nervous about it, but I couldn't say no and we went into the bedroom and, when she got undressed, I could see that her legs were like just skin and bone. Not like the way they were before. And I remembered that she was limping when I knew her and I thought back then that it was an injury she'd picked up in her tennis training, but it was really the first onset of the muscular dystrophy.

The Tearaway

It was strange being in bed with Paula again. It wasn't like before when she was all over me and I had my head stuck between her legs. It was more subdued. I didn't like being there because of Nicole and also because of Paula's legs; she didn't have no control of them and they just sorta flopped around like deflated balloons. It made it difficult for me to do it to her – like it's not something good to be talking about, but it happened so I have to say it. It was a bit embarrassing for both of us and I gave up in the end because it just wasn't any good, I was never gonna be able to do it and I'm not even sure if she still wanted me to. I think she was just trying to turn back the years and get to what it was like before, when we were both younger and she was so fit you could bounce pennies off her arse. But that wasn't gonna happen and she realised it in the end. So, we just lay there for a while and smoked a couple of cigarettes. Then I got up and went back to Sandy's. It was the last time I ever saw Paula.

Nicole had already gone back to France and it was time for me to follow her. I was on the coach at 7.00 a.m. the next morning and back in Paris by the evening. As soon as I saw the skyline, all my troubles seemed to disappear and the noise stopped humming in my head. I was so glad to be back to eating croissants and horses and drinking Pernod and playing chess. Nicole's apartment was small, with a window and a single bed and a desk and a small wardrobe. I mostly slept on the floor, because it was more comfortable. Money was tight. Nicole's parents were still sending her some cash, but they kept reminding her that they'd be very upset if their hard-earned was being used to entertain guests – and that meant me. For sure! I just carried on like before; when Nicole was in college I read books and met up with people or just slept off hangovers from the night before.

There was this club called the Le Cirque in Paris where I'd been before and it stayed open all night and was mostly a gay venue – with a breakfast bar just across the road where we'd go at six in the morning after coming out of the club. Anyway, it was coming up to my twenty-first birthday and there was this guy called Tony who was gay and who took a shine to me – see, this is what I was talking about, why were the gay people attracted to me? Was it because they recognised me as being gay as well? This is what bothered me in Grimsby, but it didn't bother me in Paris cos no one knew me there. I had a clean slate.

Anyway, everybody knew I was with Nicole, so I didn't worry about going places like Le Cirque and this Tony said he'd take me there to celebrate my birthday. Nicole couldn't come because she was cramming for an exam and she said she'd have a drink with me back at the apartment later. So I went there with Tony and Boy George music was playing and he gave me an E to take. Now, I'd never taken Es before, mainly because I wasn't really into the rave scene that hit the UK a few years previous, but I'd done the acid and speed and weed and gas and booze, so I figured what could it do that I hadn't already seen?

Le Cirque wasn't strictly a gay club, lots of women hung out there too, maybe because they knew they wouldn't get stalked by morons all the time and they could let their hair down without having to tell blokes to fuck off every five minutes. But it didn't take long for me to find out it was a mistake going there with Tony instead of Nicole. The first bugger to accost me was a Naomi Campbell lookalike. She-he grabbed me as I walked past and spoke in French:

'*Vous êtes la mienne.*'

He-she was about six foot two and wearing ten-inch platform shoes and I couldn't get away from his-her grasp. Then Madonna and Audrey Hepburn and Marilyn Monroe came over and started pulling at me as well.

'*Vous avez un cul gentil.*'

'*Vous êtes à nous.*'

'*Vous aimez le grand robinet?*'

Like, I was being pinned down by this lot and the E was kicking in at the same time. They were running their hands all over me and I was feeling weird and Naomi Campbell was saying this French word over and over and over:

'*Jeu . . . jeu . . . jeu . . . jeu . . .*'

And it sounded like she-he was saying 'shoo' and I thought he-she was talking to the others and trying to shoo them away from me, so I started saying 'shoo' as well and they were all laughing and tickling me and trying to take my clothes off and I was on the ground with the four of them on top of me when Tony came over.

'*Laissez-le seul!*'

Tony shouted and they all got off me and sulked away, showing their teeth to him like cats and making scratching gestures. Now, most normal guys would've freaked out at all this, but I wasn't freaked, I just needed to go for a piss and I was trying to figure out if I should go in the *Hommes* and risk getting assaulted by the trannies again, or go in the *Dames* and have the butch brigade bash me up.

I went to the women's and was thrown out by someone who looked like Dorothy from *The Wizard of Oz* and, when I ran in the gents, this midget bastard grabbed me by the dick while I was pissing and wouldn't let go. I was trying to punch him, but he was too short and I had to kick him in the kneecap to make him stop. It was bloody surreal and I didn't know if it was all an illusion being caused by the bloody E or I was really experiencing all this weird shit. Tony disappeared again, so I went and sat on this wooden bench that was about a mile long and arched round the dance floor. The E had fully kicked in now and my heart was jumping out of my chest and back in again. I was flipping out, I couldn't focus and my head was ruined, like it didn't belong to me, and my eyes were like tennis balls. I tried to stand, but couldn't. It was like I was gonna fall over, so I sat back down on the bench again.

I had my head in my hands when some bloke tapped me on the knee. I looked up at him and he made a gesture towards the exit with his head. I didn't know who he was or what he meant, so I stayed where I was. The crowd on the dance floor was going crazy, jumping all over the place and I thought maybe I should get up and dance. But I knew I'd be like Bambi on ice, with the rhythm of a dog scratching at fleas, if I did.

Next thing, some other bugger tapped me on the knee and walked off towards the door, looking back at me, like, to see if I was following. I couldn't work out what was going on and I was all over the place. A third guy tapped me on the knee and stood there looking at me, so I told him to piss off! Then this other lad sitting next to me said something to me in French that I didn't understand.

'*Parlez-vous anglais?*'

'*Oui.*'

'Why they keep tapping my knee?'

'*Ils vous veulent* . . . they want you.'

He told me in broken English that this was the pick-up bench where I was sitting. They tap your knee and you're supposed to follow them outside to their car or a room or somewhere to do the business.

'You should now go . . . he will pay you.'

I jumped up and bolted out onto the dance floor, doing a good impersonation of someone with St Vitus's dance having an epileptic fit and sweating like Pavarotti in a sauna from the E. It was the first and last time I ever took ecstasy or molly or mandy or whatever the hell they call the stuff.

The next day was my twenty-first birthday. I was a man at last and it was 1993 and I was being 'kept' in Paris by a girl's parents who hated me. I had no job and no money and all that was waiting for me back in Grimsby was a bankrupt alcoholic who sat around all day in a sleeping bag to save money on the heating, and who probably thought I was still living in his house.

But I loved Paris and didn't want to leave it. I read Jack Kerouac's *On the Road* and learned how to juggle with three balls and I was mixing with people who talked about art and philosophy and literature and things I'd never heard of and couldn't understand, but still fascinated me. Nicole took me to places like Le Louvre and Montmartre and Sacré-Cœur and up the Eiffel Tower and the along the Champs-Elysées and down the River Seine and under the Arc de Triomphe and she explained the history of those places to me and I felt ashamed because I didn't know. Grimsby was like another universe, a dark, depressing place where there wasn't any hope and you were sinking down in black quicksand that you could never get out of. Nobody there would've understood how I felt, not Andrea nor Bob nor any of my mates. They'd all just say how I must think I'm better than everyone else and I should be on the tugs or trying to get a survival ticket so I could go work on the rigs and not be idling around in frog-land like a big bent jessie! It was above my station in life and I didn't deserve it and I knew it would have to end – sooner or later. My life felt richer and I wanted more, to go live in other cities and to find out other things and read other books and learn to juggle with five balls instead of three.

But it just wasn't right, I mean, living on the money Nicole's parents sent – especially as I hated them and they hated me. It just didn't feel good. I couldn't get a job without being able to speak the lingo and I didn't like having no money and Nicole paying for food and drinks all the time when we were out. Made me look like a right ponce altogether and I ended up stealing francs from women's handbags in nightclubs and trying to flog bits of stuff from other people's apartments in the flea markets. And that wasn't

right either! Nicole's exams were close and she was cramming and stuff and couldn't come out places with me and I
didn't want to be a distraction and get blamed if she failed.
And after the Le Cirque shit, I was wary of going anywhere
on my own, in case the Paris gays thought I was one of
them. So I went back to Grimsby and I knew as soon as I
arrived that I'd made a mistake. I tried to get a job in a
chicken-processing factory and as a tyre fitter and a dustman
and a fire-extinguisher salesman, but there was nothing
doing. I was desperate for some sort of income, other than
the dole, and I thought all that talk from Mam and Alan
when I got the apprenticeship, about having a skill and
being a craftsman and qualified for gainful employment,
turned out to be a load of old bollocks.

I had mixed emotions about being home, at first. It was
familiar, like where I belonged – slow-paced and gloomy
and factories closing and people down in the mouth. Not
like Paris; not bright and optimistic and sophisticated. I
moved back in with Sandy and it was like I never left,
drinking super-strength lager from the supermarkets and
cheap vodka and slipping down somewhere dark and
lonely. I'd drink the lager first thing in the morning, then
fall asleep and drink the vodka when I woke up and I was
turning into Sandy, living in his dark bubble and I probably
could have lived like that and not gave it a second thought
and maybe still be living like that, if I hadn't met Nicole
and she hadn't shown me the things she did. Anyway, I
hadn't been to the Horseshoe since I got back, mainly
because I was too stupefied and lethargic to be bothered.

But one night I ran out of mind-numbing booze and decided to go over there. Dan was on duty and immediately the free stuff started coming my way. We had a lock-in after the pub shut and played pool and listened to the jukebox till about three in the morning. Well, I must've drunk so much I passed out, or maybe it was because I wasn't eating properly, but I woke up on the floor of Dan's flat above the pub. It was still dark and I felt like I couldn't breathe, like my chest was caving in. I could remember dreaming, some kind of erotic dream about being back in Paris and in bed with Nicole, and I had this big hard-on and it felt good.

I was still drunk and I thought I could see Dan sitting on top of me and forcing my cock up his arse. He had his back to me and his hands were behind him, leaning on my chest and he was kinda squatting and sliding up and down on my dick. I thought it was a dream and then I knew it wasn't, but I didn't do anything, like shove him off or shout at him or nothing. I don't know what he was doing before I woke up, maybe molesting me while I was dreaming about Nicole, and I wanted to kill him and stab him and shoot him and strangle him, but I did nothing. My stomach turned and I started gulping so as not to throw up and then I just turned to stone – like I left my body to get on with it and I flew away. My dick went down and he had to get off me and I still did nothing, just felt a tear running down my face and I curled up into the foetal position and waited. I stayed awake until he left in the morning, then I got up and went back to Sandy's.

The Tearaway

The humming noise inside my head started on the way home, like a dull ache, and I couldn't figure out why I just lay there and did nothing. The voices in my head kept saying if there was ten lamp posts I was gay and if there was only nine, I wasn't – if the car in front of me turned right I was gay and if it turned left, I wasn't – if I just imagined what happened in Dan's flat I was gay and if I didn't, I wasn't. But it was too late for all these mind games, wasn't it? There was no way I could redeem myself or start a new game to make it all square or pretend to myself any more. I was gay and that's all there was to it. I could hear someone saying 'I told you so' over and over and over and it was what I deserved, because of the stuff I did when I was younger.

I took a long cold shower when I got back to Sandy's, but it didn't matter. Dan had give me some sort of STD and I had to go to the VD clinic and have a swab shoved down the eye of my dick and then take medication to clear it up. It was the last thing I wanted to have to cope with. But I had no choice.

Chapter Fifteen

If I thought that was the worst of it, I was wrong. What I didn't know was that bastard Dan took a letter out of my pocket on the night and found Nicole's address in Paris. He wrote to her, saying:

> Dear Nicole,
>   Just to let you know, Dean is in a loving caring gay relationship now.
>   I will look after him. We've had sex and we love each other.
>   Sorry you had to find out like this.
>   D xx

I knew nothing about this until I got a letter from Nicole, with Dan's letter inside it. She wanted to know what was going on and what had I done and she always suspected I was gay. The house was falling in on top of me again and the sky was falling in on top of the house. I rang Nicole, but she wouldn't answer the phone and I thought about going over there to explain, but I had no money. So I wrote her a letter. And while I waited to see if she'd reply, I died inside and the days got darker and darker and I just wanted her to be beside me, to be beside me and give me a hug – like my mother used to give me a hug when I was a little kid and Bob had gone back to sea. But I wasn't a little kid no more and my mother was gone and so was Nicole. Drink was the only thing that silenced the noises in my head and I spent all my dole money on rough cider and one-star brandy and mixed the two together and the mixture took me away from my life.

Now, most people would say I was just feeling sorry for myself and I should've pulled myself together and been a man about it all. That's definitely what Bob would've said if he knew –

'Man up, you little queer!'

But I wasn't in the mood for pulling myself together and one night when Sandy went to bed, I went to the medicine cabinet after drinking a litre of cider and a half-bottle of brandy and I took all the pills in there – Anadins and aspirins and antibiotics and some other stuff and then a load of Rennies tablets so I didn't get indigestion from the OD. I mean, I'm trying to kill myself and I'm worried about it giving me bloody indigestion – that's how off my head I was. Anyway, I got Sandy's shotgun and just sat in the kitchen with it, rocking backwards and forwards and the motion must've stirred up the booze with the Rennies and foam started to come up my throat and out of my mouth and I was choking. You'll say that was the whole idea, but I started panicking and rang 999 and, instead of saying 'ambulance', for some reason I said 'casualty'. With all the foam spewing out of my mouth, my voice sounded weird, the operator couldn't understand me and she must've thought I was saying some kind of crazy lunatic stuff or something –

'Has I all what?'

'Casualty!'

'I'm sorry, I can't understand you.'

'Casualty!'

'Has I all tea?'

'Casualty!'

'Is this an obscene call?'

Then she hung up.

Next thing I knew the cops were outside the door and I'm standing there frothing at the mouth with a shotgun in my hand. But I was coughing so much and being sick that I dropped the gun and they quickly took it away and found out it wasn't loaded. They got Sandy out of bed and gave him a bollocking for not having it locked in a cabinet and it was lucky for me, or maybe unlucky, they hadn't called up the armed response unit and shot me dead and then I'd have got what I wanted. The coppers called an ambulance and I was taken to hospital. The nurses gave me something called a witch's broth, which was like black syrup in a little 20ml cup and it tasted like the stuff you find at the bottom of a sump. I had to knock it back and they gave me a cardboard bowl. It only took a couple of seconds and I was going into spasms of vomiting. It turned out I hadn't taken enough tablets to knock out a small rabbit and the Rennies amused them no end. But the gun was a different matter and I was sectioned after that.

I spent the night in hospital and, the next day, a liaison officer came to see me and asked me why I tried to kill myself. I told him about the rape and the noises in my head and the voices and the depression and the low self-esteem and everything and he wanted me to press charges against Dan. But I couldn't do that, because I didn't want the whole thing coming out in court and I didn't want to see Dan again. I was transferred to the psychiatric unit of the hospital for assessment and the shrinks came and asked me more questions and evaluated my mental health and said they wouldn't lock me away. But I'd have to become an outpatient and attend every week for ongoing assessment.

So, once a week I had to go spend an hour with a trick-cyclist going over the questions again and again – why I wanted to overdose and why I felt I had no options left and how it wasn't a real suicide attempt because you can't kill yourself with Rennies, just a cry for help. It was the end of the road for me inside my head – I had nowhere else to go and it felt like my brain was mocking me, laughing at me because it got the better of me. *Ha ha ha ha ha – stupid div!* In a way, it was a relief that I didn't have to argue with myself no more and it was a relief to have someone to talk to about it.

Gradually, the shrink began to unravel the spaghetti of my mind, separating what I thought was true from what was actually true. She isolated the shame and the disgust and the sorrow and the anger and the pain. Before, they were all jumbled up and joined together, but now I was seeing them as individual emotions, one caused by the other and then causing another that caused the first one to get worse and on like that in an expanding circle that was full of black shit. She told me that Dan was a predator and it wasn't my fault – I didn't encourage him. It wasn't my fault either with Peanut or with the bullies and perverts at school or the molesters in the car or the trannies in Le Cirque. She explained how predators work and how they groom people and prey on insecurity and manipulate situations. She told me that most people who are abused blame themselves; that it wasn't uncommon to feel the way I did and getting the STD made it worse and just reminded me of what happened and made me feel dirty and scummy. She taught me to cope with all that and I got to realise the world hadn't stopped and there was tomorrow and maybe Nicole would write back and things would be all right again.

She gave me this exercise to do, like if I had a bad thought I should put it in an imaginary box and put it to one side somewhere. The next bad thought I'd do the same and lock it away. And when the time came and I was stable enough, I should take each thought out of its box and look at it and try to make sense of it and deal with it.

To be able to bring every shit thought to the front of your mind and then put each one in a box is a bloody hard job in itself, without going back and taking them out and looking at them again, but I learned to do it and it made me mentally stronger. I realised that some things weren't my fault – maybe a lot of things were, but not everything. And

I also came to accept that I wasn't gay, I was straight, and that there was nothing wrong with being gay – if you were gay. So I figured a gay man would have the same problems as me if he kept thinking all the time he was straight, even though he didn't like girls and was trying to make himself into something he wasn't, just because voices in his head were telling him to. It's like, you don't need to constantly ask yourself what you are; you don't need to be reassured all the time, you just have to be it – like, just *be* it! Anyway, that might not make much sense to you, but it made sense to me and I started to get better.

It wasn't like a miraculous recovery or nothing like that. I came to depend on the sessions and I'd turn up when it wasn't my day if I couldn't get one of the bad thoughts into its box, or I'd turn up drunk and wanting attention when I was lonely and needing to talk to someone and they'd send me home and tell me to come back on my proper day. And it was strange, because I'd always been told that, if you were a man you kept your thoughts to yourself and you couldn't just go up to somebody and say 'I've been molested' because you'd be made to pay for that – for telling the truth. If you tried to express any real feelings, you'd be ostracised and all the head-shaking and nose-snorting and finger-wagging and mouth-shouting would start. But now I couldn't stop saying things, all the things I wasn't allowed to say before. And it didn't feel like I was any less of a man for doing it, it felt like I was more of a man than I'd ever been before.

I started playing football again and training in the week and I was playing for Westlands and the fire brigade and I even got to play for Barton Town again in the Lincolnshire League, alongside guys like Mickey Czuczman, under floodlights and in front of a huge crowd. I liked being around people again, going to matches and training, it was the only way I could function and keep the bad thoughts in their boxes until I felt well enough to take them back out. Sometimes they got out without me knowing and I'd hear the humming in my head and I'd have to go grab the buggers and stick them back inside their boxes and lock them up.

One time, I remember, I confided in one of the football wives about what had happened with Dan. I don't know why I did it, I was probably feeling a bit shitty and she looked like my psychiatrist and I thought she'd be OK – I mean, I tried to make a joke about it like I used to do before when I was embarrassed or exposed. I could see her face twist in disgust and she said why did I just let him do it, why did I just lie there and how come I got an erection and why didn't I punch him and I couldn't explain. Later in the bar when we were all sitting round having a beer and a banter and someone got on her case and started making cracks about her taking drinks from blokes or something like that, I can't remember, and she said:

'At least I don't let them shag me, like Dean.'

And all the fucking bad thoughts jumped out of their boxes at the same time.

Nicole came back from France for good after doing her exams and it was inevitable we'd meet up. She didn't want to talk about the letter and I just told her it was a bad joke, a lie, and she believed me for some reason. It wasn't much of a conversation, just a look she gave me and I knew what it meant and that's what I said – it was a bad joke, a bad lie, and that was it. We never mentioned it again. I was still seeing the psychiatrist, but I didn't have a job and I'd heard nothing from Andrea since she broke up with Sandy.

I ended up walking away from the therapy because I didn't like the homework they were giving me and they started to go deeper into the rape and into the things that happened in my childhood and I just couldn't face that. Not in the detail they wanted. I figured I'd climbed a mountain and turned my mind around and I didn't want to rake up the past. I regret that now, mind you. I should've stuck around and dealt with everything once I started. Maybe if I had, things wouldn't have worked out the way they did. One of the easiest ways to deal with pressure in your head is to talk to someone about it, but an even easier way is to keep it inside you. You do that and you think you're winning the battle, but you ain't. The thing stays in your mind and it festers there and sometimes you can't see straight for the poison. In the end, it can wreck your life, just like it did to me. I thought I was mentally strong after the therapy, but I was only strong as long as I was having the therapy. Once it stopped, the strength stopped with it and the bad thoughts were still in the boxes locked away and I hadn't got round to taking them out and making sense of them and dealing with them.

Me and Nicole spent the summer together and Mam got back in touch after a while. She went to live with my grandparents first and then she met someone else and she seemed happy enough. We used to meet up at a garden centre and have tea and scones. It was hard trying to rebuild the relationship we once had; I'd pushed her down the stairs and she'd deserted me and it was tragic how we'd been so close and how we were so distant now. She didn't introduce me to her new boyfriend and I didn't want to be introduced to the wanker anyway. It was a strained, awkward, arm's-length reunion and I thought it was better left like that. I guess she did as well.

Nicole left to go back down to Cambridge to finish her education. I followed her down and we lived in a shared house together. Her parents paid the rent and gave her an allowance, but I didn't want it to be like Paris, scrounging off her all the time. At least I had my dole cheque here in England, but that wasn't enough. There was a garage opposite, owned by the Co-Op and they advertised in the free paper for a mechanic. I went for the job, even though I was a diesel fitter, not a mechanic. The pay was £250 a week, with a discount card and a pension and a decent funeral rate – but I didn't get it. I didn't get a job on the council dust-carts either.

Going to the SU bar every night became a routine of cheap pints and baked potatoes, and the students watched rugby, not football. I was at the university more often than the people I was hanging round with and the campus started to resemble the Grimsby town centre where I used to hang out with the GHS. Then I got a break. I went for an interview in Cambridge, wearing my best Benetton shirt and chino trousers and we discussed pay and hours and terms and conditions and they said they'd be in touch. Three hours later they phoned me and told me to come collect my gear – I'd be starting on Sunday at 10.00 a.m. I told Nicole and we went to the SU bar to celebrate.

Sunday came and I was up and ready at 9.00 a.m. Trousers nicely creased and short-sleeved shirt with burgundy stripes and a clip-on tie. I looked the dog's bollocks. When everyone left the house, I legged it out of the toilet and collected my hat. It was raining and the place was locked when I got there and I had to bang the door to get them to let me in before anyone saw me. They took me through the routines – my title was DC, a position where I would be working in close contact with the public, meeting and greeting and offering help where necessary. Then they opened up the Burger King and gave me a mop to keep the floor dry and an anti-bacterial spray for the tables and wipes for the trays after I'd emptied them into the bin. A good life, as they say, if you don't weaken!

Burger King wasn't exactly where I thought I'd end up working when I started my apprenticeship, but it kept the peace between me and Nicole as far as money was concerned. I mean, I'm not running down people who work in fast-food places or nothing, you gotta do what you gotta do, but I just expected more after four years of low-wage slog. And, as bad as it was for Nicole to have a boyfriend who was a diesel fitter instead of a lawyer, a boyfriend who was earning £56 a week in Burger King at the age of twenty-one wasn't exactly good for her social status.

Our relationship was getting edgier by the day – we were kinda chipping at each other all the time and, to be honest, the abortion had affected Nicole more than I realised. She wasn't the girl I met nearly four years earlier and I guess I wasn't the same lad either. We had a bit of a turbulent history together and the turbulence was turning into a tornado. The money I earned didn't go very far, it was more of a gesture really, a token to pretend I was paying some of the bills like rent and whatever, but it mostly went on nights in the SU bar. The relationship was getting unruly and living together in the same house was becoming a strain. We were more like a tired old married couple than the lovers we used to be. Then she got pregnant again and we had to go thought the whole abortion thing again. She had it done in Cambridge this time, but it was another setback. It was another birthday that would never be – another day to remember and forget. I couldn't handle it this time and neither could she.

Nicole threw me out and I went to live in another student house with some friends. All I had was a bed and a mattress, no covers, no pillows, nothing. My heart was broken and I turned to the old routine that served me well in Grimsby – Tennent's Super in the morning, vodka in the afternoon. Up to then my career at Burger King had been going from strength to strength – I went from sweeping and mopping to preparing the vegetables like lettuce and gherkins and tomatoes and, not long after, I was cooking the burgers and stopping the students from shagging each other in the toilets. I was making the most out of a bad situation, just like when

Ken put me on the wire wheel cleaning nuts and bolts at the fire station. If that taught me anything it was how to turn a negative into a positive, so that's what I did. Vegetables were chopped to the right dimensions, decks cleaned fast and burgers done nice and neat – I was the fastest and the neatest and got more down the chute than anyone else. I was three months into it and looking at an assistant manager position when Nicole ended things. Then I just sat in my room for days on end swigging and sniffing butane gas and listening to Roxy Music and U2 and Simply Red, over and over and over. I couldn't be bothered to move or get moti-vated or anything and I thought the best thing to do would be to just die. And if I could have died by just sitting there drinking neat vodka and inhaling the gas I would have, as long as I didn't have to do anything else. As long as I could hallucinate myself into the grave.

When I did finally get up and stagger over to the SU bar, looking for Nicole, I was bollocksed drunk and falling all over the place. She was there, talking to the rugby lads who never spoke to her when she was with me, for fear of having to fight me. When she saw the state of me, she just took one look and walked away. I wasn't even capable of talking, so I dunno what I would've achieved if she had spoken to me. The blokes in the SU bar were a bit wary of me because I had a reputation for being a bit of a tearaway around the campus. This came from the time when I had my MZ motorbike and I was pissed up and drove it round the campus with two other drunk guys on board with no helmets and no lights on and Security chasing us all over the place. Until I smashed the MZ into a ditch and we all got thrown about twenty yards over the other side. Security didn't know who I was, because I wasn't officially at the university and nobody grassed me up because they knew enough about me to keep their mouths shut. But that was just physical stuff. I was no threat to them verbally, being educated as they were. I only had sarcasm, which they said was the lowest form of common wit. Even though I thought it was the highest form of put-down shit. But they weren't bothered about me now, laughing and pointing at me as I staggered round the place like a drunken down-and-out.

Everyone left the house and went home for the Christmas holidays, including Nicole. The whole place was sad and empty and there was nobody left but me. I don't remember much about it, because I drank and slept my way to New Year's Eve. Then I got up and broke into the house I used to live in with Nicole. I didn't want to rob the place or nothing like that, I just wanted to be near something familiar – I lay on the bed and pretended she was beside me and I know it sounds freaky, but I didn't feel so alone there. Then the phone rang and I answered it and it was Nicole. She said she was ringing to check if one of her friends was back – on New Year's Eve? We talked and I asked her to give me another chance, because I still loved her, but she said it was over for good and she told me to get out of her house – which, I suppose, wasn't unreasonable. I knew it was the final goodbye and I ended up scaling a flagpole in the forecourt of a nearby garage and taking down the flag that was on top of it. Maybe it was supposed to be symbolic, I dunno. It probably made sense to me then, but it don't now.

Then I got a break. I was down at the Joke Shop, which is what we called the Jobcentre, reading the wanted ads in the newspapers, when I saw an advert placed in the *Sun* by an agency in London. It was for a HGV fitter and the pay was £9 an hour. I went to the library and faxed a copy of the CV one of the students had done for me to the agency. They faxed me back, giving me a starting date to go work for Haringey Council – a forty-five hour week at £9 an hour and I wondered how come getting the job was so easy. But it was a bit better than Burger King, eh? The only problem was, where would I live? I'd accepted the job, I mean I had to – it was a way out of my misery. I contacted Andrea and she arranged for my toolbox to be sent down to Cambridge. I rang Sandy's house in Humberston to see if he could help me and whoever answered told me he didn't live there no more and they were renting the house. They said he was working in London, in a place called Balham and he had a job same as before down there, as a dispensing ophthalmic optician. They gave me his number and I called the old bugger and he said he had a flat above the spectacle shop and I could come and live with him. Haringey was in north London and Balham was in south London, but I could get to work on the tube, which I had experience of before, from the time we came down to see Grimsby play Wimbledon and we stayed out at Heathrow.

Dean Williams

It was perfect: back with Sandy again in a job that was paying £400 a week and a flat and everything. Just goes to show you, when you least expect it – the dark clouds blew away and all I could see was blue skies, stretching all the way down the A12 to dear old London town.

Chapter Sixteen

Me and my toolbox got dropped off at the new workshop in Tottenham and London was all snazzy and strange and bigger than Paris and more intimidating. It was like being in a foreign country again, only one that spoke the same language as me, in a different accent. As well as that, in Paris I'd spent most of my time on campus and not mixing it too much out in the city, and in Grimsby you didn't get that cosmo mix you got in London. I mean, we had the usual quota of Asians up there, in the 7-Eleven Spar shops and the doctors' surgeries, but we didn't have Ugandans and Somalians and Arabs and Chinese and Russians and all sorts and it was a bit of a culture shock for me. I left my toolbox at the council depot and walked over to Tottenham Hale tube station which was on the Victoria line. Then I took a tube down the twelve stops to Stockwell, where I changed to the southbound Northern line for the last four stops to Balham.

Sandy's flat wasn't a flat at all, just a single room with a shared kitchen and toilet. Sandy had the bed and my place to sleep was on the floor, in a sleeping bag. There was a pub a short walk away and that's where we headed after I dropped off my Head bag. It was a Wetherspoon's pub called 'The Moon Under Water', where the beer was double cheap and all the dossers on the dole hung out. But not me, I was starting my first full-paid job and Sandy was also earning again, so we were in good shape. He was down in London about six weeks and didn't have many friends, so he was glad to see me. I was only in the pub a few minutes when this scruffy-looking woman with greasy hair and brown teeth came over and introduced herself as Babs.

'Arite, laav? You new here then?'

'Yer.'

'You drinkin' wiv the Scottish fella?'

'Yer.'

I put my hand out to shake hers, but there was nothing only half a sleeve.

'Lorst me arm, laav. But the uvver one works OK.'

So I switched over and shook her left hand and when she went back to the bar Sandy said they called her 'The Bandit' and she was in the pub all the time. There was a lot of characters like that in London and I was gonna meet a few of them.

I started at the council on a Tuesday morning at 10.00 a.m. and there was a few things I didn't know about the job. Like I was employed by the agency, not the council, and I was on a month's trial and the regular council workers referred to us agency lads as 'cockroaches'. I was put on a shift with three or four other agency workers and we were given all the shit jobs to do – like working on the dustcarts which were full of gunge and stank bad. If I asked for a bit of advice or help the council full-timers pretended they were deaf and what made it worse was I might as well be speaking a foreign language. Now I knew why getting the job was so easy – the hard part would be keeping it.

I was twenty-one and the youngest they'd taken on, apart from their own apprentices. But I kept my head down and got stuck into the work and I never complained and just did what I was told. If overtime came up, I'd ask for it and the more I was around the council guys, the more they accepted me. The foreman called me into his office after a couple of weeks and said he liked my attitude and he was gonna keep me on after the month's trial. He said I'd be an 'improver', which worked well for me, because it meant I wouldn't be thrown straight into ripping out engines on my own and I'd be helping one of the senior technicians. The other cockroaches didn't like it, because they were getting paid the same money and having to work on the scummy dustcarts. It gave me a massive confidence boost.

After a couple of weeks, I got friendly with this barman in the Wetherspoon's pub. You're probably thinking 'That was a bit stupid, Dean' after my experience with Dan at the Horseshoe. But I knew this guy wasn't gay, because I'd seen him chatting up the women a few times. He was South African and one Friday night he asked me if I wanted to carry on drinking after closing time. I thought he meant a lock-in, so I said 'yer', but the pub closed at the regular time and he took me up to Shepherd's Bush to an Aussie pub called the Walkabout. It was a trek to get there, because

Shepherd's Bush is in west London and we had to go north again the four stops to Stockwell, then five stops on the Victoria line to Oxford Circus and another seven stops west on the Central line.

The place was heaving when we finally got there and the South African had no money and he asked me to loan him a bullseye, which is £50 to anybody who don't know their money slang. We got in the place and he was nowhere to be seen for most of the night and I got bollocksed drunk on Castle beer, which is South African lager and fairly strong at 5 per cent, especially as I'd been drinking in the Wetherspoon's pub before. It got to about 1.00 a.m. and I thought I better try to find my way back to Balham, because I didn't have a bloody clue where I was. But the barman reappeared when I was staggering towards the door and he said it would be better if we got a black cab, because the tube stopped running at midnight, which I didn't know, by the way.

Anyway, he flagged a black cab that was being driven by a Rastafarian bloke, with long dreadlocks down his back like I'd seen on TV and the South African insisted on going via King's Cross. He asked if we were looking for 'Toms' and the barman said we were. I didn't have a clue what a 'Tom' was, all I was bothered about was the meter running and it was already on £14. The last thing I wanted was to get hammered for the fare as well. The next thing I know this bird gets into the cab and speaks to the driver.

'Where?'

'Balham.'

'I ain't gaan Balham, no fackin' way. Hand or marf in the back, fifteen quid each.'

'Nah, I wanna shag.'

After the South African said that, she got back out and buggered off. I didn't know what the hell was going on. The only experience I had with prozzies was once with a mate called Elliot in Hull – and she threw a brick at the van we were in. The driver looked at us in his rear-view mirror.

'I know a brass in Tooting, she does homes.'

Tooting was on the way back to Balham, so it didn't seem so bad. We pulled up on Tooting Common and a girl came out of a side road and got into the cab.

'Thirty quid up front . . . fifty for the pair. Full sex.'

She was mixed race, with a gold tooth and a short skirt and leather boots. We went back to the barman's flat on Balham High Street and he'd spunked all the money I gave him, so I got lumbered with a £27 cab fare. As well as the £30 up front for the brass. We all went upstairs and she hitched up her skirt and bent over and told the Bok to 'stick it in'. This was new to me – no kissing, no cuddling, just smash it straight in. While the barman was doing her from behind, she threw a condom from her handbag to me and told me to put it on. Now, I could barely walk, let alone get a hard on and then the barman started shouting at her:

'You stink of kippers! You smell bad, woman!'

I was doing my level best to get the rubber on and rise to the challenge, but after I heard that there was gonna be nothing doing. He pushed her away and told her to go wash, but she just came over to me and told me to 'stick it in'. I had my trousers down round my ankles and I asked her if we could kiss or something first, just to get the blood flowing. I mean, I really didn't want to waste my money. She just shouted at me to get it up, but it was a lost cause, so she buggered off and the last thing I remember was trying to chase her across the room like a penguin as she bolted with the cash.

I'd done about £200 in all that night, but the South African promised he'd pay me back the money he borrowed and go halves on the expenses as soon as he got paid on Sunday. So I suppose it wasn't too bad and I'd had an experience. I staggered back to Sandy's place and just crashed on the floor until the next morning. Sandy worked Saturdays downstairs in the opticians and, as soon as he left, I climbed into the bed. There was a fire escape on the back wall that led down to a Chinese restaurant and beside the pub was a burger shop we called 'Tricky Dicky's'. It was close to the railway bridge on Balham High Street where the pigeons used to gather in the hoarding and shit on the meat because, a couple of times a week, I'd get deli-belly from eating there. But the guy was good for credit and, after a skinful, the half-pounder with cheese and egg and onions and garlic sauce and pigeon shit tasted like something that was made in heaven.

Anyway, I got up at midday and went down to The Moon Under Water with my newspaper and my coupons from Ladbrokes. I settled down with a pint to work out the fixed odds and to see the barman and make sure he was gonna be good for the money he owed me the next day. The guv'nor asked me how last night went and I said I couldn't remember much, but I had a hangover from hell, so it must've been good. I asked him what time the South African was coming on and he just shook his head, like he was talking to one of the winos.

'He ain't, mate.'

'He's on tonight, then?'

'He's gone. He finished last night.'

'Finished what?'

'Finished up. They do that, South Africans, Aussies, New Zealanders . . . work for a while, get a bit of money and move on. They like to travel the world.'

Welcome to London!

Lots of things were different down here and I told you there was lots of characters as well. Sandy and I were becoming regulars in the pub and people talked to us, usually after being introduced by 'The Bandit', who was always mouthy and pissed and in the middle of every conversation. One night I got hand-shook by a group of men who included Scotch Jimmy and Irish Brian and One-Eye Tom and another bloke called Clifford who was a south Londoner. They were contractors or painter-decorators or something and they seemed OK, until this other geezer came in and whispered something into Jimmy's ear and he started going mad, effing and blinding and trying to get out the door. Brian was holding on to him and trying to keep him in the pub and Clifford said to me a 'situation' was developing and would I like to lend a hand. I was drinking with them, so what could I do?

We left the pub and went to another place called The Nightingale, just off Wandsworth Common and One-Eye told me I had to stand at the door once we got in there and not let anyone out. It was a Saturday afternoon and there was about thirty people in the pub and I didn't know who any of them were. I mean, they might have been related to the Krays, or the Richardsons or been soldiers of Diamond Jack Sloan, for all I knew, and I half expected the bullets to begin flying any bloody minute.

Well, Jimmy walked up to the bar and picked up a pint glass and smashed it. The other three were covering the exits like me, and One-Eye was telling me not to move. In a split second, it all kicked off. Jimmy stuck the broken glass into some fella's face and the next thing there's chairs flying and kicking and punching and screaming like in a Wild West film. Bottles were smashing through the window and breaking on the street and it was all pandemonium everywhere.

Now, I'd been in a few rucks with the football gangs, but my knees were starting to wobble because it was like something from *The Long Good Friday*. It couldn't have lasted more than a couple of minutes, but it seemed a lot longer than that. In the end, Jimmy picked up an empty glass and, as he walked past me in the doorway, he turned and launched it at the bar, hitting all the clean glasses in the racks above and showering splinters down all over the people there. We walked out of the place and someone hailed a black cab and we piled in, with me still shaking, and nobody said a word for a few minutes. Then it came out that one of the blokes in The Nightingale was a loan shark who got Jimmy's bird to pay off her debt with sex and Jimmy took offence to that. Then they all patted me on the back and congratulated me for not scarpering and for standing my ground with them and they told me I was one of them now and they'd look after me. Now, you might think this was just another bunch of mouthy bloody street-arabs who were up for it after a bellyful of beer – just like I did.

But it wasn't!

Back at Haringey, I was getting up to my old tricks like I used to do at the fire station in Grimsby – like pulling pranks and getting too cocky for my own good. I was working all the hours available and the more I worked the more confident I got, and the more confident I got the bigger the jobs they trusted me with, and the bigger the jobs they trusted me with the cockier I got. Because the workshop was so large, most of us cockroaches had our toolboxes mounted on shopping trolleys. We'd cut away the sides and the front of the trolley and fix the toolbox to the shelf bit. But I had to customise mine, didn't I, like I fitted a 12-volt battery to a washer bottle and some jets and a twin-tone horn. I used to take the trolley round and spray people with the jets or wait till someone was in a tight space then go up behind them and let the off the horn. This didn't endear me to everyone and my first major cock-up came by way of a timing belt, which drives the main components of an engine, if you want to know. I'd done three similar jobs before and I was tearing up the times – six hours down to three-and-a-half hours down to two hours. I wasn't even bothering to use locking pins to secure the engine and stop it from moving. So, on this job I had plenty of time to spare and I made the mistake of going out into the workshop and leaving the job halfway through, so I could go round with my customised trolley annoying people.

When I came back to finish the job, I put the new timing belt on and fixed the engine back together and turned the key. The engine sang, and when I say sang, I mean it made a tune it wasn't supposed to. It meant that something had moved while I was out pissing about the workshop and the engine had seized up and it was serious. Now I had to go and explain this to someone. I went to one of the senior guys first, someone I'd just blared the horns behind and made him jump and bang his head. I simulated the noise the engine was making and asked him what it meant. He smirked.

'Engine's facked, saan!'

I had to go to the foreman, the one who'd told me he liked my attitude.

'Think I've made a mistake . . .'

'Wot yew dan?'

'Seized the engine.'

'Yew're too cocky by alf, Dean. Yew facked the engine cos yew're gaan araand actin' the fool and not concentratin'. Now fack orf aat o' my sight an' sort it.'

I felt like I'd let him down, after he gave me a chance, just because I couldn't stop being the joker I was since schooldays – showing off, looking for attention. This was the first time I took a good look at myself and saw what everybody else was seeing. I thought I'd be sacked, but the technician who was my mentor as an 'improver' came over and told me to look on it as a lesson – a learning curve, an experience. He helped me sort out the engine and it wasn't as bad as I thought. So, a couple of things got fixed that day.

It was a lesson that was to save me from the sack a few times after that. The full-timers at Haringey were massive union men and everything was health and safety, so me going round with my trolley of tricks was a definite rule-breaker and I had to dismantle it. These guys would down tools at the drop of a hat if there was any disrespect of the proper procedures. Anyway, one of them got the bullet for something one day and the next thing everything stopped. I hadn't joined the union yet because I hadn't been invited, as I'd only just stopped being a cockroach and I had no protection if I downed tools with the others. This union guy came over and I told him I couldn't afford to get involved because I'd already blotted my copybook with the trick-trolley and I'd get sacked and the union would do nothing to help me. He started calling me a scab and telling me I was out of order and if it'd been a month or two earlier I'd have taken the piss or maybe hit him or told him to bugger off or something. But I thought, if I didn't support them I'd lose the mateyness of the other guys and they could make things difficult for me in the workshop. So I said OK.

'What you want me to do?'

'Stop working.'

'I have stopped.'

'OK . . . that's OK then.'

'OK then.'

And he walked away, happy that he'd won the argument. I went back to what I was doing as soon as he was out of sight, but I'd used a little diplomacy to get me out of a no-win situation, something I hadn't done much before. I saw it as a watershed or a divergence, like a turning point in my life – like I was learning something for a change, instead of thinking I knew it all.

Talking about a divergence, or is that a digression? Anyway, I forgot to tell you about when I went moonlighting in a mortuary – it lasted one night only. It was when I was eighteen and I wasn't earning enough as an apprentice, so one of the firemen gave me the number of a local undertaker who paid cash-in-hand for casual work, mostly at night. I gave the guy a call and it wasn't long before he came back to me and said he had a few jobs for me to do. He was about forty or fifty or something and he lived alone above the funeral parlour and that worried me to begin with.

It started with me doing a few, like, handyman-type jobs around his flat and he used to watch me and make comments and innuendos all the time, like if I was struggling to get to an awkward place, he used to say he liked to hear me groan. I thought 'Bugger this' and it's like what I was saying before about these irons coming on to me. But I needed the cash, so I kept on. Then he took me down to the mortuary to help prepare a body for the Chapel of Rest. We walked through the chapel to a room that was cold and had what looked like bunk beds made out of stretchers. There was body-bags on the bunks and the undertaker guy left and said he'd be back in a minute. There was a heavy smell of disinfectant, or maybe it was the smell of something else, but I was petrified with fear. I stood still, next to a marble table that had grooves on the outside edges and holes in the corners and the middle. I was trying to work out what it was for, when one of the bags moved and made a noise like a thud and I nearly shit myself.

I wanted to run out of the place, but I couldn't move. All sorts of things were going through my head and then the undertaker came back. I pointed to the bag, which was hanging off the stretcher-trolley thing and he went over and opened it. He told me that rigor-mortis sets in first, but then the bodies loosen up again and so the arm had dropped down. He wheeled in an old lady and we moved her onto the marble slab. She looked like she was asleep and he told me we had to bung up the cavities and put make-up on and sew her lips together to stop her tongue from sticking out. As he was moving the body, she let out a noise – it's hard to say what it was like, maybe a groan or something and I was shaking in my bloody shoes. Then he laid her down and she farted. That was enough for me, I was gone out the door. I wanted the extra money, but I didn't want it that bad and I never went back to get paid for the few hours I'd already put in. I could've handled lifting the bags, as long as I couldn't see them. But I wasn't keen on spending a night in the mortuary with them farting and croaking and waving their fucking arms at me.

Anyway, back to London. I was becoming more and more involved with Jimmy and Brian and One-Eye and their crowd and we were drinking together every night in the pub. They all wore these pin badges with strange writing on them that I didn't understand and they had these sayings when they were drinking, like they'd all clink glasses together and say things like 'chucky our law'* and 'quinnig nineteen-sixteen' and other stuff that made no sense to me. They were all Celtic fans and I thought it was something to do with the football, so I clinked my glass with them and learned to mimic what they were shouting and they all laughed at me and I laughed back at them.

One night this copper came in and he was a Glaswegian like Jimmy, but that's where the similarity ended. He was also a Rangers supporter and I thought there'd surely be trouble. But, instead, someone piped up about there being a football night in The Swan at Brixton on the Saturday and the group told him to come along. They said it'd be a great night altogether and he should wear his Rangers colours and be there at 7:30 p.m. and not be late. Me being into the football and all I said I wouldn't mind coming too. They went a bit quiet and I wondered why they didn't want me there, but after a while One-Eye said to the others:

'Let the boy come. It won't do him no harm.'

There was heavy security on the door when we got to the venue and we were all searched and patted down for weapons, but I thought nothing of it, because it was football and it might kick off. But when we went down the stairs, the first thing I saw was the flags, Tricolour, IRA, Bobby Sands, Celtic flags, banners – all over the place. Everyone was drinking Guinness and the atmosphere was rowdy, with people milling around and pushing and shoving. There was

---

* Tiofaidh ár lá – Irish language phrase for 'Our day will come'.

a pool table with young lads about fifteen or sixteen playing and a stage and a bar and the music was hard-core rebel stuff. We'd only just got ourselves a drink, when the Rangers policeman came tumbling head-first down the stairs. The doormen had searched him and found his warrant card and he was also wearing blue-nose colours.

Well, that was double bad news for him in a place like this. The minute he touched the bottom, he must have thought a boot shop had fell on him. The young lads were the first in, kicking the bejaysus out of him, then the older men. It was sickening, even to me, and I'd seen a few things in the gangs that you couldn't show on the telly before ten o'clock. Fortunately, it didn't go on for long and he was dragged back up to street level and I suppose he was flung out. I dunno what happened to him after that, I never saw him again. I half expected the place to get raided later on, but it didn't happen – don't ask me why.

Now I wasn't political, even though Nicole told me some things when I was with her. But I didn't understand what was going on in Ireland and, to be honest, I didn't care all that much. They were bombing us and we were shooting them and half of London was a no-go area with stop-and-search points and barriers and gates and a ring of steel round the City to protect the investments of the rich. The group I was with knew all the words of the rebel songs and I just stood back, not wanting to get too involved, but also not wanting to have some of what the copper just got. So, when they came round collecting for their comrades in Belmarsh and The Maze and the bloke on the stage said

Williams

every pound was another bullet for a British soldier, I threw my change into the box like everyone else. I stood looking at these men who were supposed to be my mates and who said they'd 'look after me' and they were all cheering and jeering and I couldn't wait for an excuse to get the hell out of there and back to Balham.

Chapter Seventeen

Next night in The Moon Under Water, the group was asking me how come I'd left the thing in Brixton so early. I just said I wasn't political and didn't want to get involved in stuff like that – it was OK for them because they were Irish and Scottish, but I was English and I didn't like contributing to English soldiers being attacked. They tried to explain that the same English soldiers were propping up a bunch of Orange bastards that didn't want to be English, Irish, Scottish or any bloody thing else, but just wanted to lord it over other people and be the big 'I am' in someone else's country. I said I didn't really understand the ins and outs of it and I had enough problems without getting arrested for bloody treason and sent down for ever and never seeing the light of day again.

But I also didn't want to make enemies of this group because I liked it in the Moon and I'd have to go somewhere else if I fell out with them. I think, in the end, they agreed I was a stupid Sassenach gobshite, but I was still OK and we could be drinking mates without being on the bloody barricades together. And that suited me fine. It was the second time I used my noggin to get me out of a no-win situation, instead of resorting to either violence or clowning, and it was like I was finally growing up and becoming a man.

Or so I thought!

The thing about it was this, I was encountering things in London that I'd never encountered in Grimsby, like different points of view and different situations and different attitudes to a lot of things. You had to learn to roll with it a little bit or you'd be in trouble all the time. Like, nobody can just live alone and keep in their own views and keep out everybody else. If you try to do that, you never learn nothing and you just stay the same, you never change. I suppose some of you will say it's better not to change at all than to change for the worse – but that's a kinda negative attitude to have, don't you think? You gotta look at everything and if you don't like it, you got the option to walk away, but if you don't even bother to look, then you never know if you were right or wrong and maybe you missed something important that could make your life more worthwhile. Grimsby was all about Liverpool FC and Man United and Town and getting a job and making a few quid and finding out whether you're gay or not and being loved by someone – and don't get me wrong, those things are important, but they're not everything that's in the world. In London I was made to think about why someone would want so much to kill someone else and what made people feel so passionate about things that were remote before – and I had to think about whether I agreed or disagreed with things that never were an issue before. Living in London made Grimsby seem like a shoebox, where I could walk from one end to the other and not see anything new. In London, there was something new no matter where you went – all kinds of people believing in all kinds of things and it seemed like anything was possible. But you still had to be careful.

One night, I was coming out of a pub called the Dragons Puzzle on Balham High Road and, as I walked across to a 7-Eleven to get something – I dunno what – I noticed some people smashing up a bicycle that was chained to a lamp post. Most of them were young kids, but one of them was my age and he seemed to be the ringleader. I didn't go get involved, just stood back. But the bike owner came out and they jumped all over him, smashing him to the ground. Well, you just can't walk away from that, can you? I ran over and cracked one of them and two others grabbed me round the neck and tried to drag me down and this gave the bike owner a chance to get up. But, instead of helping me, the bugger legged it down the road and left me to fend for myself. I wouldn't go down, but this ringleader bloke was standing in front of me and he was wearing a three-quarter-length leather coat and screaming at me, like, who do I think I am and I'm a dead man and the kinda stuff shitheads are always screaming at people. I'd heard that sort of bollocks before and it didn't impress me and some of the Asian shop owners were coming out with baseball bats in their hands. Then this ringleader opened his coat and I could see a sawn-off shot-gun hanging down the inside of it. The others let go of me and they all moved off, giving me and the shop owners the finger and shouting abuse back at us.

After they went, a sort of aftershock came over me. I mean, why did the guy I was helping out run off and leave me? And why did the Asians come out when it was nothing to do with them? And if they hadn't come out, would the ringleader have shot me? Was the gun even loaded, or even a real gun? Would he have had the balls to pull the trigger? Would I have died there on the street, been killed for nothing, for trying to help out someone who left me there to be killed? All kinds of questions filled my head and I just stood there on the street for a long time, even after the shop owners had gone back inside and it was all quiet again. The thing is, I wasn't scared or shaking in my shoes or nothing like that – I was just thinking how things happened, how things could happen just out of the blue.

It was the same when I went to a football match with this lad I knew called Mark, who's dad ran a paper stall outside Balham tube station. It was Chelsea and Millwall, like arch rivals, but the hooliganism had died down a lot and it wasn't like it was a few years earlier. After the game, we went over to the Old Kent Road or Kennington or Camberwell or somewhere to meet with his mates. Well, there was a crowd of Millwall in the pub we went in and one of them had a Stanley blade on him and was going round chivving geezers' arses at random with it – I mean, cutting straight through cords and denim and a lot of howling going on. It was time to go and we legged it out of the pub, straight into a bunch of the same gang. Everyone just scattered, being chased with bats and pickaxe handles and one of Mark's mates got a blade rammed right up his arse and they pulled it up towards his back and he dropped to the ground immediately. We jumped on a passing bus and we could see him lying on the ground in the distance, being savaged like he was in the middle of a pack of wild animals. I heard later that the bloke ended up in hospital and I think they said he wasn't gonna be able to walk no more. And I thought about all the violence I'd been involved in and it made me see the complete stupidity of it all. I mean, all this supporting a football team and fighting for a colour or a flag, whether it was blue or red or green or purple or whatever – hurting people and crippling people and all for what? Who really got anything out of it? It makes you think, don't it? And it made me think back then too.

Like I said, everything was totally different from Grimsby; sort of outside my comfort zone, if you know what I mean. Everyone said hello to each other in Grimsby, especially the older people, whether they knew you or not. If you said hello to a stranger in London, they'd probably call the bloody cops and have you arrested. Everyone was out for themselves and it was hard to get on the inside, so being part of a group that would back you up was good, even if that group collected money to buy bullets to shoot soldiers. And it wasn't like they were out-and-out terrorists or anything, mostly all we did was drink and sometimes they'd sing and talk bullshit and pretend they were doing something worthwhile for the 'cause'.

The Moon Under Water was our base. We'd never arrange to meet or nothing, we just knew that's where everyone would be. And at closing time we'd shoot over to an illegal out-of-hours drinking den on a nearby housing estate. It was a basement flat converted into a 'shebeen', which is what the Irish called a dive and the bloke who ran it was Irish as well. Three knocks on the door and then down to a makeshift bar, where you could play poker and drink duty-free and buy cheap cigarettes and tobacco. The only problem was, the place got raided a lot and, if you were inside at the time, you got hauled into court and fined. As well as that, the more people knew about it, the more popular it became and it got to the stage where regulars like us were being turned away. So we started going to another place called The Tropicana instead. It was a Jamaican restaurant by day and a 'blind pig' by night, which is what the Jamaicans called a speakeasy. It was invite only and lights off, with candles on the tables and drinking till dawn on the weekends and geezers outside on the lookout for the Old Bill.

And that was my life in London, at least at first. Sleeping on Sandy's floor and feeling the vibration of the tube trains through the floorboards, and I never needed an alarm clock because the first tube started rumbling past at 6.00 a.m. I was doing well at work too, other than going there smelling like a brewery on Monday mornings and falling into the pits on a regular basis. I was a full-timer for Haringey now and not working for the agency no longer, but on a rolling one-year contract. And I must've been doing OK, because they made me shift foreman. I was now dishing out job cards to the cockroaches and working 2.00 p.m. till 10.00 p.m., which kept me out of the pubs on the weekdays. I also had the keys, which meant it was my responsibility to lock the whole place up at 10.00 p.m., before I went home. It was a huge building and I had to start locking up at 9.45 p.m., to get it all done by 10.00 p.m. It was good, being a shift foreman. I could sit in the office and give orders to the agency guys and I was still only twenty-two. But, like I said before, there's always some stupid divvy to mess things up for you – ain't there?

There was this Nigerian cockroach called Naidoo who was older than me and he reckoned he should've been given the full-time job before me. Anyway, we were teamed together this night on a welding job. The dustcart we were working on was the newest in the fleet, only two years old and £50,000 worth of kit at least. Naidoo's job was to make sure the hopper and compactor were clear of any waste that could catch fire, while I got up on top of the dustcart with the welding gear. It was a twenty-minute job and all the bollocks had to do was stand by with a fire extinguisher while I did the work. I had the full face mask on and was welding away on the plates and brackets that had cracks and I noticed that the soles of my safety boots were getting hot. I took no notice, knowing that Naidoo was close with the extinguisher and carried on. Then the backs of my legs and my arse started to get hot and I kept patting them to get some air in. But I had welding gloves on and couldn't feel much through them. Then it felt like the sun was shining on my back and the heat was getting a bit fierce, so I turned round to see what was going on. The bloody dustcart was alight, with flames coming up through the gap where the hopper hinged and shooting up my overalls. I looked for Naidoo, but the bastard was nowhere to be seen. I was twenty feet up in the air, with a moveable stairs up against the dustcart, and I had to rip off my burning overalls quick as I could then climb down the stairs after them to get away from the inferno.

Well, the burning overalls set fire to something else and it was spreading. The whole workshop and yard were filling up with thick black smoke and the danger was the diesel would catch light. Even though it's not flammable, it only needed a catalyst like a spray of oil in the chassis or something. I was the foreman on this late shift, remember, and responsible for what happened. I called 999 and the fire brigade came and I thought it was ironic that I used to work for them in Grimsby and now here they were again, trying to save Haringey council depot after I'd set it alight. They put the fire out, but there was a lot of damage, including the £50k dustcart, which was a complete write-off. At the inquiry afterwards, it came out that it was Naidoo's tea break and he'd buggered off and left me alone. He got reprimanded, but they didn't sack him and there was bad blood between us after that because I said he was incompetent.

A condition of my job was that I should pass my driving test. I reckoned I could drive well enough to do this, so I didn't have any lessons, apart from the one en route to the test centre at Wood Green. The examiner wasn't the most talkative of blokes and it was hammering down with rain as

The Tearaway

I drove round Tottenham, an area I wasn't familiar with. As I overtook a parked dustcart, of all things, a bin-man walked out in front of me. I slammed on the brakes and skidded to a stop, but controlled the car. The examiner bolted forward and I could see a look of irritation come over his face and I thought I've bollocksed it now for sure. The forty minutes went by and we pulled back into the test centre and he asked me about stopping distances. I didn't know the exact numbers, like in feet and inches, so I thought I'd tell him in a different way:

'Safe stopping distance in the wet?'

'From here to that car.'

'In the snow?'

'A bit further.'

'In the dry?'

'Not as far as my first answer.'

Then he gave me the top sheet of his form and it said I'd passed. It was Halloween and I thought maybe he was having a little joke. It turned out later the instructor I drove there with was a mate of Sandy's and the examiner was a mate of the instructor's and he hadn't reached his quota of passes or something. But it didn't matter to me. I was now legal to drive after five years on the roads.

The reason I'm telling you this is, because of the rolling contract, I had to re-apply for my job. Haringey had also been criticised for not employing its fair share of ethnic minorities, which meant they now had to advertise everything and Naidoo was applying for my job as well as me. My superior said it wouldn't be a problem, because he was on the interviewing panel. It was a points scoring system and there was a written test and, after about a week, I was told I'd been reappointed to the job and Naidoo could go take a jump. But the bastard objected and said I cheated and he told them I'd lied on my application form. Question 40 on the form asked if you had any driving convictions and I had one from Peterborough. Question 39 on the form asked if you had a full driving licence and if you hadn't, you could skip question 40 and go straight to question 41, which is what I did. I mean, I'd only just had my licence, like, for maybe five bloody seconds so it wasn't as if I was committing perjury under oath or anything, was it? The investigation board didn't see it like that and I was sacked, one week before my wedding to Michelle.

But I ain't told you about Michelle yet, have I?

Remember I said one of the blokes in The Moon Under Water was called Clifford? Well Sandy only went and took up with his sister, Pam, who lived in South London, and he started staying at her place more often that he was in the flat. This was OK with me, because I got to sleep in the bed when he wasn't there. Anyway, I met this girl called Michelle when I went round Pam's with Sandy one Sunday for a roast dinner. To be honest, she wasn't my type, like she had a shaved head and a nose piercing and she looked like she'd be at home on a protesters' picket line. But women were hard to come by in Balham; it wasn't like back in Grimsby where you could pull a lot easier. In London they were suspicious of blokes and I suppose they had good reason for that. And you couldn't just get off with a one-liner like 'If you don't want your hole, can I have it?', which is what they used to say in Gy – not in a nasty way, but in a laddish way that sometimes worked with the birds up there. But down here you had to do a bit more work, you had to have a conversation and let them get to know you and most nights I was too pissed to be capable of anything like that. So sexual intercourse with anything other than my hand was pretty scarce.

Michelle was just that, I'm ashamed to say now, and I didn't want a relationship or any hassle. She lived in Basildon and she came over on Saturdays when Sandy went to Pam's and sometimes I got invited to her place for the weekend. It didn't last no more than six weeks, because Nicole got in touch with me and there was a chance we might get back together. I took a train up to Cambridge and read *Philadelphia* on the way, because that's the kind of effect Nicole had on me – she inspired me to be better than I was, as you know. All her friends had left university and she was doing her final year alone and we spent the night together and I was in love again – like the time we'd been apart hadn't existed. It looked like we were destined for each other and Michelle faded into the background. The only problem was the distance between us, but we reckoned we could sort something out and we weren't too worried about it and I went back down to London with all kinds of plans in my head for the future.

It wasn't long after I passed my test that I got a phone call from Michelle telling me she was pregnant and she was keeping the baby. My head just sorta caved in. I went down to Sandy's shop and I had to sit down. I'd gone all white and couldn't take it in that I was gonna be a father after two abortions, and to a baby whose mother I didn't particularly like. And just when I was getting back with the mother I loved who'd got rid of the kids. It was like God hated me, I was sure of that. I felt sick and spaced out and light-headed and I didn't know what to do next. Michelle knew I didn't want to be with her and, to give her credit, she didn't ask me to. But I couldn't just walk away if she was gonna keep the kid. I still remembered the birthdays of the other babies who didn't live and their birthdays were the same as their deathdays and now I had a chance to make up for that in some weird way. But it would be the end for all time with Nicole – or would it? I started to form a plan in my head how I could sacrifice the next two years of my life and stay around with Michelle until the baby was grown a bit. Like, I wanted the kid to have my surname and I'd work my arse off to pay for stuff and take responsibility and build some kind of future. Then I could do the off and go back to Nicole and things would be all right again. Michelle said the baby would only have my name if I married her, so I agreed.

And then I told Nicole about my plan and I never ever heard from her again.

I sorted all the forms out at Wandsworth Town Hall and we got a wedding date for December and by that time Michelle would be five months pregnant. It was 1994 and Blackburn Rovers were top of the league and Brazil won the World Cup and Nine Inch Nails and Bone Thugs were in the charts and the Channel Tunnel opened. I arranged the registry office and the flowers and the reception at The Wheatsheaf pub in Tooting and bought the wedding rings at a shop in Basildon and worked like crazy to pay for it all. Then, a week before, I lost my job and the stupid thing was that Naidoo didn't get the bugger either. So it was all for nothing. The only good thing about it was I'd spent the best part of a year working on dustcarts – like compaction and hydraulics and electrics and operations and all the other stuff and not many people specialised in them. So I knew it wasn't gonna be too long before I'd get a job with another council, if the bastards didn't blacklist me. Which they didn't. And just a week after the wedding, I got taken on by Lambeth council at Shakespeare Road depot in Brixton, which was closer to home. The owner of Sandy's bedsit had kicked out all the tenants because he was turning the place into self-contained flats and, anyway, Sandy had virtually moved in with Pam by then and I was the only one left in the building. I had no electricity and no heating and it was like a squat, really, and the owner didn't even know I was there.

My mother decided not to come to the wedding, but my father, Bob, and his brother, Dave, were on their way down. So was Nimbus who was gonna be my best man. I was disappointed that Andrea turned down the invitation, but I didn't have much contact with her at the time and I reckoned she must've had a good reason. Maybe it was because Bob said he was coming, which surprised me. I mean, I wasn't gonna ask him, but I thought that would be wrong and the past was another place and time for me then. But I wondered how he'd get on with The Moon Under Water crew, especially if they started singing their rebel songs at the reception. I went out with them and Sandy the night before the ceremony and I told them my dad was coming down and they said they looked forward to meeting him – before we all done a runner from an Indian restaurant and left a £200 bill behind us.

I woke up next morning on One-Eye's sofa and changed into the suit I bought at Next in Oxford Street. The wedding was at 11.00 a.m., but the pub opened up early for us and we had a few whiskies before we made our way to the town hall. A big crowd turned up and, for once, I was glad Bob and Dave were there, because they were the only family I had to support me. All Michelle's family were present and the place was packed as I walked up to the registrar. More people than I thought turned up, like some from Grimsby and even one of Nicole's friends from university and Balham's finest, like 'The Bandit' Babs and 'Brain-Dead' Phil and 'Alky' Glen and you get the picture. The only one who wasn't there was Nimbus, and he had the bloody rings.

They played the usual churchy-funeral music while I was standing there waiting for Michelle but, when she turned up, it changed to Eric Idle singing 'Always Look on the Bright Side of Life', from the Monty Python film *Life of Brian*, which is what I chose. I didn't do it to be disrespectful, like Michelle's parents thought, but just to express what I was feeling at the time. I guess they wanted their daughter to have a big fairy-tale church wedding and this is what she got, as well as being married to me – which must've been a huge disappointment for them. Nimbus turned up late and I had to use my dad's wedding ring for the ceremony and we made the vows and signed the register and were pronounced man and wife. We made our way to The Wheatsheaf in Tooting where I did a free bar for an hour, which was all I could afford, and I noticed four people who didn't fit in well with the other wedding guests, because we were in a function room at the back of the pub. They were friends of the McCardles, who owned the majority of South London, along with the Richardsons and they were all suited up like they'd been invited. I mean, these were shave-headed, muscle-bound geezers who you didn't go up to and ask for their invitations. Anyway, they left after a short while and the reception was in full swing – until the police surrounded the pub at about 6.00 p.m. and said nobody was to leave.

There was a Ladbrokes betting shop next door and it'd been turned over by four armed robbers wearing suits and wedding buttonholes and the police had to question every-one and that put a bit of a dampener on the party. Most of the guests went back to the Moon and the Republicans behaved themselves and Bob and Dave didn't play up and everything went good from then on. One of the barmen from the Moon had left to work in a hotel up in Kensington and he got us a room on the cheap for our honeymoon for two nights.

It was cold outside the hotel, so we didn't do much or go nowhere, just stayed in the room or in the bar and the baby was moving round in Michelle's stomach and she was quite large by now, so we kept our distance in the bed. Afterwards, she went back to Basildon and I carried on squatting in Sandy's bedsit until I could get some more money together. I'd done the 'honourable' thing and it all went off well enough.

Apart from the armed robbery.

Chapter Eighteen

The Lambeth job was shit! Sandy drove me up to get my gear from Haringey and drop it at the new place. It was a 6.30 a.m. start and, what with all the drinking that was going on, I was lousy for getting up in the morning, especially on a Monday. The gaffer was ex-army, and I was allergic to authority. The bastard reprimanded me on my very first morning and gave me a 'stern warning' and how he wouldn't tolerate this and how he didn't like that and there wasn't to be tools left all over the place and clean overalls every day. He was like a cartoon character in a comic to me, with speech bubbles coming out of his mouth and the words made of polystyrene, like when I was a little kid and people used to go on at me. I just switched off and said 'yer, yer, yer' to everything.

Then there was all the bloody rules and regulations – one supervisor to sign off my time, another to inspect my work, another if I was doing electrical, another for seized nuts and bolts, another to check my arse after I'd been to the bog. It was crazy, and it took me longer to track down all these divs than it did to do the bloody job sometimes. So, in the end,

I just went and did the job first and then got the red tape sorted. But they didn't like that, because it upset their little cushy routines and I was all the time being dragged into the gaffer's office and told what the bollocks expected and what he didn't expect. It all came to a head in February, two months after I started – the ex-army bastard called me into his office and told me he didn't need me no more and he gave me the sack.

In a way, I was glad to be out of the bloody place. It was 7.00 a.m. in the morning and I went back to Balham and onto the piss. But when my head cleared the next day, things looked different. I was married and my wife was pregnant and I was still living like a single man. As well as that, I was fed up of the cold, damp bedsit with no shower and the gas had been cut off and the builders were moving in. So I asked Michelle if I could come live with her and she agreed. It wasn't ideal for either of us. She was only a couple of months off giving birth and I scoured the papers every day for a job, but there was nothing doing in Basildon. The local council wasn't using outside contractors for their dustcarts and there were no HGV-fitter jobs going.

I would've done anything to get out of the flat away from Michelle – quick-fitting or tyre-fitting or mending bicycles on the street corner. But they all said I was overqualified and I'd only bugger off as soon as something better came along. I had to go sign on the dole to make sure there was some money coming in at least. Michelle had an old 1972 Cortina and that got me around and, after three months of driving it with no tax or insurance, I finally found a job. It was working for a coach company and I was given a van and I had to sleep in the workshop three nights at a time to cover the RAC breakdowns they were contracted to do. It wasn't unusual, either, to be sent abroad to replace a gearbox or something on a coach that had broken down, so I wasn't seeing much of Michelle and she was up against having the baby.

The first day on this new job, I opened my toolbox and found it full of gritting sand. The bastards at Brixton depot had nicked all my tools and I didn't bother to check it when I picked it up after being sacked. The foreman said I could use his tools until I got some more of my own, just as long as I cleaned them every Friday – not just the ones I used, but all of them. But I didn't mind that much, it was a job and I was bringing in money and the baby was born on 3 May.

It wasn't an easy birth, because the umbilical cord was wrapped round the kid and its heartbeat was dropping off fast. Michelle was rushed to the operating theatre and given an emergency caesarean section. I waited outside because she wanted to be anaesthetised and they wouldn't let me in. It was nerve-racking, because there was all sorts of nurses rushing in and out and I was praying for everything to be OK and for the kid not to have to die, like the others. But she didn't and Amie was born and we took her home to the flat after a couple of days. We qualified to go on the council housing list, but we were told it could be three or four years before we'd get a place and then we'd have to take whatever we were offered. I didn't like that, because I planned to be off in two years and I wanted Amie to be out of the damp flat before I left.

A few months later, Michelle rang me at work to say that Amie's leg was hot and swollen and she wouldn't stop crying. I came home and saw the swelling for myself and I thought her leg was gonna burst open. We took her to the doctor and he sent us straight to the hospital and they took X-rays and did all sorts of tests and they stuck needles into the poor little kid and she was crying from the pain and nobody seemed to know what was wrong with her. The swelling stopped, but it never went back down and they said Amie's knee was being eaten from the inside. I didn't know how the hell that could happen, but they said she could lose her lower right leg. I went bloody crazy and said no way was that happening and I wanted a second opinion. Just as luck would have it, two days later a paediatrician from Jimmy's Hospital in Leeds was down there and he took a look. He thought Amie had something called osteomyelitis and he changed the medication and the swelling went down. Tests confirmed he was right and there was no amputation, but we were told Amie's leg wouldn't grow at the same rate as the other one and we were referred to Great Ormond Street for observation.

Things weren't going too well at the coach company either. We'd just finished doing about £1,000 worth of work on a big truck and everyone was out on breakdowns or road tests or something, except me. Two Irish blokes came in and told me Lee, who was the reception guy, said they should ask me if I'd give it a wash down before they picked it up. I always got a tip for doing a wash down, so I got the keys and they drove the truck up onto the wash ramp for me. I spent an hour cleaning off the chassis and tilting the cab and doing the engine as well, for good measure. Then they pulled it off the ramp and gave me a tenner and drove off. I was happy with that, because it meant nappies and formula milk for the kid. But when everyone came back, they wanted to know where the 28-tonne tipper lorry went to. Lee wasn't on reception and the bastards took advantage of the fact I was on my own and they didn't pay for the work and had a free truck wash to boot, which normally would've cost them £50. I was just a fitter, so how was I to know they were pulling a fast one. And it was no use reporting them to the cops, because they were Travellers and the lorry was probably in Ireland by now. The boss went mental, screaming and shouting and calling me all the names under the sun.

But it didn't stop there. A couple of weeks later another gypsy came in the workshop flogging 14-inch TV sets and saying how they'd be perfect for the coaches. I took him to the boss and he checked out a few of the TVs in the office and they were all working perfect. He paid cash for six sets and I ordered a 32-inch to replace the one we had in the flat and gave the bloke £30 deposit. He told me to come to his van to get new sets, because the ones he showed us in the office were display models and they'd been knocked about a bit. I carried the six boxes from the van and they were heavy and the boss opened them to make sure there was TVs inside. They were all cushti and the bloke said he'd be back with my 32-inch in an hour.

Anyway, an hour later all hell broke loose. TVs were being fitted to the newest coach before it went out that night on a trip to the Alps and the sets weren't working. We took one of them down off its brackets and plugged it into the mains – still nothing. Then the supervisor stripped down the back of it and there was bugger-all inside but a lump of concrete where the workings should have been – just a screen and a lump of concrete, nothing else. I got blamed again, even though it was the boss who checked the boxes. Needless to say, the gypsy didn't come back with my 32-inch and I was £30 down the swanee as well. Next day at tea break, some of the arseholes were calling me a northern twat and a wanker and stuff like that and the boss's son came over and started circling round me. He was waving a can of thinners and asking me what I'd do if he poured it down my overalls.

'Remember when Michael Jackson got burned doing that Pepsi advert? I'm gonna make you dance like him.'

I didn't think he'd do it, but he did and then he got out a lighter and was right up in my face with it.

'What you gonna do now, northern boy?'

He flicked the lighter and the vapour from the thinners caught afire. As I stood up, it engulfed the front of my whole body and I could smell my nose hair burning and I could see the orange flames in front of my face. I was running round in circles and struggling to breathe when one of them tripped me up and rolled me onto my front and extinguished the flames. I never wore trousers under my overalls and when I got them off, my legs were red raw and my stomach and chest as well. I was a bit pissed off by this and I just went toe-to-toe with the boss's son, even though he was in his thirties, and I would've probably killed the fucker if the others hadn't stood in between us. The upshot was I got paid leave till the burns healed, which weren't that bad, only like sunburn, but I milked it for all it was worth and made the tossers pay. When I went back to work, the boss's son had been kicked off the site, but I was asked to resign. I didn't want to go, but they said they'd pay me a month's wages and give me a good reference and I knew they weren't really asking – they were telling.

Amie was too small for the specialists to be able to do anything for her at Great Ormond Street; she needed to be six or seven before they could tell how much damage had been done. But they predicted the shortage length would be about one or even two inches by the time she was a teenager. There would be a choice of lengthening the short leg or stunting the growth in the good one, but that was ages away and we didn't have to decide anything yet because she was still a little baby. But I hated being with Michelle and I'd make excuse after excuse to stay out every night, like I was doing overtime or shifts or football or something – anything rather than have to go home. Don't get me wrong, I loved my little girl and I told her when she was asleep that I was sorry for what I was gonna do. But I knew my time with Michelle was coming to an end and, as soon as I could get us a decent house and have it furnished and all, then I'd be off and get my life back on track. I was still travelling down to Balham and drinking with the crowd and often driving back pissed to Basildon. The voices in my head came back too, telling me this was no good and that was no good and picking fault with everything and shouting into my brain.

We were offered a house that came available due to the previous tenant dying and the floorboards were stained where her body had decomposed and I didn't like the area. So I turned it down on medical grounds. I said I was an alcoholic and it was next to a pub and I got a letter from my doctor backing me up. I also said I had mental issues and had been in a psychiatric outpatient's ward. But it cut no ice with the council and they said I'd lose points and slip down the waiting list if I turned it down. Then I saw where they were building a new complex in Laindon that was part council and part housing association, so I went to their offices with a sob story about how I was slipping into depression and wouldn't be able to work and would be a drain on the town's resources. It took a bit of wrangling and several visits by health officials, but I pulled it off.

It was a brand-new house, not even finished, and I'd go round and talk to the builders while they were working and tell them that my daughter was severely disabled and could they put decent fittings on the doors and turf the garden for us and give us a patio. It was wrong, I know, bringing Amie into it, but it was only words – and it worked. We moved in after a couple of months and it didn't take me long to get a loan and furnish the place and get real pine flooring laid and everything – banks were throwing money at people back then and I'd got a job at Newham council, so I was earning and could pay them back. It was 1996 and I was one step nearer to the end of my plan and clearing off back to London.

Then I lost my driving licence.

I'd been down to Balham on the lash and I was acting the bollocks in the car on the way back, like seeing how I could do a braking stop at the fastest speed – I could only do it drunk, that's how stupid a thing it was. Well, the blue lights were flashing behind me and, when I stopped, a young copper opened the door and dragged me out. He had me up by the side of the car by the time his sergeant came over and asked me what I thought I was doing. I knew if I spoke they'd smell the alcohol, so I just stood there like a dummy with a weird smile on my face. The young copper kept asking me questions and I kept ignoring him which made the bugger angry. They were waiting for a traffic car to come with a breathalyser and the young copper spun me round to put the cuffs on, so I shouted at him:

'Hang on . . . I ain't been nicked yet!'

But he was an enthusiastic little bastard and he kept trying to wrestle my arms away from my sides and I kept resisting, until I got a dig into the kidneys – then another one. That was it, I swung round and grabbed the arsehole by the throat and the older copper then got me in a headlock and we all fell to the ground and I was trying to gouge the young copper's eye out, I was so bloody angry.

Then another cop car screeched to a halt and, before I knew it, I had six Old Bill on top of me, trying to get my hands behind my back and I was screaming at the young copper under me. It took them about five minutes to bring me under control and I was bundled into the back of a van and taken to the police station, where I was booked in for drunk-driving. I claimed I'd been assaulted and they sent the two coppers who arrested me down into the cell to talk about it. I told the older sergeant he knew the young one had dug me in the kidneys and he was covering it up and I thought they were gonna get nasty and give me a few more whacks. But, instead, they sent the duty sergeant to my cell and he said if I carried on with the claim of assault, they'd charge me with GBH on the young one. So I calmed down. But I was still charged with both drunk-driving and a Section Four public order offence. I got a three-year ban and a fine and probation.

This wasn't good, because I had to be able to get to work. I sold the car to Sandy and Pam, because I was the registered keeper and the Old Bill would be checking to see if I was driving it. I bought an old Sierra Estate and took a chance. Once Michelle and Amie were set up in the house, I asked Sandy to look out for a place for me so I could move back to Balham.

I liked the job at Newham. I was back as a cockroach again, but the East End blokes there were all pranksters and always up to stuff, like pressurising the oil drainers so that when the cleaners opened them the oil would shoot up like a geyser – and putting pigs' heads and other stuff they found in the dustcarts in people's lockers. I got on real well with them. The dustcarts used to come back with all sorts of appliances that were just chucked out by people in the rich houses – like TVs and microwaves and toasters and fryers and music centres and stuff. We could take them home with us because they worked perfectly well and were only thrown out because they'd been upgraded and the rich people didn't want them no more.

Meanwhile, a full-time job came up with Redbridge council and I went for the interview and got it. The manager at Newham wished me well and said if things didn't work out I could always come back and all the lads were sorry to see me go. The money was better at Redbridge, but it was 6.30 a.m. starts and that was never my strong point. It was also a place where unions ruled and I wasn't allowed to weld or do electrics or anything that was specialised. But I just did like I did before, not waiting for the proper people and just getting on with the job and causing chaos and putting people's noses out of joint, and it was obvious that my card was being marked from the start.

I was a back-end specialist at Redbridge, and that might sound funny but it meant I was working purely on the compactors. The thing about this place was all the fitters went drinking at lunchtime – they'd take a minibus to the Moby Dick pub in Romford and come back half-pissed. And they all had spirits stashed in their lockers and you could get a plastic glass and do the rounds in the workshop. Like, a whisky with this one and a brandy with that one, and you'd be half hammered by the time you'd done a single circuit. But it wasn't the booze that done for me, it was my timekeeping. I was always late and I started getting one of the apprentices to clock me in and then I'd sneak in the back way with my overalls already on and slide into the back of a dustcart. The workshop manager was always running round trying to catch me and he gave me warning after warning until, in the end, he sacked me. But luckily for me I left Newham on good terms with the gaffers and they took me back there after Redbridge.

It was too risky to drive over to Balham to drink, so I joined a club that was just at the entrance to the estate where the new house was – only a three-minute stumble home. That's where I met Georgina. The Sierra didn't last long either – no insurance and no licence, all it had was an MOT, and I was driving from Newham in a downpour with the wipers on full throttle and I couldn't see much out the windscreen, going along the Barking Road. It was dark and I wasn't doing any more than 30 mph when I felt a thud. I braked immediately and tried to see out and a split second later the windscreen came smashing in on the passenger side. I almost shit myself and I didn't want to get out of the car, but I had to. There was a black geezer laid out on the road and the whole street had come to a standstill. There were people round him and I moved the car out of the way – I knew I'd be sent down for driving on a ban and I was shaking and my legs were wobbling and my heart was racing. I was hoping the bloke wasn't dead and I kept saying to myself 'Please be OK, please be OK'. I thought about doing a runner, but the windscreen was buggered and I'd have to leg it on foot and they were bound to find the car.

The Tearaway

After getting the motor out of the way and out of sight, I raced back to where the man was and he was saying 'Sorry'! He'd come out from between two buses and straight into my path. I played on this and said he'd have to pay for my windscreen and a bus driver was calling for an ambulance and the police, but the bloke said he was all right and he got up and walked away, apologising. I think he was happy to get away without having to give me any money and I was happy to let him go. I kicked the windscreen out completely and carried on home in the rain. I sold the car the very next day.

Anyway, I was telling you about Georgina, who I met at the club and she was on her own and we made eye contact first and then we began chatting over a game of pool. She was tall and blonde and fit and I hoped the voices would like her and they'd pipe down and leave me alone for a while. She seemed to be on my wavelength and we had a good night together and arranged to meet again later in the week. She told me she was single and I told her I was divorced. She lived in a rough area over in Pitsea in a council house and she had a boy who was just a little bit older than Amie who was a big lump of a lad and his dad must've been a big lump too – whoever he was. She said I could move in and I said yer, I would, as soon as I sorted a few things out. Me and Michelle had been rowing and I thought this was as good a time as any, so I told her enough was enough and I was off. She said if I left, I needn't bother coming back – ever. That was good enough for me. She threw all my stuff out the window while I was saying goodbye to Amie and I stuffed it all into my sports bag and called a taxi and headed over to Georgina's. And that was that.

It was September 1996 and she thought it was a joke when she opened the door and I was standing there, on her doorstep. Then I showed her the Head bag and all the stuff I needed to survive in there – toothbrush, socks, boxers and a few clothes. We quickly got to grips with each other and I was happy again – like a massive weight had been lifted from my shoulders. I arranged to see Amie on the weekends and we were OK together and I was in a kind of heaven I hadn't been in since Nicole. Georgina was just fine; she liked going to football and doing the things you imagine a normal couple doing and I thought I was falling in love with her. I encouraged her to get a childminder so she could go back to work as a legal secretary and she was earning more money than me and we travelled into London together on the train in the morning and back again together in the evening. Everything was working in sync and we made each other laugh and I had a sex life again. We were like kids together when we went out shopping or drinking or whatever and it seemed like we didn't have no cares like other people had.

I even started playing football again. It was a while since I'd kicked a ball and I found a Division Nine team playing in fields not far away. I asked them if they wanted anyone and they invited me for a training session. I gotta be honest, they were useless and a far cry from my days at Barton, playing under lights and being paid and getting free alcohol.

The Tearaway

The lads I played with in Grimsby were good players and the teams were in the top flight. So it didn't take long for this new lot to make me captain and I guided them to six wins on the trot and was then asked to trial for the Essex representational side. We had blazers and everything and won our first game and I was asked to take the captaincy. After playing a couple more times for the Essex side, I was asked to play for a team in Southend called Eastwood; it was a Saturday League Division One outfit and it was like being back in Grimsby, playing top-flight amateur football. Things were going good – it was bound to go wrong, wasn't it?

Anyway, I was playing up front and jogging back to the halfway line after scoring, when a defender I'd skinned started telling me what he was gonna do and how I was gonna end up in hospital. It made me all the more determined to take the bollocks on and dance round him and nutmeg him, which is what I did. Next thing I felt a stamp on my left ankle, right on the Achilles tendon and it was hard enough to drop me to the ground. Nobody knew why I went down; it looked like a sniper had shot me from the stand. Play resumed after water and the magic sponge and I was limping a bit and trying to run it off, when the bastard did it again, this time higher up on my calf muscle. Well, I spun round and we went nose to nose and, all of a sudden, he was on the floor. I thought he'd just dived and was playing for the referee, but I turned so quick I'd inadvertently headbutted him and he was out cold on the ground. Everyone came running over and people were shouting to give him space, that he'd swallowed his tongue and they set about reviving him. The other team started trying to fight me and the referee was a full-time copper and he arrested me. An ambulance came for the dickhead and a cop car came for me and I was taken to Wickham police station, where I gave a statement and was released pending further investigation.

I played two more matches before being hit with a charge of violent behaviour by Essex FA. To cut a long story short, I was banned for five years from playing football and that put an end to my glorious career in the game.

Anyway, getting back to Georgina, it was during one of those last two games that I got a phone call from her asking me to come straight home and not go to the pub after the match. I thought something serious had happened but, when I got there, all she said was people were talking and she couldn't carry on working. I was confused and she wasn't making much sense and kept saying things were gonna change – but she wouldn't say how.

Chapter Nineteen

Next day was Sunday and the house phone kept ringing, but every time I answered it, it just went dead, like whoever was on the other end hung up. I just thought it was some div dialling a wrong number and didn't take much notice. Then her mother came round and started going on about how wrong we were, me and Georgina, and how our behaviour was disgusting, in front of her grandson – I mean, like holding hands and kissing in public. Georgina freaked and threw her old lady out, but I was getting a bit worried by all the innuendo and started asking questions, like who the kid's father was and why they split up and who was watching us and talking about us and stuff like that. She sat down and told me the story.

It happened two years ago, just after the boy was born and she and her husband were out walking with him. Two men came up and pointed a gun into the pram at the kid's head and her husband was told to leave town. That was her explanation, and the people watching us were her husband's family. She wasn't single at all, they'd never been divorced and he'd been gone two years. I kept asking questions about him and it came out that the bloke was a hired hitman and he'd been grassed up and hunted down to his own town for something he'd done and the warning came from someone who owed him a favour. It was like I'd been shot myself – what kind of people were these? If someone who owed him a favour pointed a gun at his baby's head, what would the fuckers who were trying to find him have done? What had he done to be hunted like that? Georgina's family disowned her and stopped the care for the kid so she couldn't work and the phone was ringing incessantly and she wouldn't answer it and, when I picked it up, it just went dead all the time.

'He wants to see his son.'

'Let him.'

'It's not that simple, I'm afraid . . .'

Then one night the phone started ringing about 3.00 a.m. and it was some woman saying 'Sorry' repeatedly. I hung up and it rang again and the same voice came on saying she couldn't stop him and then 'Sorry' again and again. I hung up again and it rang again. This time I told Georgina to answer it and another woman's voice came on crying and saying how she was having sex with me on a regular basis, in the house and in the bedroom and how she was here last week and shit like that. Georgina hung up and we stayed close to each other, not knowing what was gonna happen next. I tried to make light of it and said it was probably Michelle or one of her friends – until there was a great thud on the front door. I don't mean a knock, it was more like someone hit the door with a sledgehammer and the next thing this bloke came through it like a fucking rhinoceros. He had a head, but no neck and a body like he'd been working out with The Hulk, and Georgina was screaming 'No! No!' and then it went dark and I couldn't breathe.

He had several fingers in my mouth and it felt like he was trying to reach my brain via my eye socket. I bit down on his thumb and stuck my own finger into his Adam's apple and Georgina was screaming for him to stop. He was spitting and barking that I was a dead man and he was gonna end my life and I believed him. I was turning purple from where he was strangling me, when Georgina smashed a vase over his head and he let go, but he didn't keel over, he just went for her and that was my cue to get the hell out of there. I stumbled for the back door and round the side of the house to the front, with him coming after me. I crouched behind the dustbin until he ran past, then I legged it in the opposite direction. I could see two people getting into a cab down the road and I pushed them out of the way and jumped in. I shouted to the driver to take off and I'd pay him double fare. He took me to Michelle's house and I was lying on the floor of the cab, shaking uncontrollably. I banged on the door and begged her to pay the fare and she did.

She knew what was going on, because Georgina rang her and told her the bloke said he knew where I was and he was gonna come get me. Michelle asked me to leave for Amie's safety, but I had nowhere else to go and no clothes or shoes or money or anything. And, anyway, it was too late – a car skidded to a halt about five doors down and no-neck was smashing in the door of number 35. Georgina rang again and said he had a gun, so I called the coppers and told them my family was in danger and I could hear no-neck working his way along the street and he was getting closer to Michelle's. Then I could hear sirens and he jumped in his car and drove away, just before half-a-dozen police cars turned up and, for once, I was bloody glad to see them.

Georgina told me afterwards her no-neck husband and two other men were planning to kidnap me. One of the men was involved in the killing of a drug-dealer with keta-mine and they were all involved with the people who ran the doors and got shot in a Range Rover in Rettendon the year before. I knew these were no cardboard gangsters – these guys were the real fucking thing. Their plan was to take me away and I'd never be seen again and she said I was lucky to be still alive and I knew that, because he wasn't too far away from Michelle's house when the cops came.

The phone calls kept coming and the police arranged for us to move to a safer place in Leicester and they promised protection, but we had to leave immediately and never come back. I couldn't do that. I knew I'd never see Amie again and I'd have no job or friends or anything – so Georgina left without me and I never heard from her again after that. I went to live with a mate from football for a while and commuted to work and I never knew if no-neck or his mates were watching me or not. It was a twenty-minute walk from Barking Station to the job and part of it was over wasteland, which was a perfect place to be taken out. It got too much for me in the end and I moved back to Balham.

The Tearaway

I just drank all the time and got wrecked and woke up in other people's houses – women's houses, people's houses who I didn't know, weird houses, crack houses, squats, all kinds of places. I eventually moved into a flat with this black bloke called Danny who had sickle-cell anaemia, he gave me the front room and it had a futon and I used to spike his tea with Tamazepam and have drinking parties when he fell asleep. But I was getting nowhere fast. Twenty-four years old and I'm a drunk and sleeping on floors and working as a bloody cockroach after all the years as an apprentice and all the expectations and all the broken promises and cock-ups and shit that I caused to happen to myself and other people.

I left Newham and got work at TLS, a vehicle rental company, over Cricklewood way. They gave me a van and I became a mobile fitter, even though I was disqualified from driving. I still had my driving licence, even though it was worth bugger-all – I kept it rather than produce it to the court and took the £100 fine for not producing instead and, to be honest, there wasn't stop and search like nowadays, nor the automatic number plate recognition that detects banned and non-insured. It was a cream job, the van was full of kit and I made a packet out of doing private work and at night we'd all go round from the workshop to a pub in Kingsbury. That's where I met Emma – she was from Glenrothes in Scotland and she was a nurse in Paddington. I just remember talking to her in the pub one minute and waking up in her bed next morning. She rang me a couple of days later and we began seeing each other. In 1997 we moved into a flat together.

The only reason I mention her is because she was a bit weird. She had these M&S carrier bags everywhere, like some sort of fetish or obsession or something. She had to sleep with them, so in the bed there'd be three or four carrier bags and I'd wake up and she'd be clutching them. She wet the bed as well and I never found out why – she was twenty-five, same as me, and every week or so she'd wet the bed. But the worse thing about it was she made me start wetting the bloody bed as well. I mean I'd be asleep and, when I felt the warm sensation on my legs, I started dreaming I was having a slash in an alley and the pair of us would be pissing the bed. What a bloody state!

Anyway, I was sacked from TLS nine months after I started, for flicking a cigarette butt down some dickhead's throat. There was this apprentice kid mouthing off at me while I was drawing on a fag – I ignored the wanker and just flicked the butt in his face as I walked off and said 'Suck that, you prick.' But he was yapping so much with his big gob open, it flew into his mouth and stuck in his throat. He was going into convulsions with the butt burning his tonsils and I was summoned to the gaffer's office and sacked. It wasn't too much of a problem though, because I was leaving anyway and I'd already got myself another job with Iveco in Alperton and I used the TLS van to transport all my stuff over there before I handed it back.

I was an instant hit at Iveco and they made me workshop foreman, doing thirty-six-hour shifts straight, without going home or sleeping or nothing. But the sole on one of my feet peeled off in my sock and I was told I had trenchfoot and had to go on the sick. Iveco paid for all my time off and I spent most of it in a new pub that had opened in Balham called the Eclipse. The prices were double dear, to deter the rabble from the Moon and they soon barred all the undesirables, but it was a cool place to hang out and me and Sandy took up residence and got friendly with the guv'nor, who was called Andy.

Christmas was coming and Emma buggered off back up to Glenrothes for the holiday. I was back working at Iveco and covering the Christmas shifts, but with a promise of time off in the New Year, so she bought me a ticket to come up after her when I finished. In the meantime, it was nearly Christmas and I was on call and drinking with Andy. After about five or six pints of Guinness, he decided he wouldn't have enough glasses for Christmas Eve – it was a big old place, on three levels – cocktail bar, public bar and dining bar. He could get some over on Tooting Broadway, from another Regency Inn pub, but he didn't want to drive because of the beer. Things like that never bothered me, so I said I'd take him. It was only a five-minute spin, so I took the call-out van, which was a big old bus with an extra long wheelbase. I parked right outside in the High Street and we went in and had a few more pints of Guinness with the landlord before collecting the glasses. When we came out there was a parking ticket slapped on the van, because it was on chevrons, which I didn't realise. It was a fixed penalty and I looked at it and threw it away. But as soon as I drove off I could see the flashing lights behind me and a copper pulled me over just after the right turn into Upper Tooting Road.

I shoved three Extra Strong mints into my mooie and I knew this would mean prison for sure if he breathalysed me and took me in or even sat me in his car and ran a check on me. I thought about running off if the copper turned his back or spoke into his radio, or maybe give a false name or say I was an escaped lunatic and not responsible for my stupid actions. But I knew he wouldn't listen, or take any mitigating circumstances into account, like alcoholism or child-abuse or suspected homosexuality or attempted murder or anything else for that matter. It was windy and I hoped he'd be able to hear me without having to move in too close and smell my breath. The reason he stopped me was because I wasn't present with the vehicle and then I showed contempt for the law by tossing the parking ticket away. He asked me questions about why I was parked on chevrons and who the van belonged to and he rang through a check on Alperton Trucks and who was I and where was my licence. I told him it was in the office and I was making a collection as I'm on call and sorry, officer, about the chevrons – and the parking ticket. I was just glad I was down-wind of him and he gave me a producer and a fixed penalty and let me go. Touch!

I was off the hook, for Christmas, at least. But I only had fourteen days to produce all my details, like licence, insurance, MOT and the MOT was the only thing that was kosher. Driving while disqualified was four months in prison and no insurance was six points and a hefty fine – and I'd lose my job into the bargain. Was it worth it for the sake of a few pints? Sure it wasn't, but I only said things like that to myself when I got caught. It's kinda like cheating on your wife – 'I'm sorry I did it', but you ain't sorry you did it, you're only sorry because you got caught. And the same with me, that's how I lived my life. You could say it stemmed back to when I was a kid, with nobody to tell me what was right and what was wrong, but I dunno – it's more a selfish thing, where you put yourself first and to hell with anyone who gets in the way of what you want to do. I didn't say that to myself then, I was too busy looking for a way out and hoping I'd get a stretch of community service rather than a custodial, but it seems like the truth to me now.

I didn't worry about it for too long and took the train from King's Cross up to Glenrothes when I finished my Christmas stint. Emma met me with some friends and it seemed like she didn't want to be alone with me for some reason. I let it go and she took me to her dad's, where I was staying in a renovated barn with a real log fire. Then she buggered off. Her dad told me she'd been spending time with her first love since she got back and he had his own car sales showroom and was loaded. Her old man told me I wouldn't be able to compete with this bloke, so me and him watched a load of recorded Pink Floyd concerts together and drank whisky and it was all right until Hogmanay.

We went round all the houses and sampled the haggis and all the different neeps and tatties and after that to a large community centre for a hooley and I was good and enjoying myself and doing the Highland Fling and dancing up and down like a lunatic. But it was like a high and it only lasted till Emma came in with her bloke and that's when it started to affect me. I don't know why. I mean, I wasn't in love with her, at least not like I was in love with Nicole or even Georgina, but it took me by surprise and sent me into a depression and the darkness came over me again and the voices started calling me a clown and a cuckoo's arse. It was like I'd been rejected again, and I felt like I was a little kid and not a grown man and all the bad feelings came back out of their stupid boxes. I couldn't stay there, in the leisure centre, so I went off on my own and trawled the bars in the town centre and ended up with a pint glass and a bottle of vodka. I couldn't get in when I went back to the barn and I had to break a window in the conservatory and this didn't endear me to Emma's father, even though we'd had the chummy drinks. And my return ticket wasn't for a week, so I had to stay there on my own, with nobody to talk to and nothing to do except drink myself down into the dust.

I used to sleep with the radio on – still do sometimes – and I can remember the nights in Glenrothes in a drunken dream-state – listening to dour music with no commentator – sad music that I didn't know if it was real or inside my dream. Half-asleep and half-awake – three o'clock and four o'clock and five o'clock and all the sad love songs you could imagine playing on the radio, over and over, repeating themselves every hour or so. And the time passed real slowly.

But the black mood left me when I got back and I was too busy thinking about what kind of a sob story I could conjure up for the judge and the duty solicitor, as I went down to Tooting nick to face the music two weeks later. I walked in smoking a cigarette that might be my last for a while and I saw a sign that said: 'The Reception is Closed Due to Staffing Shortages'. Woo-hoo! All I had to do was prove I'd turned up, so I nicked the sign. But nothing's that simple, is it? The court sent me a letter and the charge was parking on chevrons at a crossing and that was it. Nothing about failing to produce my licence and insurance or anything. I had to appear at Croydon magistrates and I went before a lady judge who looked like she had a red-hot poker stuck up her arse. They read out the charge and the parking offence and I admitted to it and she told me to hand in my licence to have it endorsed and then dismissed me from the witness box. I stuck my hand up.

'S'cuse me, your lordship . . .'

'I'm a ma'am, not a lordship. What is it?'

'I don't have a licence to endorse.'

The magistrate was confused. She went into one. What did I mean? Why hadn't I got a licence? Didn't anyone check?

'S'cuse me, ma'am . . .'

'Yes, what is it now?'

'I'm, eh . . . banned.'

How can he be banned? How can a parking contravention be issued and not know he's banned? Why haven't charges been brought? Off with his head!

The prosecution people were summoned backstage to her chambers and the court was adjourned. I was led back to the main area and told to wait. I waited forty minutes before they came back out. Poker-arse addressed the court. When I was stopped, the copper should have checked me there and then but, because the van came back clean, he assumed I would be too. I mean, what company is gonna employ a driver with no driving licence? As the reception was closed when I came in to hand in the producer I didn't have, it hadn't been established that I had no licence and the mandatory twenty-eight days for notification of charges had expired – blah, blah, blah. I was told I was very lucky and was free to go – with three points and a fine. I was about to skip out the door when the magistrate called to me:

'Mister Williams . . .'

'Yes, ma'am?'

'People like you will always end up before people like me. I look forward to the next time.'

But it wasn't a warning I was gonna take much heed of. The result in the court meant I was still employed by Iveco and I'd still be driving without a licence. But I couldn't go any higher than workshop foreman at the job and I was getting bored. I wanted to be a manager and I was getting fed up with the whole diesel scene and I was taking time off left, right and centre to drink with Andy in the Eclipse. He owed me for the trouble he'd caused with the glasses and he was happy to fire up the free booze to make it up to me and let me drink after hours till three or four in the morning and then sleep on the sofa in the staff quarters. Sandy drifted back to the Moon for the cheap prices and, slowly, Andy showed me the ropes of the licensed trade, asking me to do the door now and then and collect empty glasses and come behind the jump to pull a few pints when it was busy and take in deliveries and do the cellar.

I was soon mixing cocktails and brewing up our own brand of real ale that was sold cheaper than the others and learning the spirits and the legal stuff like minimum age and licensing laws and stocktaking and how the computerised tills worked. In two months or so, I pretty much knew how to run a pub. Andy spoke to the area manager and put me forward for a job with the brewery and gave me all the answers to the questions I might be asked. I passed the interview and was offered the job of assistant manager at the Eclipse, with accommodation and food and expenses, but the package was still only worth about £15,000 a year, like, in my hand. I was earning £500 a week as a fitter, but I took the job anyway and it changed how I got on with people. You see, all my mates at the Moon came round when they found out and expected me to freeload them and let them have afters and sub them when they were broke, but I couldn't do it. I had to throw them out at closing time and I couldn't sit and chinwag with them and loaning money was against company rules – not that that would've stopped me, but I knew I'd never get it back and it would have to come out of my wages and I'd be working, like, just to supply the freeloaders with booze. I had to separate myself from off-duty and working and it's funny how people change their attitude to you when you won't do what they want you to do.

For instance, Jimmy's parents were coming down from Corby for a visit and he got me in a corner and he didn't ask me, he told me he expected four free meals and a hundred quid to be available to him.

'Don't ya be lettin' me down now, Deano. Don't ya dare!'

I was in two minds at first whether to knock him out or tell Andy. In the end I did neither. I waited for Jimmy to come in and, when he did, there was more than four, there was about ten of them. He came up to me and asked me for the ton and I told him to go fuck himself. He started laughing in his Glaswegian accent.

'Yer windin' me up, ya wee bollicks, ain't ya?'

'No, Jimmy, I ain't.'

He raised his fist and I pointed to the CCTV cameras all over the place.

'What'll a tell ma family?'

'Tell them the kitchen's closed, due to a burst pipe, and the Moon's closer to your pocket.'

It wasn't long before I had no mates left at all.

But I had new friends now. My time was spent socialising with other people in the trade and I actually drank less, because I was working seventy hours a week and I was usually knackered at night by the time we closed up and cleared up and had a quick staff drink. Deliveries were at 5.00 a.m., so I had to be up earlier than I'd ever been before, apart from the time when I used to nick the stuff from the milk round. It was hard work but it was a good time. The World Cup again in 1998 and Beckham lashing out at Diego Simeone and getting the red card and me setting up a little tickle with the postman.

Chapter Twenty

The scam with the postman was to get him to feel the envelopes for credit cards. Don't forget, this was a time when all the banks and supermarkets and fish 'n' chip shops and soup kitchens and lunatic asylums were giving away their own credit cards. They were just sending them out in the post to people whose names they got from the phone book and, once the postie found a card, I had three days to spend as much as I could on it and split fifty-fifty with him. The cards were insured and the issuers were insured and the insurers were insured and I'd go get cigarettes and tobacco and ask for cash back while I was at it. All I had to do was sign the name on the front of the card on the back. They didn't have chip-and-pin and they had them machines they slid across a docket thing and it was easy-peasy. If we got two or three cards a week we were making money. We could either sell or use the goods and spend the cash.

But I stopped dead in my tracks when I was buying some clobber in Tooting and the shop manager got suspicious. He took the card out the back and left me in the shop and he was talking on the phone to someone, but I couldn't hear who, or what he was saying. He was only gone a couple of minutes, but it seemed like an hour and a half and I was about to run out of the shop when he came back. He didn't say nothing, just put the card and the docket in the sliding machine, got me to sign and gave me the gear. I was out the door and gone and I cut the card up and told the postman I couldn't do no more because I'd joined the Jehovah's Witnesses and they told me I'd never get into God's kingdom on earth if I kept doing it. It might've been nothing with the shop manager, but I wasn't gonna take a chance. Organised credit-card fraud was serious shit that could've cost me a long spell inside and I wasn't gonna risk it again. Maybe I was growing up?

I stayed in the pub game for eighteen months. I was looking to get my own establishment or become a satellite manager – like a relief manager going round filling in for people when they were on holidays and stuff. The problem was, I couldn't get a liquor licence because of my criminal record and that meant I was stuck as an assistant, earning £15k and trimmings and I wasn't all that happy with it. Then, one night, I went on the piss with the chef from the Eclipse and that kinda put the tin hat on it. We did a tour of all the Regency Inn pubs in the area and got hammered and were out of order with the staff and then went back to the Eclipse and fell all over the place there as well. Andy didn't want to do it, but other staff complained and it got me sacked and barred out of all RI pubs in the world and I couldn't exactly go back to the Moon after falling out with all the arseholes there, now could I? But as soon as I got sacked, I walked straight back into a job as a fitter, working for London Ambulance. I was also homeless again, because I got chucked out of the pub's accommodation. Luckily, Danny was still alive and his front room was still unoccupied, so I moved back onto the futon.

The months that followed are a bit of a blur. I spent all my money on booze and I couldn't keep a job because I was taking so much time off. I went from London Ambulance back to the council and here and there and everywhere, working for whoever would put up with me until they couldn't any more. Sitting in pubs, randomly picking a place from the tube map, then going there and getting slaughtered. I even went down to Brighton and ended up nearly drowning in the sea and the lifeboat had to be deployed to save me – they dragged me out, spewing up beer and seawater.

I'd stay on it for six or seven days at a time, until the money was all gone, then back to work to earn more, then back on the booze again. I was drinking twenty to thirty pints a day and pulling two-baggers, which was the name for dodgy women – one bag over her head and one bag over mine, in case hers slipped off.

I'd met someone else while I was working in the pub; her name was Jennifer and she was working for the DSS across the road. But the long hours meant most of the time I was working and we just talked from either side of the bar. I called her one night and we began to see each other, but she made me go for an AIDS test before I could sleep with her. The place was heaving when I went down there. Don't forget, AIDS was scarier then than it is now, and they gave me a blood test in the morning and told me to call back at 5.00 p.m. for the results. There was this therapist or shrink or something there when I went back, saying how to cope if you tested HIV positive and where to go and what help you could get and I thought this don't sound too comforting to me, because I never used condoms with the two-baggers or with anyone else for that matter and I was worried. It's like I was saying before, you don't feel sorry until you think there might be repercussions from your actions – I wasn't sorry I didn't use condoms; I was sorry I might have caught HIV.

I had to wait for the nurse to call my name for the results and the crowd gradually started dwindling down, until there was only me and this geezer in a suit left. We were both sweating and the cleaners were walking past and giving us dirty looks, like we were some kinda scum they'd just shaken off their shoes. The next thing, this special counsellor turned up and that meant someone had HIV – either me or him, or maybe both of us. I was trying to think who I might have caught it off, but I couldn't remember most of it, so it could've been anybody. The suit was looking worried as well, so I guessed he'd been up to something he oughtn't to and maybe he was married and he could've passed it on to his wife or anything. Didn't bear thinking about.

Then the two of us were called into separate rooms and the nurse looked at the results in front of her and paused, like she was a judge and was gonna deliver the death sentence or something.

'Your results have come back negative, Mister Williams.'

I was ready to collapse crying onto the floor because I thought she was gonna say 'positive' and I couldn't believe it when she said 'negative' and I still collapsed crying onto the floor. Then I got up and hugged her. As I walked out of the clinic, I could hear the guy in the next room screaming and my heart went out to him. There weren't the drugs around then that they got now and it was looked on as the end of the road. But I was OK and that's what mattered most to me.

Jennifer and I got a house together. It wasn't easy; she scammed the council under the 'right to buy' scheme, saying she'd been living there for three years and she got the mortgage in her aunt's name and we sorted out the auntie some way, I can't remember how, and the house was ours. We split all the bills fifty-fifty and it was good while it lasted. Then I got caught driving her car while disqualified and there was no way out for me this time. I was back in court again and I suppose I was lucky again – I got eighty hours community service instead of a custodial, along with a year's probation and a fine and a six-session course on why not to drive while you're disqualified and an extension of the ban. All that, even though I pleaded guilty! I said I couldn't do the community service because I was working six days a week to pay off a mortgage and I'd rather go to prison. The judge went berserk and told my solicitor to take me to one side and give me some good advice – which he did. It took me a year to do the community service and a load of court appearances. The probation was just as bad – it started off with weekly visits, but the officer changed it to monthly, because he couldn't deal with me telling him about my past all the time. He even asked to be taken off the case.

Jennifer left me for her childhood sweetheart, just like Emma, and I thought I must be doing some good in the world, getting all these people who'd lost each other back together again. It's like, they didn't realise what they had until they met me. The reason she left was because I couldn't get out of the bad habit Emma had started me on – that sometimes when I felt warm in bed I started dreaming I was taking a slash up an alley. She woke me one night screaming: 'Stop it! Stop it! Stop it!' and I thought I must be snoring or something, but I was taking a piss up her back and she didn't understand that it was psychosomatic.

After she left, I started doing the chatlines – you know, like it was £1.50 a minute and you listened for messages in an in-box and you had a code and, if you liked the sound of someone, you left a coded message in their in-box. It cost me, like, £100 just to sort out the code and figure out how to use the bloody thing, and my messages were all rubbishy and weird and I never got no replies. Then this bird from Reigate contacted me and I got her phone number and we began calling each other. It was a bit of a turn-on, because I imagined I was talking to Cindy Crawford and then she asked me if I'd ever had phone sex before. I didn't know how you could have sex with the phone, but I also didn't want her to think I was stupid or unsophisticated or something, so I said I had – loads of times. She told me she looked like Princess Diana and I asked her if that was before or after the crash and she hung up and never called back.

I had one more response before I gave up on the chatlines and that was from a woman up Tottenham way and we got to the stage of swopping photos. I sent her one of me that I'd had taken when I went to Mexico with Jennifer, before the incident in the bed, and she sent me one of Dani Behr. Anyway, she sounded good-looking and she had a right husky voice and I got my best gear on and aftershave and underarm spray deodorant and I found her flat and knocked on the door with my heart pounding. This woman answered in a leather suit and I thought it was her mother –

'Is Dani in?'

'I am Dani. You are Dean?'

I didn't want the whole evening to be a waste of time, so I went out with her and she showed me the local nightspots and we had a few orange daiquiris together and went back to her flat. It wasn't the most romantic of nights when we went to bed, because I was hammered on the daiquiris and could hardly stand up, never mind get anything else to stand up, and she was a bit disappointed in the morning when I left early – before she woke. I cancelled my subscription to the chatline after that.

I couldn't keep up the mortgage on Jennifer's house and socialise like I wanted to as well. It was all right when we were together and she was paying half and I was working all the hours and earning. But some bastard stole my toolbox and I had to start from scratch and it was embarrassing for a while, turning up to work with less than the apprentices and borrowing tools for weeks on end and I had to spend £2k just getting back to where I was to begin with. It was the year 2000, when all the computers were gonna go haywire and planes were gonna fall out of the skies and the world was gonna come to an end. But it didn't and it was kind of a letdown. I watched the VCR and the alarm clock and everything else that was digital, but nothing stopped or blew up and I realised that life was just gonna continue as normal – nothing was gonna change.

I had a mate called Darren and we sorted out a flat together and I gave up Jennifer's house. The problem with me and Darren was, we were too much alike and it was difficult living with the wanker. We were trying to outdo each other all the time and each of us had to be better than the other – better at drinking and gambling and better with women and fighting and every bloody thing. It was like two ten-year-old kids living together with no supervision. It came to a head one night after we'd been drinking over at Crystal Palace and he pulled this bird and brought her back to the flat. He took her into his room, but I kept knocking the door and interrupting them, just for a laugh, but he didn't see the funny side and went mental at me. We had a punch-up in the front room and I gave him a good dig and knocked the bugger down. I turned round to go get a drink of water and he ran back into the bedroom and came out with a handgun and the bird screaming after him.

'Put the gun down, Darren. Put the gun down!'

'You think I'm a mug? You think I'm a mug?'

That's all he kept saying and the bird was going hysterical screaming at him to put the gun down and I was shitting myself because I could see the fucker wasn't in a stable state.

I tried to reason with him – like, telling him not to do anything stupid and how we were mates and all. Then he put the barrel in his own mouth and tears were coming down his face. I was sobering up rapidly, saying anything that came into my head.

'Don't do it. Don't do it.'

He took the gun out of his mouth and pointed it back at me and I was sorry I told him not to do it, but he started going on about how he felt suicidal and he didn't want to live any more and I felt like saying 'Put the gun back in your mouth, then.' But I didn't – just in case. I eventually managed to get close enough to take the gun from his hand and he broke down and collapsed on the floor. I took the clip out while he was crying about how he wanted to join his dead father, who'd also shot himself and he'd been charged with attempted rape on some bird and the bank had closed his account and a notice had been served on the flat and he had nothing to live for. Thanks for telling me. He stood up and came over to me with his arms out for a hug – so I knocked him out.

Darren and I were served with an eviction notice and I was wondering where I was gonna go now. Then I got a job as a mobile mechanic where this woman called Ashlee worked in accounts and it wasn't long before I got her to come out with me. We went to the company Christmas do in a hotel near Gatwick and, even though we booked separate rooms to stay overnight, I was feeling confident. The only trouble was, I'd had a few drinks with crazy Darren in the afternoon and I'd had to pick Ash up from her house, which was in the middle of nowhere. First thing, I nearly crashed into a Porsche on the way out of her place in the wilderness of Kent and, if that wasn't bad enough, I got lost in the grounds of the hotel and couldn't find the car park. I mean, I could see all the cars parked away across the lawns and stuff, I just couldn't find the way to get there. So, the obvious thing was to drive across the grass. Which I did, until the car sank up to its axle in soft mud and I couldn't get it out.

Now, Ashlee was looking a million dollars and I was looking like I'd just played eighty minutes of rugby in a quagmire and all these people were looking out the windows of the function rooms. There was only one thing to do, leave the car where it was and carry Ash over my shoulder to dry land. It sort of put a dampener on the rest of the party and I ended up spending the night in my own room and my plans for a night of sexual gratification went awry. Next day, it required two service vans to pull me out of the mud and we took out a lamp post while we were at it.

It was a month before I was to have my way with Ashlee. Normally, I wouldn't have bothered, but there was something special about her, so I persevered. She had her own house and her own mortgage and two daughters and I moved in with her the day before the bailiffs moved into Darren's flat. Close shave. But I knew even then that this relationship was going to be different. Ash had the measure of me and there was no use turning up to the picnic with just a napkin like I was used to – this time I'd have to bring the whole spread, and the cutlery too.

The tearaway years were over.

But I was getting fed up working for this company and that company and I wanted to be my own boss. So, when this geezer called Nelson asked me to come work with him, it looked like a good deal. He was having a new workshop built and I'd have my own office with a leather chair and the latest this and that and I could name my own salary and bullshit, bullshit, bullshit! What I didn't know was this Nelson was a gypsy and, now, I ain't got nothing against gypsies – just as long as they got nothing against me. I ended up working at the back of his house in a tiny freezing unit and, like, fourteen-hour days, seven days a week. When the new workshop was finally built and we did move, I never got what was promised to me, just more bullshit. The fucker was treating me like I was his personal serf or something. But Ash was pregnant now and I needed to be earning, so I was trapped.

Then, out of the blue, a genuine opportunity came to me to start my own business. It was a big risk, setting up in my own mobile servicing vehicle – I had to have some start-up money and customers and a business plan and I had bugger all. But Ashlee saw how I was working for Nelson and she told me it'd work and I went for it. '*Carpe diem*', as they say in France. Nelson nearly had a heart attack when I handed in my notice, because he thought he had me by the balls – and he would've, if it hadn't been for Ash's support.

Anyway, things worked out OK and I won't bore you with the details. I've been my own boss for the past ten years and I love it.

I always wanted to write a book, I dunno why – maybe to get rid of the anger and hate and resentment inside me. Exorcise the demons. Finally take all the bad stuff out of the boxes inside my head and try to make some sense of it. I'd sit at home tapping away at the laptop, not telling Ash what I was doing when she asked me because I was too embarrassed about it. Then the kids infected the computer with a virus and I lost it all and I thought maybe it wasn't meant to be written down – maybe it was meant to stay inside my head, stored away safe. Or maybe my story might be some help to someone who went through or was going through the same? I tried to get some advice on how to write it and hooked up with people who were making films and writing screenplays and stuff and it was another world. And it just happened bit by bit – someone asked me if I ever did any acting and I laughed and they said I should try it.

I signed up for Paul McNeilly's acting classes and it wasn't long before I was getting parts as an extra and little bits and pieces and I found out I was good at this acting lark and people liked me. *The Sky in Bloom*, featuring Bill Thomas, was my first experience on a set and I was buzzing after getting an email asking me to play a bodyguard. They told me I needed to build up a show-reel and get myself an agent and a couple of credits under my belt. Anyway, I got to the set and it was a restaurant in north London. I was two hours early and nobody else was there and the waiting outside was nerve-racking – just like the old days with the GHS when it was gonna kick off with some other firm. I didn't know who was who or what was what so, as soon as I saw some geezer coming towards the restaurant, I started talking to him.

'Yo, I'm Dean.'

'I'm Tom.'

'I'm the security guard.'

'Oh, right, you're the security guard.'

'Where do you want me?'

It transpired that this Tom bloke was nothing to do with the film and was only out looking for a place to have a meal. He shuffled off down the street, looking back at me like I was some kind of creepy crimshaw.

The crew and director and everyone turned up eventually and I got to know who were actors and who were extras and the difference between the two and they were all real nice people. There was trades there too, like me, electricians and lighting guys and sound guys and I told them I was a diesel fitter and they laughed at that and we got on OK – until the director came over and told me I was a waiter, not a bodyguard. It seems there was some sort of mistake and the bodyguard scene was next week – today, I was a waiter. My nerves were jangling and I thought how am I gonna do this thing? I'm a diesel fitter, not some poncey actor – then I thought, what about all the times I was acting the fool at school to stop getting beat up, and all the times I was playing the joker so's not to be rejected?

Acting came natural to me, I'd been doing it all my life. They changed my role again, to the restaurant manager, and I wondered if all film shoots were this chaotic. But I did it, re-shoots, over and over and over – wides, two-handers, three-handers, close-ups. But I did it!

And that's how it started, just bit roles – bits and pieces. Boring, mostly, and I'm sure you don't want to hear about hanging round all day doing takes, over and over again. I thought the life of an actor was a glamorous one, but mostly it's just hanging around, waiting for something to happen. But I kept meeting great people – actors, directors, people who gave me advice and steered me along the path of this new part-time career, which I was doing along with running my own servicing business. People like Ronnie Fox and Seb Castang, who've both done big films – and Billy Zane in *Mercenaries*, where I was two different people and they started paying me for my time. I got my first proper acting job as a gay bouncer in a piece for the London 48 Hour Film project, working with Geoff Bell and Vas Blackwood. Would you believe that – a gay bouncer, of all things? The film was called *4play* and I got to go to Leicester Square for the showing and rub shoulders with some of the great and the good. The audience laughed at me, which they were supposed to do. You see, I was still playing the fool – acting the idiot. Only getting paid for it.

Paul McNeilly involved me in guerrilla filming on the streets of London on weekends. We just went out with a camera and some actors and shot little situations that he'd written. It was all very improvised and a great way to learn the skills. He told me the worst actors were the ones who actually had to act – the best were the ones to whom it came naturally. Paul also got us to perform in a theatre in front of a paying audience and I owe a lot to that guy – he's one of the best teachers I've ever met. He borders on genius – and you know what they say about genius. But I guess I'm the one who's been sectioned, not him. Ha ha ha.

I was also getting invited to a lot of 'networking' sessions and parties in London. Now, my social skills probably ain't the best. Trying to force conversations with total strangers done my head in a bit – unless I had about ten pints of Stella down me first – and then I got bolshie and sarky like I used to do at school, because most of these things were full of people who were only interested in you if you could do something for their careers in the film industry. And I was no bullshitter – I may've been a lot of things, but I wasn't an arselicker or a bullshitter.

'What are you?'

'I'm a plus one.'

'OK dear! Really . . . only a plus one?'

Which meant I wasn't officially invited, just the guest of someone who'd been invited. Then they'd walk off and try to collar someone more important than me. But I did meet a fantastic agent who organised my show-reel and signed me up with a management deal and I was now a professional actor – as well as being a professional diesel fitter, of course.

But it wasn't all plain sailing – it was nights out till 5.00

a.m., lost days servicing vans through alcohol, tear-ups with Ashlee, getting felt up the arse and French-kissed by every gay producer in London, fights in pubs, being thrown out by bouncers – it seemed like the bad old days were coming back again and I'd never amount to nothing in this game. But then I got the deal to write this book, plus the lead role in a major movie that's in production right now, as I write, and much more. So, all the French-kissing might have paid off and my film and TV career is something that seems to be on its way for the future, not the past. So, I'll have to tell you how it pans out some other time.

Epilogue

I'm still living down in darkest Kent with Ashlee. It ain't
been an easy time and we've had our differences and caused
each other heartache – but we're still here. I still do the
diesel repairs when I feel like it, while I'm waiting to become
a big star, just to keep my hand in. Ashlee is the only woman
for me, she gave me a great son, Sam, who's nine years old
now – same age as I was when I went to Crosby Juniors and
was eating the soggy cereals and Bob's lardy fry-ups and
dodging the bullies and winding up the teachers. Lot of
water under the bridge since then and it's a different world
for Sam – I hope. He's what life's about for me now – him
and Ash and my lovely stepdaughters Maisie and Lauren.
The voices are gone – been gone a long time and I don't
think they'll be coming back. There ain't a battle every day
to make my head work in sync with my body and the booze
ain't as important to me now as it used to be. Don't get me
wrong, I still go on the lash every now and then, just for old
time's sake – but I can take it or leave it and I never let it
interfere with my life like it used to. I know for sure I'm not
gay, not that there's anything wrong with being gay, like I

said, but it just ain't for me – and it's like the fella said when he kissed the turkey, 'each to his own'. Ha ha ha.

One regret is I don't see much of Amie. She's got a new dad now and they fitted a halo to her leg and extended the bone by an inch and a half and she's a beautiful teenager now and I love her deep down – deep, deep down.

I go back up to Grimsby every now and then and I still keep in touch with some of my old mates. Nimbus went into the carpet shop business and Matty McCourt is a writer – the 'Hooligan Poet' – and he's had several books of his own published. And Fazza's making a name for himself in the world of graphic novels. It's a far cry from the days of abuse and suffering when we were young. People say your childhood days should be the happiest of your life. Maybe they should, but it's not like that for a hell of a lot of kids – at least, it wasn't in my day and I'm sure the world ain't changed all that much since then. All I'd say to those kids is, I was a right little mammy's boy, and if I could come out the other side of it and make something of my life – you can too!

Bob got bowel cancer and I go see him in hospital. I don't know how much he remembers or what he thinks about his life and how it affected me when I was a kid, but we've kinda come to terms with each other and I'm the man in the prime of life now and he's maybe close to the end of his, I don't know, and there ain't much point in being enemies and I've still got his name tattooed on my arm that cost me £1.50 all them years ago. I carried my gran's and grandad's coffins when they died and I remember the holidays in Scotland and the refuge they gave me when I was a kid with nowhere else to go.

Andrea lives on her own now and I think she prefers it like that, after all she's been through in her life. The last bloke she was with stamped on her head real bad and that's why she never came to my wedding – I only found that out after the bastard died. She don't come down to visit us because she can't drive and she likes her privacy, but I go see her and she keeps in contact with the kids and life's quiet for her now after the turmoil and she deserves it to be like that. We don't talk about the cupboard days or the violence or the bad things, but I guess she's got her memories – just like I got mine.

I lost touch with Sandy and I wish him well, wherever he is. You might say he wasn't the best influence on my life, but he took me in when I was being shat on and he was always good company and you need something when you're down, don't you? You need someone to be your friend. I've got other friends now, some close and some not so close, some famous and some infamous, I've been loved and loathed, touted and threatened and life's like that, ain't it, one man's meat is another man's poison, as they say. I like meeting the film people and it's nice to be invited to the premieres and charity dos and stuff, but I'm still a Grimsby boy and I never forget where I came from. My goal is to go half-circle, from a tearaway to a top-notcher, but I won't be the judge of that; it'll be the people around me who'll say what they think and that's how it ought to be.

Thing about it is, I ain't never been a conventional bloke

and I've always done things my own way, right or wrong. If it was right, fair dos – if it was wrong, I took the consequences and only whinged a little bit. I like to help people if I can, whether it's with advice or work or charity or whatever. That don't make me no philanthropist, I've been a selfish bastard all my life, but I'm trying to change – trying not to repeat the mistakes of the past. And the whole point of this story is to say to you that you never know when a black cloud's gonna come over your head – and you never know when it's gonna blow away and the sun comes out again. No need to commit suicide, or drink yourself to death, or think things are never gonna be any better. Life changes all the time – you ain't even met the man or woman you're gonna be in ten years' time – or five years' time – or one year's time. And, you never know, you might even like that person.

Sometimes someone comes along and lifts you up to another dimension and, for me, that was Ashlee. If I hadn't met her, I guess I might still be a cockroach and drinking myself to death in the dives of London. Who knows? I hope this book will explain to her, and maybe some others, just who I am and why I do the things I do and I hope she'll understand and excuse me for being me. A wise man once said these words and I'm not even sure what they mean, but I know they mean something:

A starlit or a moonlit dome disdains
All that man is,
All mere complexities,
The fury and the mire of human veins.

Thanks

To my beautiful soul mate and partner of 13 years, Ashlee. I appreciate the dark times you have endured with me, yet stuck by me – you deserve a stick of rock . . .

To my mum, Andrea, who gave me support and advice, and also to my father Bob – you can never stop loving your father, and this is no different.

To all at Kings College Hospital on Christine Brown Ward, nurses who cared for me in the darkest hours and made it possible to stay focused.

To Matty McCourt, the inspiration to write this book.

To Darren Page for continued support and keeping me entertained with his split personalities.

To Fazza, for sharing his own experiences with me and being brave enough to allow me to share them.

To Marc Dennis, for being my accomplice in many mad escapades.

To the women I've met in my life who were angelic enough to put up with me. Love!

To all my mates from Grimsby and London who I haven't mentioned here – you know who you are. I salute you!

To all who encouraged me to keep travelling forward, I appreciate your private messages.

To Grimsby Town, the place I love.

Finally to my son, Sam – you are my best friend and everything good I do is for you.

'We were never meant to succeed.'

Deano x